THE BUSINESS OF BAKING

The book that inspires, motivates and educates bakers and decorators to achieve sweet business success.

Michelle Z Green

THE BUSINESS OF BAKING:

The book that inspires, motivates and educates bakers and decorators to achieve sweet business success

Published by: Good Egg Publishing, Melbourne, Australia

ISBN: 978-0-9945241-0-2

Cover design by: Michelle Lorimer

Cover photo by: Cathy Worsley

Author photo by: Jeremy Blode

Dedication

For the sweeties who taste-tested a lot of cakes, delivered thousands of cupcakes, tolerated many late nights and still inspire and encourage me daily:

David, Alexis, Julian and Claire

How To Use This Book

I never intended for this book to be read cover to cover. I meant it more to be as a cake business bible. It might be the kind of thing that sits reassuringly on your shelf until the time you need some advice and inspiration. Perhaps one day you'll be procrastinating about getting work done, so you'll pick up this book and randomly pick an article to read. Like a decent bag of potato chips, you might find that once you get started you find it hard to stop. Maybe something about your business is bothering you – someone asked for a refund, or you're not sure how to deal with a situation with a supplier. In those instances, pick this up and find the topic and article relevant to you and read it. However you choose to use it, know that each page and each word is infused with my philosophy about small business: we're in this together.

One more thing – as most of the articles in this book were originally published on my blog, you may find things that say "Today, I'd like to write about," and "Recently, you guys said," - this is because new articles are published on the blog weekly, and it's got quite the active online community around it. I invite you to join me there at **thebizofbaking.com**

For further resources related to this book, please visit the website:

http://thebizofbaking.com/BestofBoB

The Best of The Business of Baking

Contents

Introduction	1
Before You Begin	4
• And You Are ...?	4
• A Typical Small Cookie Company Story	7
• Just One Little Cake Please	10
• The Final Cake Design	12
Chapter 1 – Getting Started In Business	15
• Don't Run A Baking Business If You Don't Want To	16
• Before You Open A Business	19
• Ten Things You Need To Spend Real Money On In Order To Succeed In The Baking Business	22
• You Make Awesome Cake. And. Now. What?	24
• How To Name Your Cake Business	28
• The Dog Ate My Figurine	31
• Elephant Bites	34
• The Right Time	37
• What Is A Business Plan?	39
• Writing A Business Plan Part 1	42
• Writing A Business Plan Part 2	46
Chapter 2 – Home Based Business	51
• Work Versus Effort	52
• Planning Your Home Based Cake Business	55
• Setting Boundaries For Your Home Based Business	58
Chapter 3 - Day To Day Running Of Your Business	61

- Boring But Important   63
- Confused in Cakeland – Your Telephone Number   67
- Sign On The Dotted Line   69
- Signing The Lease   72
- Well Equipped   75
- Confused In Cakeland – Buying Cake Tools   79
- Like A Cake Boss   81
- Make More Money, Spend Less Time   84
- Friends With Benefits   91
- Your Business. Your Rules   94
- Delivery Etiquette   97
- Hiring Versus Outsourcing   100
- Dealing With The Cow Down The Road   103
- Taming The Email Beast   106
- I Have No Life. Only Cake   109
- How To Make Friends.   113

Chapter 4 – Products   117

- Why Be Standard When You Can Be Generous   118
- Confused In Cakeland – Allergen Free Baking   121
- Cakes And Copyright   123
- Inspired by   126
- I'm So Clever, I Bought It All By Myself   129
- No Bake Cake   134
- Confused In Cakeland – Choosing Ingredients   137

Chapter 5 – Money   139

- Working For Free   140

- Being Charitable   146
- Your Dirty Little Secret   149
- Confused In Cakeland - Making A Living From Selling Cake   152

Chapter 6 – Pricing   155

- Charge What You're Worth   157
- Educating Customers About Pricing   161
- Getting More Sales   164
- Pricing Cake Is Not Just About You   167
- Let Me Tell You A Story About Pricing   170
- The Promise Of Future Work   173
- Confused In Cakeland - Pricing For Wholesale   177
- Should I charge A Last Minute Order Fee?   179
- Confused in Cakeland – Show Me The Money   182

Chapter 7 – Customers   185

- Finding The Right Customers   186
- Buy. Repeat. Share   190
- Promises, Promises   195
- Confused In Cakeland - How To Deliver Cakes Via Plane   197
- You Need It WHEN?   199
- I'm Just Not That Creative   201
- Ugly Cakes   204
- Confused In Cakeland – Giving Out Samples   207
- Confused In Cakeland – Sneaky Peeks   210
- You Couldn't Pay Me Enough   212
- You Couldn't Pay Me Enough Part 2   215
- Close The Deal And Make The Sale   218

- Hater's Gonna Hate, Cakers Gonna Eat (Oreos)   221

Chapter 8 – Marketing   227

- Marketing for Bakers   229
- Confused In Cakeland – Best Marketing Idea Ever   231
- Five Steps To Writing A Marketing Plan   234
- The Table   238
- Not The Bad Cake Lady   242
- I Spy With My Little Eye   245
- How Do I Find More Clients   248
- Who Is My Ideal Client   250
- Where Are My Customers Hiding?   254
- How To Sell Without Feeling "Yucky" About It   258
- MMM Business   262
- First, Best, Only   268
- Confused In Cakeland – Using Pictures From The Internet   271
- Eventful   273
- Selling At Markets Successfully   277
- Wedding Fair Vendors – How To Become An Awesome Vendor   281
- Networking For Cakers   284

Chapter 9 – Social Media   287

- Social Media 101 For Bakers And Decorators   288
- Confused in Cakeland – Is A Website Necessary?   292
- Website Essentials   296
- Breaking Up Is Hard To Do   298
- Social Media Overwhelm – My Social Media Experiment   302

- Marketing Your Business On Social Media   306
- Confused In Cakeland - How Do I Deal With Trolls On My Facebook Page?   309
- Social Media Etiquette   311
- What NOT To Share On Social Media   314
- Do I Need A Business Newsletter?   316
- Starting Your Business Newsletter   319
- Does My Cake Business Need A Blog?   322

Chapter 10 – When You Really Need A Hug Of Understanding   327

- When Life Happens   328
- We're In This Together   331
- I've Lost My Mojo. Now What?   334
- Should I Quit My Business?   338
- Unsupported   347
- Confused In Cakeland – Parenting While In Business   349
- Family Time   351
- The Importance Of Self Care   353
- Who Is Riding In Your Sag Wagon?   356
- How To Avoid Making Mistakes In Your Business   359
- Don't Waste Good Chocolate   366

Chapter 11 – When You Need Some Tough Love   369

- Five Thousand Macarons   370
- Detours Not Roadblocks   373
- Feel The Fear And Do It Anyway   377
- Feeling Inadequate   381
- In It For The Love AND Money   385

- How To Be Stubborn   389
- The Stories You Tell Yourself   392
- You And Beyoncé   394
- Timing Is Everything... Or Is It?   397
- How To Lose Weight and Still Eat Chocolate   400
- Stop Multitasking   403
- Healthy, Wealthy and Wise Part 1 - Healthy   406
- Healthy, Wealthy and Wise Part 2 - Wealthy   410
- Healthy, Wealthy and Wise Part 3 - Wise   413

Conclusion   415

INTRODUCTION

I've always loved to cook and bake. From a very young age I was making strange creations for after school snacks, begging my Mum to buy box mixes for me to try and flicking through cookbooks for fun. That being said, it never really occurred to me to consider food as a career. I grew up in a culture that values food very highly as it's a central part of our customs and traditions. That same culture didn't value the profession of food though – my choices seemed to be limited to becoming a doctor, lawyer or accountant. As I grew up and realised the "doctor, lawyer, accountant" plan wasn't for me, I found myself more and more drawn to the idea of becoming a cake maker. I only started to pursue this once I was in my late twenties and already a mother to triplets (because that's the BEST time to decide on a career change, right? As though triplets wasn't enough of a challenge). Some friends got together and bought me a Wilton Level One Buttercream class as a birthday present. Each week I'd go along to class carrying my plastic toolkit and my heart was filled with anticipation and excitement about what I might learn that week. Frankly, I was also grateful for the break from the happy chaos of a trio of toddlers! Very quickly I learned that cake decorating was my happy place, and in addition to just loving the experience, I was pretty good at it. (Although now, looking at those early efforts, I'm not sure how good they really were but I was certainly proud of them!)

At that time, the online learning world was still new so my only option to progress my skills was books, some limited live classes, and culinary school. With my new found enthusiasm for cake decorating bordering on obsession, I pursued all three of those avenues at once. I learned to pipe freehand from several books, took short courses in all things cake, and applied to become a pastry chef. Looking back now, it all seems a bit mad really but at the time it just seemed like I'd found my calling in life. It did not take long for friends and family to encourage me to start a business, in part because they were supportive and in part because they needed cakes for their own celebrations and events.

Ultimately I finished two culinary degrees (I'm nothing if not thorough) and pursued a career as a pastry chef. My love of cake decorating never left me though, so while rolling hundreds of croissants at 3am was my "day job" by night I was still making custom cakes. As time went on, my skills improved and my dreams did, too. It was no longer enough to be a cake maker – I wanted to own a store front and make cakes full time. I pursued that with the same passion and obsession as I pursued my decorating skills – learning from books, taking business classes, creating endless spreadsheets and coming up with logo ideas. I did all of this while operating my business from home, in an unregistered kitchen, figuring things out as I needed to. Eventually I transitioned to part time pastry chef work and moved the business to a commercial kitchen, and then I let go of the chef work and operated the business full time from my dream store front.

Around that same time, thanks to myriad cake shows on TV, the cake industry exploded – suddenly I had a whole lot of competition, incredible sugar artists were getting notoriety globally, and my little cake business was booming. Not long after moving to my store front, my phone started to ring with people wanting to "pick my brain" for business advice. They too had taken a class or two, and they too had friends and family encouraging them to sell their creations. They were in the same place I had been many years earlier, only with the advantage of online learning for their cake skills. Where they struggled was with the business side of things. There might be a YouTube video for piping, but there wasn't one for dealing with irate clients or coping when the cake you're delivering falls over! These phone calls and coffee dates made me realise that there was an industry need for business information – so much like my obsessive pursuit of decorating, I started to get excited about helping the industry with the business side of things.

I developed a short, 3 hour class on "How to Start a Cake Business," and offered it locally. Four people came to that first class, but those four encouraged me enough to believe there was a need for these kinds of classes, so I kept going. Six people came to the next class. I kept teaching it and each time the numbers grew alongside my confidence that I was on the right track. Once I realised that there had to be a need for this information beyond my home city, I started the Business of Baking blog (http://thebizofbaking.com). I was shocked (and rather nervous) with how quickly the blog resonated with other cake makers, people who like me suddenly found themselves in a business they had no idea how to run. We knew all about cake (or could find a tutorial to help) but marketing, budgeting, pricing? Totally clueless. The blog grew into a 2 day business skills class (which still runs - http://bizbakeontour.com) , and today it continues to evolve into online classes, webinars, books and more.

In keeping with my original plans and aspirations, I became the cake maker I wanted to. I owned the dream store. I raised my family. I achieved a whole lot of things I wanted to achieve. Before opening my business I knew it was not going to be the "forever job," and that eventually I'd want to move on from cake to something else; I just had no idea what that "something else" would be. Every day I get emails from people all over the world, thanking me for my honesty, my guidance, my "no bullshit" attitude to cake, business and life, and every day I am grateful to those friends who bought me that basic buttercream class. Without all of that, I'm not sure I would have gotten to here – and right here is exactly where I am meant to be. I'm not able to adequately express just how honoured and grateful I am now to help guide, mentor and encourage the next generation of cake decorators who are pursuing their business dreams.

I still very much love the artistry of cake, the science of baking and I'm fascinated by the incredible leaps the cake decorating industry has taken in the creation of new tools and techniques. I'm incredibly proud to be surrounded each day by innovators, creators and artists. My life philosophy is, "All things are possible," and daily I see this in action in our industry. I hear of the cake decorators who run a business with the challenges of a young family, compromised health or limited resources. I see the cake decorators who make edible pieces which look nothing at all like edible items that push the boundaries of "edible" and "cake" with each new creation. Mostly, I witness the women who didn't think they were good at anything finding themselves able to support their families through the money they make via cake and in turn, inspiring another generation of women to do the same.

In this book, you'll find a selection of the articles I've written on the blog (for the full archive, visit *thebizofbaking.com*) as well as some new content. Each article was written with the intention to guide, motivate and inspire you to take steps towards that business dream which right now, might only live in your head.

All things are possible.

Sometimes, though, you need someone else to show you how to get it done.

With love, gratitude, and plenty of sweetness,

Michelle

April 2016

P.S. One last thing- while I was born and raised in the United States, I've lived in Australia for the last twenty years, so you might find some very Australian expressions scattered throughout this book. I considered changing them, but then to do so would change the flavour of things and that didn't seem quite right! **Once you know a recipe works, stick with it.**

BEFORE YOU BEGIN

The first three articles in this section pretty much explain:

1. why you should read what I have to say,
2. what the industry is like at the moment (a bit awesome and a bit crazy), and
3. a story about how we all got into this business.

All of these should sound familiar on some level – because while we all might have different artistic skills, our business paths often start out the same. We all start with passion and enthusiasm for our craft, which is exactly the best way to start most things in life – with tons of passion and enthusiasm.

The last article in this section is one that is so important that I reference it many times throughout this book. Therefore I decided it needs to go here at the front, just so you read it now. You may find that you need to come back to it several times before it fully sinks in.

And You Are ...?

If you're reading this book and you're a skeptical sort, you're probably wondering, "Yeah, but who the heck are YOU?", "What makes you think you know everything there is to know about running a cake business?" (and, in my mind, you have a slightly aggressive tone to your voice. Which of course is *ridiculous* because everyone knows that the people who are into cake are all sweetness and light ALL the time. Except of course when it's 7 pm, the party is at 7:15 pm, and you noticed that because of the humidity, all the wings have fallen off the sugar fairies you spent ALL WEEK making).

The fact is NOBODY knows everything there is to know about running a cake business - because each business is unique (and yes, we'll talk about how to figure out your point of difference.) If you've come here thinking you will find the get rich quick template to running a cake business, let me burst your bag of cornflour right now and tell you this isn't it.

However.

I've been running my own successful cake business for several years now. I've worked as both a chef and pastry chef in businesses ranging from small cafes to large catering companies. I've consulted with a number of small businesses on everything from starting up a pastry kitchen to making cookies for sale in a cafe. I started my business exactly how you did, right there on my kitchen table, shortly after some friends bought me a Wilton Level One Buttercream course for my birthday. One night I would come home from my (boring, but well paying) office job and be eating dinner and watching television next to my husband. The next night, I suddenly found myself with no time for dinner and 300 itty bitty flowers to make ... and I'd never made a single sugar flower in my entire life. Of course, how I came to find myself needing so many flowers and having no real clue how to do them ... yes, well, once again that's because I'm running a cake business and I didn't even know I was doing it.

I'm also a mother. A daughter. A friend. A wife. A woman who would never in a million years have called herself an entrepreneur (and please god, not that awful expression "mompreneur") but now I know that's exactly what I am. (I still feel weird about that word. Seriously, it seems like such a conceited word to describe who I am and what I do. I make cake. Maybe I should be called a cakepreneur? Yeah, NO.) I've managed to get this far running my business while being all of those things. Some days I'm awesome at it, some days I want to pull the blanket over my head and pretend that people can't see me. But - yes - I know a heck of a lot about running a cake business. And about being a decent mother, wife and friend while doing it. I also know a fair amount about giving great customer service. About taking it personally when someone says something not-so-nice about something I slaved over. About the things I wish someone had told me when I started out in business (I feel the same way about parenthood. Why did nobody warn me about smell? And the noise?)

So - I've got so much information to share with you, my brain feels like it's going to burst.

Before we take this friendship any further, though, here are two things you need to be aware of:

1. Nothing I say is a substitute for legal or financial advice from the people who went to school for a very long time to be able to give you legal and financial advice. Everything I say here comes from my education-based knowledge, my experiences in life and in business, my learning from other people, my living each day doing the same things I'm going to tell you to do. The fine print is this: it's worth paying the men in suits for actual legal and financial advice.

2. I'm American, but my business is based outside of the US., The things I'm going to talk about are important and will matter regardless of where your business is based. Occasionally I might reference local things or use local slang (because I write the same way as I speak) so if you don't understand,

ask me via email to clarify. However - no matter where you are in the world, cake is cake and customers are customers.

Okay, are you ready?

slides cake into preheated oven

Let's get this cake business party started!

* Q: What's a party without cake? A: Just a meeting. I became a cake maker so as to never have to attend a single meeting EVER again. I hate meetings. Boring places where people talk over each other, the catering is generally crappy and nothing gets achieved except the scheduling of more meetings.

A Typical Small Cookie Company Story

Today, I want to tell you all a story.

Recently two lovely women contacted me, asking if I would teach them a private cookie decorating class because they were keen to improve their skills. A few days before the class, one of them emailed me a four-page corporate style agenda (including names of attendees, location, duration of meeting, etc.) outlining what they wanted to learn from me. The agenda included items like, "provide a list of recommended wholesale suppliers," and "provide recommendations for fondant brands, " and so on. I'm not going to lie. I was seriously peeved. At the same time, I generally try not to judge people for what they do not know, so I wasn't going to be unprofessional about it. I contacted them to clarify that they had asked me to teach them how to decorate cookies, not give them the details of my business - so we would be concentrating on the cookies part. They understood that but also made it clear that they were coming to me specifically because they wanted to get into the business of selling cookies.

The showed up for their class, and as is my style, I asked them to tell me a little bit of their story - why were they asking me for business info, what excited them about making cookies, what were they hoping to go away learning, and so on. So it turns out their story is much like many of ours is. They are sisters, working in corporate jobs, mothering young children, and they learned to bake at their mother's knee. They've always wanted to work together, and both of them want to get out of the corporate world - they want more flexibility, more time with their kids, more time to have a life outside of their work. With the current popularity of all things baked, they thought now was a perfect time to get into business.

As we chatted, I asked them a little bit about the particulars of their business, as they live on opposite sides of the city to one another. They told me that they've already had a number of orders, have set up a Facebook page, have registered a business name with the appropriate government agency, and have approached several businesses asking them to carry their line of product. When I asked them where they were producing the cookies from, they said they were doing it from home - and when I asked if they had much trouble with registering their kitchens and homes as a food business, they gave me a blank look. "What does that mean, a registered kitchen?" they asked.

I went on to explain what a registered kitchen meant, and then went on to tell them they needed to be insured, they needed to have done the proper food handling qualifications, and so on. "But nobody ever gets sick from a cookie, surely!" they said, "I mean, really, it's just a cookie."

Yeah. It's just a cookie. Just like this is just a blog I write.

At this point, I could feel my heart sinking like a stone thrown into a bowl of still-warm ganache: it made a slow, painful, sticky descent as I realised that these two well-meaning women might have some idea of how to run a business, but no real idea how to run a *baking* business.

Like I said, I don't judge people for their lack of knowledge - and after all, in the beginning, I didn't know what a registered kitchen was, either. At the same time, my sinking heart was also about the fact that they didn't seem all that bothered by my assertion that they needed to do things properly.

I decided that perhaps (to save my battered soul) I should move onto the task at hand, which was teaching them how to decorate cookies. I asked if I could look at their work so far, to get a feel for their skills and what I could help them with. They showed me lots and lots of pictures on their phones ... of nice, beautiful cookies they had made. Cut out ones, stacked ones, ones with patterns - really just a whole lot of beautiful cookies with a bunch of different finishes on them.

Were they perfect? No.

Were they sellable? Yes.

Would they rival a lot of other cookies I've seen online, in terms of both design and apparent quality? Absolutely.

So I started to ask a bit more (I'm nosy, what can I say?) - I wanted to know about their skills, what they wanted to learn from me (from a decorating skill point of view) and where they wanted their product to end up in terms of looks and finish. Their answers pretty much left my heart in tattered shreds. They'd learned how to do it all via free tutorial videos they found on Google and YouTube. Neither of them had ever done a single class anywhere. Just played in their kitchen and watched (in their words) "a heck of a lot of YouTube videos." The best part? They'd only been doing it for about a month when I met them. Until they got to my kitchen, they had really only used fondant a half dozen times.

A month of watching videos.

A MONTH!

And yet ... they are in business. They don't have any idea about registered premises, insurance, or even much about the actual product they're going to sell ("You mean I can freeze cookie dough?" "How do I colour fondant?" "What's the best way to attach the icing to the cookie?") but make no mistake, these two perfectly nice women <u>are in business</u>. What's more, on some level they are my competitors. And they are coming to ME to teach them how to make their product and on some level, how to run a business in the first place. Let me be brutally honest here. After they left, I fell into a bit of a funk about it all and for several days afterwards I couldn't get their story out of my head. I let it roll around in my brain a fair bit. They were nice, polite, enthusiastic students. I had a good time teaching them. I really do hope they're going to be successful. So why on earth was I (and if I'm really honest, still am) upset about this?

Here's why - because I started like they did. I liked to bake and was pretty good at it, so I had in my head this dream of owning a cake business, which I then turned into a reality. It took me YEARS AND YEARS to do that though. Not a mere month of YouTube video watching. I researched the heck out of the industry (including the health regulations) so that when I started I was starting the best way I could, even if I was under charging. I went to school, formally and informally - not only to get my culinary degrees but also did lots of seminars on boring stuff like keeping correct tax records and marketing for dummies and how to package food properly.

These girls? *One month of YouTube and Google*.

Truth is, I've got no idea if they're going to be successful and I've got no way of predicting that, either. The only thing I know for certain is, this industry is FULL of people exactly like these two sisters. Their story is not unique at all.

I write this blog - and I started the whole idea behind the courses I teach - because I felt that the industry needed someone to stand up and say to these sorts of people: be enthusiastic, be creative, be passionate. Be all of that, but please ... BE SERIOUS about your business.

I started with the same dream these girls have - to leave my corporate job and have a life of flexibility and creativity. Why am I so heartbroken then, by these women who really want no more than what I wanted when I was at that stage?

Because they did not seem to appreciate that there is *a lot more* to starting a baking business than can be found in just one month of Googling and 3 hours spent with me learning to roll fondant.

The heart breaker is that convincing them - and people like them - of that is by far the hardest work I've ever done.

Just One Little Cake Please

You're the owner of a cake business ... only you never had any grand plans to be the next Cake Boss. It just sort of ... happened.

It went something like this.

Your friend saw a cake you made for your son's birthday. She was impressed (because she can't even figure out a box mix). She asked if you wouldn't mind making one for her daughter's birthday which is coming up in a few weeks. "I'll happily pay you for it", she said.

"Sure", you said. After all, making Lachlan's cake was quite fun and you enjoyed it (never mind that you were finding blobs of blue icing around the house several weeks later).

You made the prettiest, pinkest, sparkliest cake for her daughter. You were up until 2 am making sure it all looked as good as you could make it. You took it (and your son, a bag with a change of clothes for your son, sippy cups, wipes, water bottles, a spare sweatshirt and your very large handbag) to the party. You prayed the entire way there that the cake would stay in one piece and that the birthday girl would love it.

The cake remained perfectly intact, even when you went over those speed bumps in the car park of the play centre. The birthday girl loved it. She even squealed. What's more, her Mum loved it. The guests loved it. Everyone fawned over you. Right there, in that slightly stuffy, noisy, smells-like-toddler-feet, home of a thousand lost socks, sounds-like-a-war-zone play centre, you were a CAKE GODDESS.

You went home from the party.

You had some cash in your pocket that the birthday girl's Mum paid you.

You've got the voices of the party guests in your head saying how talented you are, how clever, how you can be making money off of this.

You are dreading going back to work on Monday morning, even though you know that without your job, you can't afford your living expenses.

The phone rings.

It's one of the guests from the party, gushing with praise and her voice just slightly hysterical. "Jane," she says, "I need a favour. I was going to bake Isbaella's cake for her party this week, but I've got no time, the oven is broken, my hair is a mess, Dylan threw up in the back of the minivan, there are lollies stuck in the couch and I just won't be able to do it. I know, I know, I'm the worst Mum in the whole WORLD but I've just got to get a cake for this party. I saw the cake you made for Jennifer. it was AMAZING. I just need one little cake. Please, please will you make one for me for Saturday?"

You can remember the feeling of being a goddess. It felt so good you could almost taste it ... and it tasted exactly like a bar of Lindt Special Milk Chocolate which you don't have to share with anyone else. In other words, almost intoxicating. You can feel the cash in your pocket. It's practically burning a hole through your jeans (which need replacing). (Good thing you've got that spare cash with which to go on a little shopping spree.)

You find yourself agreeing. "Sure, I can do that."

"Oh THANK YOU! I'll totally pay you for it, I promise. I'll call you with the details in a couple of days, right now Isabella can't decide between a 12 tier fairy castle and a 3D ballerina with fairy wings. Catch up soon. You're a lifesaver!"

Did you hear that? That was the sound of you opening a cake business ... and you didn't even realise you were doing it at the time.

Sorry? What did you say? You don't know anything about owning a cake business?

That's where The Business of Baking comes in.

I'm here to hold your hand through the process. To listen, encourage, help, and occasionally give you a dose of the not-so-sweet side of cake business ownership (because not every attempt at sweet art is a success, is it? Even I can claim some spectacular failures, and I like to think I'm pretty good at what I do). Through blog posts, videos, interviews with other successful cake business owners, and a little dash of humour, the Business of Baking blog is going to be your best-kept secret ingredient. It'll be like having a little business guide, right there in the cupboard behind the little bottle of pink food colouring. Nobody will know when you take a little nip of it now and again (unless you choose to share with them of course.)

The Final Cake Design

Have you ever designed a cake before you've worked out how to actually make it? Sat down with a client and sketched out a concept which looked great on paper but secretly you're wondering how the hell you're going to pull it off? Looked at a picture of a cake online and then worked out how to make it yourself?

In other words, have you ever noticed that the design you're trying to achieve actually <u>defines</u> how you will go about making it?

The same thing is true for your cake business.

Here's the big question I've got for you. ***What's the final design for your cake business?***

What I'm really asking you is, why are you doing this? And by "this" I mean, why are you in business for yourself? What result are you working towards?

Are you in business because...

- You simply love making cake (and you're good at it)?
- You need a job with flexible hours?
- Your friends told you to?
- You wanted to be your own boss?
- You need to make some money while you are on maternity leave?
- You just want to make some extra pocket money?
- It seemed like a good idea at the time?
- It's way more fun than your day job?
- You want to leave this business to your kids?

Believe me, when I say, working out WHY you are in business is the single most important business decision you will ever make. Even more important than the decision to go into business in the first place. More important than your business name, the oven you buy, the people you hire, the ads you write and where you place them.

Working out the final design of your cake business is like the proverbial pebble thrown into the pond. It affects *every single business decision you will make from here on in*. The WHY needs to be way, way, WAY bigger than "because I love making cake. " Remember that cake you designed? You need to know the bigger picture of what this thing looks like in order to work out the internal structure.

Let me give you a real-life example of how knowing the end result defines the game plan.

Business Owner A's reason for being in business is that she just wants to earn enough money to allow her to afford extras for her kids, like ballet lessons. For her, it's only a little bit about the money and the flexibility. She really does not want to work full time and does not need to earn a fortune.

Business Owner B's reason for being in business is that she wants to create a full-time job for herself and she intends that this will be a family business she will pass onto one of her kids. For her, it's about the money and the longer-term legacy. She needs to earn a full time living from this.

Business Owner C's reason for being in business is to be the biggest cake business in her country. She wants to franchise her business, make a heck of a lot of money, and also develop an international reputation. She wants to give Marina Sousa AND Ann Heap AND Sylvia Weinstock a run for their money. For her, it's much more about the money and the fame than it is about the cake per se.

These three business owners are given an opportunity to advertise themselves in a major national newspaper, for a really good (but very high) price. The PR value is huge, the exposure is huge, and the opportunity will not come around again. Knowing what they know about why they are in business, should ANY of these business owners take up the offer?

Owner A - No. She's a local, part-time cake maker. She can't handle and does not want that kind of publicity or potential volume of business. Sure, it would stroke her ego but also is not in line with what her ultimate aim is. If she got the same offer from a small, local paper ... she'd take it.

Owner B - Maybe. She wants to run a medium-sized business. This would be great for her exposure and to put in her file of press clippings. She'd only take up the offer if her advertising budget had some money in it to spare and even then maybe not. If she got the same offer from a metropolitan newspaper in her city, she'd take it.

Owner C - Absolutely she takes the offer, AND she develops a relationship with the journalist writing the article. She gets some advice from a PR person on how to make this article work for her into the future. She takes out some additional, ongoing advertising with the newspaper. Her end cake business design is way bigger and so national exposure is exactly what she NEEDS if she is going to reach that goal. She absolutely takes up the offer.

See what I mean? Knowing where you are going helps you make the decisions you will face along the way. If none of these cake makers knew where they were headed, they might all take the offer - which would be a pretty big financial mistake for at least Owner A, and probably a waste of money for Owner B and a lucky break for Owner C.

It boils down to this: knowing your end <u>purpose</u> makes all the decision making much easier along the way. I am not talking about if this is going to be a shop or if it's not. I'm not talking about cake versus macaroons. I'm talking about the BIGGEST of all big picture decisions you need to make. WHY are you actually IN BUSINESS? For the purposes of this decision, I don't care if it's cake or widgets you are selling. It's irrelevant.

I want you to work out the bigger picture of your cake business. Not the pretty logo, not the menu of cupcake flavours, not the debate over a retail business or a bespoke cake company. WHY are you in business, truly? What's your final cake business design? What the heck is all this effort for?

Write it out. Seeing it 'on paper' makes it very, very real and makes you very accountable. Go on. Be brave. Dream big.

CHAPTER 1
GETTING STARTED IN BUSINESS

The beginning part of starting a business (cake or otherwise) is the most fun part. You're picking out a name, designing a logo, getting business cards printed and you are filled with hope and promise. The realities of running a business have not quite set in yet - the long hours, expenses and handling difficult customer situations ven't yet become routine. So often I see small business coaches who shout about the joys of running your own business, about the "freedom lifestyle" and they make it all sound like rainbows and sparkles. Truth is, I love running my own business – but it's not for everyone, and I think better to be a bit (painfully) honest about it upfront. This chapter is all about harnessing that enthusiasm with a pinch of reality thrown in – don't lose your passion, just remember that we're going to be in this long after that first batch of business cards runs out! A lot of the articles in this chapter are the things I wish I'd known about earlier in my business career.

Don't Run A Baking Business If You Don't Want To

At a recent cake show in Sydney, I had the immense honour of speaking to over 600 people about two topics: how to create a marketing plan for your business, and the top six things I get asked most often about pricing. At the start of each presentation, I asked for a show of hands: how many people owned a baking business? In any given group of 100 people, about 8-10 raised their hands. I then asked, how many of you WISH you owned a baking business, or intend to start one? Not surprisingly, the remaining 90 people in the room raised their hands. So roughly, over the course of 3 days, in a relatively small city in a far-away country, I met 560 people who wanted to start a baking business.

FIVE HUNDRED AND SIXTY PEOPLE.

Here's the scary part: relatively speaking, I had a very small sample size I was looking at. Compound that sample size globally, and ... whoah. That's A LOT of people wanting to get into this industry, or who already have one toe dipped in the ganache.

Here's the thing about that experience I found most interesting - that all these wonderful people felt that they had to attempt to be in business AT ALL. What about the current global culture is out there telling us that we can't just enjoy something for the sake of enjoying it, we've got to make money out of it? We live in a time where 20 year olds can become billionaires, it's easier than ever to get into business, and there are thousands of people out there making thousands of dollars without having ever worked a "9 to 5" job. So I wonder if we all feel as though what we do has no value unless it's earning us a buck. Spend an hour or ten browsing a website like *Etsy* and you'll see literally thousands of talented artists who now find themselves as business owners. Is there anything wrong with selling your talents? No. Of course not. But why do so many people feel like they HAVE to sell their talents?

Why are the artists of the world feeling as though they cannot just be ... artists?

At the show, I also met an intensely talented cake decorator (who was there as a presenter, so you know she's pretty damn fantastic) who told me that when she saw me in the line up of people presenting, she planned to AVOID ME LIKE THE PLAGUE. Why? Because (in her words) she's no good at the business side of things, she's terrible at pricing, doesn't keep up with her paperwork (etc. etc.) and she thought if she met me, I'd be all scary and business-y and I'd call her on her business failings. (Note: I'm not scary but I did kinda call her on her lack of proper pricing.) I met this warm, gorgeous, generous, hugely talented woman and

I thought ... there's someone who is working so hard at being something she's not, and feeling bad enough about it that she's actively trying to avoid me. What the ...?

The people I've met who go into business (and not just baking businesses) generally do so because they've got a business mind. They don't necessarily have a baking mind, a creative mind, or a desperate burning desire to be decorators or macaron makers. They have an entrepreneurial mind, and that's an entirely different kind of person. They're the people who had lemonade stands as kids, or who sold candy on the school bus to other kids at inflated prices, or who just seem to "get it" about the business world and who could probably sell just about anything to anybody. The creative people I've met who go into business and are successful generally hire people who have a business mind to do that part of it for them. It's why singers, actors, comedians, etc. all have business managers! Because they're great at being singers, actors, comedians ... not great at running a business.

There seems to be some sort of shame in admitting that though - like you're somehow not allowed to just make a cake (or sing a song) for someone and when they say, "Hey, that's amazing, you should sell those!" you can't say, "No, I just love doing it. I'm not interesting in selling them." It's as though we're all under this intense pressure to sell our creative souls ... even when in our heart of hearts, we don't really want to or we just don't have the skills to.

There is no shame in being - and remaining - a hobbyist baker or decorator. *Even if you're a total kick-ass baker or decorator.*

I'm going to give you permission right here and now to NOT go into business if you aren't business minded and are not interested in becoming business-minded.

Permission to enjoy being a baker without having to sell a single cookie unless it's for the Girl Scouts.

Permission to buy new decorating toys, a fancy new mixer, or attend a cake class just for the joy you're going to get out of it, not because you need to keep the receipt and claim it later.

Permission to accept that you might be really, really great at making cake, but that doesn't mean you're good at the business of making cake.

Permission to not actually care what people in cake forums have to say about your creations.

Permission to make a cake with Hershey's Kisses on it for your daughter JUST because it's fun and she asked you to.

Permission to say to your well-meaning neighbour, "I love making these, I just have no desire to do them as a business, " and NOT feel bad or guilty about that.

Permission to not compare your work to the work of the professionals.

Permission to learn, learn, learn, learn and improve, improve, improve, improve. . . with no pressure to charge less while you're going through that process.

Permission to not worry if your prices are too low or too high.

Permission to stop feeling like baking and decorating have become competitive sports (leave that for the reality TV shows please.)

Permission to understand (because I can attest to this) that when you run your hobby as a business, there are parts of it which will become seriously UNFUN just because it's a business.

Permission to *remain a hobbyist*.

Before You Open A Business

A number of people who read this blog started their business organically, ending up in business before they realised they were in business. I actually started this blog by writing about how we all got into this sweet mess in the first place. Today's post is actually for those of you are not yet in business but are thinking and dreaming about it while working a traditional day job. It's also for those of you who are in business without wanting to acknowledge that you're in business - the ones who are taking money for their creations but not really admitting to themselves that it's a business. (I know you're out there. I'm not judging you, I promise.)

I think there are a couple of things you need to do before jumping head first into the swiss meringue buttercream. Small businesses (and all businesses start out small) are risky on a few different levels, especially in the current global economic climate. So before signing the lease or applying for the small business loan, there are a few things I think you should do. I'm not talking about figuring out what equipment you need or finding some money to invest, I'm talking about the bigger picture things you need to do.

In no particular order, before you start your business I think you should:

- **Do Some Research**: Find other people who own small businesses (and it doesn't need to be in this industry) and offer to buy them a coffee and slice of cake. Sit them down and ask them to be brutally honest about what it's like to be your own boss. Most of the people I meet have a very idealised, romantic notion about owning a small business, all about a flexible lifestyle and choosing their own hours and making way more money than anyone would pay them. I'd just simply ASK people who already own a small business to tell you what it's really like. Some of them will paint a rosy picture, others will not - but you should at least start to get an idea of what the reality is like. I'd also tell them outright, "I'm thinking about going into business for myself but I don't have any real idea of what it's like on a day to day level", so they know why you are asking and they do not feel threatened.

- **Call a Family Meeting**: even if the "family" is just you and your partner, or you and your parents. This is a thing which inevitably is going to become bigger than just you. You're going to need these people to support and love you, and if they are in your inner circle, it's important that they know what you're planning. They don't have to approve of it per se, but they should at least be aware - you know, so they forgive you when you fall asleep face first into the mashed potatoes because you were up till 3am wiring 600 gumpaste roses.

The scaffolding of our lives is often made up of our family in the first instance, so they deserve to know what they're going to be holding up.

- **Do the Math**: Small business has a way of creeping into our personal finances whether we like it or not. So ... your commercial kitchen rent gets paid by your personal tax return refund (full confession: that's how I paid my rent the second month I was in business) or you throw a few extra sticks of butter in the cart with your family's weekly grocery shop. If your family is relying entirely on your income to cover the cost of daycare or the groceries all get paid from your paycheck and you have no savings - maybe right now isn't the best time to go into it. You may never have a 'best time' financially to take the leap, but I'd suggest at the very least you want to be honest with yourself about it. Do you have any savings? Do you have family or friends who you might be able to rely on if you end up in a mess? Do you have assets? How will your family survive if you cannot bring home regular profit for 3, 6 or 9 months? Exactly how much money do you need to earn to replace what you're currently bringing home?

  Money is what makes or breaks a business, even if we don't like to talk about it (certainly not as fun as talking about perfecting those wafer paper flowers.) BEFORE you go into business is a better time to have a cold hard look at the numbers than when you're in the middle of it and can't pay yourself a dime (because you already owe those dimes to a supplier.)

- **Remember You Can Choose Differently**: I wrote a post about it being okay to be a hobbyist and I stand by that post. Just because everyone around you is saying, "You should SO sell these! You'd make a fortune!" this does not mean you have to actually go into business. You can choose to enjoy your craft and just keep it a craft. My Dad once told me, "Everyone is potentially smart enough to go into business for themselves, but not everyone should, " and he was right. (By the way his next line was, "some people just don't have the balls for it, " and he was right on that front, too. Clever guy, my Dad.)

  All I'm saying is, if you've done your research and thought that being your own boss just didn't seem as appealing as you thought it would - don't feel pressured to do it. It's really okay to choose not to. Similarly, if you've already gone down the road a ways, you can actually choose to stop. You can choose to wind it back, close it down or decide to no longer be in business. I would NOT suggest you do this weekly or monthly (as some businesses seem to ...) but I'd seriously consider not going into full-steam-ahead business mode unless you really, truly want that life.

And lastly ... (and yes, you've heard me say this before):

- **Start Figuring Out the Why**: If you're considering opening a small business or legitimising the one you've already got, spend some time working out why you want to do it[1]. It's not just about the money and it most certainly isn't just because you love making things. It's about so much more than that (bbbbbiiiiiiigggggggg picture, right?) but knowing why you're doing it in the first place is what's going to keep you through the long nights, the lack of funds, and will keep you from punching in the face your well-meaning Aunt Mildred who says, "Oh you make a few cakes, dear! How ... quaint. "You may not have a definitive answer (it takes a while), but spend a bit of time thinking about it. Hint: If you struggle to get your answer beyond "I really just like making cake", then you probably aren't being very honest with yourself about what being a small business owner is actually about.

When my triplets were small, a nurse gave me the advice, "You've got to start as you mean to go on," meaning that I'd be better off putting in place systems and values that I wanted to develop in my house and my kids as they grew right from the very start. The same is true of business - start it as you mean to go on with it. That's not to say you can't catch up or change things in the future, but if you're in the position of contemplating starting or only just getting going, you'd be wise to do the above things so that you're starting from a solid base.

---

1   See *The Final Cake Design* in the *Before You Begin* section.

Ten Things You Need To Spend <u>Real</u> Money On In Order to Succeed In The Baking Business:

(Not in order of importance. They're ALL important.)

(And all of this assumes you want to own a real business which makes actual money.)

1. **A decent website**. (not to be confused with a Facebook page. They are not the same thing.) In this day and age, you have no excuse to not have an online presence, even if the website is a single page with a montage of gorgeous photos of your product and details on how to get in touch with you. Your customers might all be online, but they're not all on Facebook.

2. **Insurance**. For your business and its premises, yourself, your clients. You do not want to be caught without it. Spend real money on it, get things well covered, then hope like hell you never need to use it.

3. **Financial advice and/or support**. I've said this before, I'll say it again: numbers do not lie (the jerks. If they would it *might* make me feel better some months.) You *must* have the numbers right if you are going to survive in the long term and there are people who are better and smarter at this than you are. Hire them or engage their services.

4. **Legal advice and/or support**. Like insurance, you never want to have to use these guys, but you never want to be caught without them, either. Free legal advice is not free if it's crap.

5. **Education**. I don't just mean courses in how to make amazingly awesome cakes. I mean business courses, webinars, e-books, business coaches, whatever. You cannot afford to stop learning how to operate in the business arena and this is true for you *most* importantly in your role as business owner.

6. **Staff**. Pay bananas, you get monkeys. If you are successful enough to need people to help you, invest time and money in them as best you can. Loyal, capable staff can make a good business into a great one. The same is true if YOU are the only employee you've got (see #5 above.)

7. **Equipment**. Just don't be stupid about it[2].

---

2   See *Well Equipped* in Chapter 3.

8. **Advertising** - and not just via social media. You might make the BEST*insert product here* but if *nobody knows* your product exists, you're wasting your time. Word of mouth is wonderful but there are very few businesses who can rely entirely on that one method of generating business. Think long and hard about this one (and where to spend the money) but if your final cake design[3] is bigger than just a few cakes a week, you've got to advertise somewhere eventually.

9. **Irritating but necessary fees** - registering your kitchen with local council, registering your business name in your state or elsewhere, securing your domain name, registering for taxes, the relevant licences needed to serve food and so on. Don't get cheap when it comes to the "boring but important[4]" stuff which makes you able to operate legally.

10. **Business cards** - this one is simple and old school but wonderfully effective and is part of your advertising as a whole. Those cards are for the people who you meet when you're out and about, clients who want to refer you to a friend, local school notice boards ... business cards are a really, really useful (and fairly inexpensive) way of getting your business known beyond it's four walls. Invest in getting some decent quality ones, and in having them professionally designed (no, Vista Print's free templates will not cut it.) This might count under the banner of advertising, but I've kept it separate because it applies to every size of business, from micro to massive.

There are plenty of places in business where you can afford to scrimp a few pennies, use less expensive options until you can afford better, utilise free resources and (especially in the beginning) make use of standard available items. The above do NOT fall into that category - use the money wisely in those places, but USE THE MONEY. You can start a business virtually for free, but if it's to have any future at all you're going to need to spend some money on it.

The gist is this: you will have to spend money (whatever little you've got) at some point - the above is to help you work out where to invest it best.

---

3   See *The Final Cake Design* in the *Before You Begin* section.
4   See *Boring But Important* in Chapter 3.

You Make Awesome Cake. And. Now. What?

Now all your friends have got that bug in your ear about how you are going to make thousands ... no ... millions by selling your sweet creations. You can't stop thinking about it. While your toddler naps, you're Googling cake companies in your city to figure out who your competition is. While you're out shopping, you're scribbling ideas down on the back of the wrinkled receipts in the bottom of your handbag. You're doodling potential business names in the margins of your notepad while you're meant to be listening to your boss talk about whatever bosses talk about. You're typing "www.awesomebusinessnameidea.com" into your browser to see if anyone else has thought of it. In short, you've already designed your ideal business and all of it exists right there in your head.

You can even see the packaging, can't you? (It's probably pink.) (And it has a cool graphic which looks a bit retro.)

The thing about awesome cake is, if you're not actually selling it, you're not making any money. It's pretty simple.

NO sales = NO business

This post is not about how to make sales, it's about knowing what you sell. Why? Because no sales is a big problem, but not knowing what you sell is an even bigger issue. Everyone's telling you that you are awesome at cakes, but that means nothing unless you can actually sell it. There are a number of ways you can do this, but ultimately the way you go about selling it will depend on your product and your target market.

Wait a sec. I need a product? I make awesome cupcakes. Isn't that my product?

Well, sure. In theory, that's your product.

But you and everyone else makes cupcakes, or have you been living under a massive rock for these past few years? (In this example, you can substitute 'cupcakes' for 'macarons' if you like ...) We're going to talk about developing your unique selling point and working out your target market a but later, but for now - you've actually got to work out what it is you DO. You're supposedly going to be a mogul cake seller, but all you've got is, "I'm going to sell cupcakes!"

Yeah.

That's not a great business model.

Think about it for a minute.

- Do you want a cupcake business that has a retail shop front?

- Are your cupcakes only going to be available at markets?

- Will you sell anything other than cupcakes?

- Are you planning on having a cake business that only bakes to order?

- Have you always wanted to own a cafe that sells cakes?

- Are you going to be a company that makes cakes for the corporate market?

- Are you a custom cookie company?

- Are you going to sell wholesale only?

- Are you a company that will sell mini cakes to cafes?

- Are you really great at baking French pastries?

- Do you love making muffins?

- Are you really just wanting to make a bit of money on the side selling to friends? (By the way, this is totally okay if this is the case.)

- Are you wanting to sell Mexican cookies? Danish tarts? Vegemite scrolls?

- Are you a mixture of all of these things?

In short - _what business are you in, exactly_?

Unless you've got a clear idea of the type of business you want and the product you are going to sell, you can't go any further. Do not pass GO, do not collect two hundred dollars. Without more thinking, right now all you have are friends who think you make great cake but don't want to pay for it, and a desperate desire to leave your day job.

So.

While in your head you've got an idea about adorable packaging, cute aprons and business cards cut into the shape of a piping bag, you really need to have an idea more about the type of business. Sit down and do some planning about this business of yours. Dream. Dream BIG. Dream in DETAIL. This fantasy business of yours isn't set in stone. Things will change. The business will evolve. YOU will evolve. But for right now all I want you to do is **answer this ONE question: WHAT BUSINESS AM I IN? (or do I want to be in?)** Be as specific as you like - hey, this is *your* baby and it can be whatever you like.

You've got to do this step. It's a hard one to do. We're all afraid of admitting out loud what it is we want to do when we grow up and here I am asking you to do exactly that. We are all afraid to take our dreams and commit them to paper. It's scary to admit that you want something different for your life. Writing it down is like a confessional almost (minus the stuffy little room and the guy in the suit.) Trust me when I say, you will not regret the time you took to figure out what you're going to build. To put this in cake terms: it's a lot easier to make a cake when you've got a recipe to work from. It's a lot harder when you're looking at a pile of eggs and flour and trying to guess what you're baking that day.

Write a recipe for your business. This recipe will act as the building block to every single decision you make from here on out. This is not about a formal business plan (but eventually, you'll need one of those.) This is about thinking, and thinking hard - about where this is going to lead you. Here's the really amazing thing about this process. Once you start putting pen to paper, you'll find that the ideas will come. Sure, the doubts and questions will come to - but the creative juices will get going and I think you'll suddenly find you've got an entire HEAD full of ideas just waiting to come out. Some of you will do this and realise that the baking business isn't what you want at all. . . the business which is in your head is actually a cafe, or a flower shop, or a coaching business. Do some soul searching.

The best part about this whole exercise? It continues to have value for you every single step of the way. When I am faced with a business decision (to expand into a new product, when I'm considering a new angle for promotion, thinking about adding another service to my business) I always first ask myself, "What business am I in?" Over time the answer has been modified, expanded, and become different to what I started out with - but that I can answer the question, succinctly and immediately, every single time - that is what drives every business decision I make. It's not the only driver, but it's certainly a major factor of how I make decisions.

Have you ever wandered into a shop that sells a certain product, but they also just sell something which seems totally unrelated and thought to yourself, "What the heck is a X business doing selling Y?" Or you've met someone and asked them what they do and they say, "Oh, I'm in IT and I also sell model trains, plus sometimes I waitress, and I'm also re-training in water therapy, and on the weekends, I sell heirloom tomatoes at farmer's markets." It's the sign of a desperate business owner - or desperate person - who behaves like that. Without an idea of WHAT it is you want to do, effective decision making becomes very difficult. We're also going to talk about WHY we do what we do (which is another major part of how I make decisions), but in the meantime let me leave you with a story.

A few months ago I went to a networking event (I hate them. Truly. But sometimes there are parts of business ownership which fall under the "boring but important" category and networking for me is like that.) Anyway, this nice woman came up to me and asked me what I do. When she found out I make cakes, she said, "Oh! My partner and I own a restaurant and function venue! Maybe you can provide us with some celebration cakes when we have events?"

Sounds great, right? I could get an entirely new place to sell cakes too, and they already do several functions a month. It almost made me think that standing there in uncomfortable shoes and eating mediocre canapes was going to be worth it.

"Let me give you our brochure, " said this lady, "and we can catch up in a few days." She dug around in her handbag for a minute and produced one of those glossy oversized postcards. She took a minute or so to tell me a bit about the venue, which sounded pretty nice. I was enthusiastic and made all the right noises about the venue.

In almost the same breath, she says to me, "And on the back is all the info you need to know about my miracle anti-aging cream! It's fabulous stuff! It will truly transform your life, it erases lines, it's like the poor woman's Botox, it's just ah-may-zing and ... blah blah blah." I must have given her the "What the ... ?" look because she then said, "Oh, you know, I've got my fingers in a lot of pies. I got the anti-aging stuff printed on the back of the venue postcard because it saves money to do it that way."

Exactly what business is SHE in, I wonder? She didn't seem so sure.

Just quietly, I don't want any anti-aging cream anywhere near my creations.

How To Name Your Cake Business

So you've done all the baking and decorating classes, you've Googled "how to set up a cake business" about a million times, you've started to take better pictures of the cakes you're making and you're daydreaming about walking into your boss's office and yelling, "you can take this crappy job and shove it!" You might have even researched what the cottage laws are in your state or what your local Council needs for you to get registered. You're starting to maybe, kinda, perhaps, aaallllmmmoooosssttt think you would like to open a baking business.

First things first, what the heck are you going to name this new business of yours?

I follow hundreds of cake businesses on social media, and over the years, I've looked at hundreds of cake company websites. I love reading the "about us" page or the reasons why people have called their companies what they've called them and I must admit there are several which have made me shake my head and wonder what they were thinking. Your business name is part of your branding and part of how you communicate to your clients, so it's pretty important to get it right.

Here are a few Do's and Don'ts when it comes to naming your bakery or cake business:

DO:

- Research what names are already being used, especially in your local area. You really don't want customers to get confused with the other companies whose names are close to yours (and unscrupulous people will happily take advantage of that confusion!)

- Think about the story behind the name. Childhood nicknames, names of the city you grew up, the names of your pets, something to do with your hobbies - all of these are great sources of inspiration for your business name and can make it memorable to customers. If you've got a good (and short) story attached to your business name, potential customers are much more likely to remember it.

- Consider the option of using your own name, but only if you customise it in some way AND you're planning on being the face of your business from here on in. There are probably a lot of "Cakes by Jane" out there so a variation on your name would be a better choice: "Cakes by Jane Smith", "Cakes by Janey" or "Jane's Creations". If you intend to sell your business, I would strongly recommend against using your own name as your business name. Also, don't use your own name unless you are happy being the face of it. In the cake industry it can be very hard to sell a business called "Sarah's Sweets" if Sarah no longer owns the place and she's the one who invented the signature style. Can you imagine anyone owning Ron Ben Israel cakes OTHER than Ron Ben Israel?

- Check the online availability of that name ahead of time, both with the correct authorities and on the internet. BEFORE you settle on a business name, check if you can use it and that it's available on various platforms. It's no fun to have to add random, different stuff to the end of your business name because someone got there before you. If nothing else, it causes confusion. If you really want it, come up with a short version which you use for online accounts (e.g. the one for Business of Baking is 'bizbake'.)

- Consider names which can spawn other names – e.g. products or ideas which can be named in the same vein. Suppose your company is called 'Sweet Pops Bakery' - you might have bigger products called "Daddy Pops" and kid-sized ones called "Baby Pops" and so on (that's a super dorky example but you get my point.)

- Be witty or fun or clever, but not so much that it makes people think, "What the ...?" If you're the only one that gets the joke, it's not that great of a joke.

- Road test the name - there might better variations you have not thought of, or the name gives an impression you didn't realise it would ('Fat Lady Cakes' might sound cute to you and conjure up images of Mrs Claus baking gingerbread men, but someone else might get an entirely different image to mind.)

DON'T:

- Come up with random spellings that nobody will remember – "Kupkakez" "Kakes" "Bakez" "Phat Cakery" "Swee-Tee" "Mackeyroons" "Bake-a-rhee" and the rest of that ridiculous spelling stuff: NO. Just NO. It's hard to remember (and, therefore, hard to find) and you'll forever be spelling it to people and explaining the spelling. (Do I really need to say it ...? Ain't nobody got time for dat!)

- Put specific products in the name if you make or plan to make more than that one thing. "Jennifer's Cakepops" isn't going to get many requests for chocolate covered Oreos or cake decorating classes because the name is too specific to a single kind of product. Plus, bakery items are very trendy so your great idea for a "the awesome whoopie pie company" name might not be the best idea two years from now. Think ahead a little bit.

- Use overly common words for the whole name. Using 'sweet' or 'love' or 'cake' and words like that are okay, but if your entire business name is a string of common bakery words, you're going to get confused with too many other companies and nothing about it will be memorable.

- False advertise - don't call yourself vegan, gourmet, organic or couture if that's not your thing or that's not your style.

- Use words which, when read quickly, can be confused with other words (especially inappropriate words) ... which brings me too ...

- Don't use inappropriate words. I'm all for funny or witty names, but "B*&tch; Cakes" or "Kiss my Sweet A$$ Cupcakes" is ... NO. Just ... NO. Don't alienate people before you've even started.

Picking a name for your cake business idea is a really important step because it sets the tone for all the things which come after that. In short, just remember that there are a lot of companies in this industry at the moment and a lot of very similar sounding names. Your aim is to be memorable and descriptive without having to resort to crazy tactics like calling yourself the "Komplete-lee Fhantahstic Kahke Khompanee. "

The Dog Ate My Figurine

A question I get asked fairly often is, "Do I need a registered kitchen to run my cake business?"

Depending on where you are in the world, your mileage may vary a bit, but the short answer is: **YES**. If you're exchanging money for goods, you must be operating from registered premises. No ifs, ands, or buts about it.

When I started out running a cake business (that I didn't know I was running), I did everything in my home kitchen. Baking, mixing, making icing, decorating, making itty bitty decorative things, cutting out edible images, filling piping bags, packaging biscuits. Absolutely everything happened from my home kitchen. (Okay, that's a lie. I generally made itty bitty decorative things while sitting in front of the TV, which was in the lounge room.) At that time we didn't have a dog[5], none of us smoked[6], and our toddlers were small enough that I could put them in a playroom and they wouldn't get their grubby little hands into the boxes of sprinkles. I figured with all of that, I was pretty much good to go. It didn't even really occur to me at that time that I needed to do anything special about the kitchen itself. I made cake, I washed my hands after I peed, that was enough, right?

WRONG. Not only wrong to be doing that, but potentially a very expensive mistake to make. I eventually learned that I needed to be operating from a registered kitchen and that I needed to have a food handler's certificate. I also learned that while it is technically possible to register a home kitchen (and many a baker has done so), the local council you are in holds all the cards. I've had people tell me that the inspector came in, wandered around a bit, said, 'Yep, that's fine," and handed them the permit to sign. I've had other people tell me they had 3 inspections, spend $10, 000 installing extra sinks, taps and fridges only to be told there was no way in hell they would be granted a permit (and even hell needed an extra hand washing sink before that would get approved.)

Registering a home kitchen is a great idea but not always easy to do. Registering a kitchen (home or otherwise) can be expensive and time-consuming. Being sued by a client because they got sick from your cake (or just didn't like it) can be even more expensive and time-consuming - and you don't want to know what happens if they sue you and it comes to light that you were operating illegally. Putting your

---

5   We have a dog now. He's fabulous, but given half a chance he'd eat cake bits. I know because I've seen him do it. He once ate a red sugar rose that I brought home for one of my daughters. It eventually required that we have TWO ROOMS of carpet replaced. Expensive lesson, that.

6   We still don't. ☺

business "out there" in the wide world (also known as Facebook) while operating from an unregistered premises - now that's just plain stupid. You might as well hold up a sign which says, "I'm selling cakes from an illegal kitchen! Come! Order cake so I can pay my legal fees!"

It can be a pretty big stumbling block when you don't know if the business is going to take off, you don't have regular orders, you have less than zero money to start this business off with, and you're still at the stage of making $50 cash-only cakes for friends. Doing everything on your kitchen table is easy, convenient, and (seems) inexpensive. It makes perfect sense for most cake companies to start out that way and it's because of the nature of them (you started with making your son's cake ...) that it's where they mostly begin. It also makes sense to keep your overheads as low as is possible, but for cake companies who intend on becoming something more than a hobby, this is just not a tenable situation.

So what do you do when you're broke but you need a registered kitchen in order to take it to the next level, and your local Council are being pains in the proverbial about it?

One word: Research. A LOT of research.

How to find registered kitchen options:

- Make the call to your local council. You just might get lucky and it's easier than you think.
- Ask your council if THEY know of any kitchens for hire in their municipality
- Call local churches or other religious organisations with kitchens in their hall
- Call local sporting clubs who may have their own space at local sport arenas
- Offer to share kitchen space with friends who also have start-up food businesses (and this might be their home kitchen if they have a nicer Council than you do)
- Find out about incubator kitchens or rent-by-the-hour kitchens
- Think about some kitchens which may not be used at night (retirement homes, clubs)
- Simply googling "commercial kitchen for rent" and see what comes up
- Call local schools who do not use their cafeteria kitchens on weekends
- Share kitchen space with food businesses that does not operate 24/7
- Get the word out there. Facebook, tweet, ask friends - often it's not what

you know, it's who you know!

- Try local culinary schools, they might have teaching kitchens available or know someone with a kitchen
- Go around to local cafes and restaurants (a lot of CBD places only operate a breakfast and lunch service)
- Catering companies often have available kitchen time as they don't operate 24/7

What not to do when looking for a registered kitchen:

- Give up. This process might take a hell of a lot longer than you think and it can be immensely frustrating.

The point is, there ARE kitchens out there which will keep you and your customers safe and not cost you the earth. Yes, it's less convenient than doing it from home, but if you're serious about this business, there is just no excuse for not finding yourself proper premises to work from. Your first kitchen won't be perfect. It won't have all the bells and whistles. It might still require you to pack up your stuff in the car every time you need to bake, but <u>it's worth doing if your business is worth doing in the first place</u>.

Yes, I'm here admitting that I too operated illegally for a very short while. Once I had clients who were not in my immediate circle of friends or friends of my immediate circle, I found a kitchen. Why? Because it was an investment I had to make if I was ever going to get the business going in any real sense (and my Council were shmucks.)

I know you're reading this thinking, "Yeah right, nobody ever checks on these things, I'm sure I'll be fine, everybody does it, it's just cake and I always wash my hands."

Tell me this: after all you've invested so far in time, money, emotional energy … is getting caught really worth it?

<u>Note:</u> *Several people have written to me since this article was published to say that their local municipality does not require registration of any kind. That's fine if that's the case, however please make it a priority to check that AND get it in writing.*

Elephant Bites

I tend to get very overwhelmed by all the stuff I think I have to do and my perceived lack of progress. A business coach who witnessed this behaviour once asked me, "How do you eat an elephant?" ... and me, in my extremely annoyed and frustrated state, rolled my eyes and bitchily said, "I don't freakin' know!" to which he replied, "ONE BITE AT A TIME. "

After last week's post, you might have decided that what you want is a shop (or business in general). You REALLY want it. If you close your eyes, you can see it. The gleaming counters. The cute aprons the staff wear. The sound the bell makes when the door opens. The shabby chic cake stands which display your wares. The wicker baskets which hold the loaves of still-warm artisan bread. The adorable cake forks. But ... the timing or the money isn't right at the moment. So how do you head in the direction of the dream shop if you don't feel quite ready to take the leap *just now*?

Or - how do you get started on your home business, if right now you are a hobbyist? It all just seems so overwhelming, doesn't it?

Simple. You eat one bite of elephant at a time. I am by nature a pretty cautious person. I've taken a whole lot of insane leaps (this blog being one of them), but on the whole, I'm someone who likes to know what I'm dealing with. I research, question, test, ask, trial ... etc until I've practically beaten an idea to death, but I'm also someone who believes in having plain old faith in the plan. Things just have a way of working out - but for me, they work out because I have a plan and it's having the plan which provides the comfort.

If you're anything like me, you need and want at least a bit of a plan. You want to know how to tackle the elephant.

Here are the **top ten real life, totally essential things** you need to do in order to start a business from home, or take that shopfront out of your head and into reality:

1. Work out your product. What do you make? (This does not require loads of detail just yet. Refinement will come later)

2. Work out your target market. Who buys your product? (This does require detail - no point in having a product if you're not sure who will buy it.)

3. Decide how much money you have *right now* to invest in your business. I don't care if this is fifty bucks or $10, 000. Find some seed

money, no matter how small.

4. Do the leg work. Call your local municipality and find out what is involved in registering a home kitchen, or setting up a commercial kitchen. You HAVE to know this in order to move forward.

5. Come up with a business name. Check nobody else has it. Register it with the right authorities.

6. Register the URL for the business name, open the Facebook page, get the email address. Even if you don't use any of them for a while, take the time to gain ownership of them.

7. Open up a business bank account. Put your seed money in it. EVERY dollar you make or spend should come from that account. I can't stress enough how much having that money (however small) kept separate makes a HUGE emotional (and factual) difference to your business.

8. Work out the numbers - how much money do you actually need to move it to the next level? Where will you need to invest the money in order to be "open for business" ... Equipment? Advertising? Or have you got enough seed money and resources right now to start getting the ball rolling?

9. Develop some branding - get a logo made, think about your corporate colours, get some business cards made. Even if that business card just has your name and mobile phone number on it and is a free template from Vista Print.

10. Start talking about it. To everyone you know. Making your intentions clear - out loud - to people who will listen. Those people will move you forward because these people will become your clients, ask about your progress, and in general hold you to it. Set your intention and say it LOUD and PROUD.

And finally:

Accept that at any time, you can choose to stop. You may have lost some money (and time) by investing in doing the above things, but that's not really a huge deal at this stage. Sometimes the best thing to do is to invest some time and money in the start and then realise that it's not the right thing for you. That's okay. You don't have to go down this path - but if you don't at least start somewhere, you'll be spending all your time on Disappointment Island (and having been there, it's boring and sad and you eat FAR too many Oreos there).

There now. Somehow that elephant doesn't seem quite so big, does it?

ONE bite at a time.

You can manage that much ... at which time the second bite doesn't seem quite so hard to swallow, I promise.

Just FYI: You don't need to do all of these today, or even this week. But this list of things should be your 'to do' list which drives you that little bit further forward. They should ALL be done, one at a time, in the time you have available to you. Don't be daunted by how much is there - but DO set yourself some goals about the time frame in which you'll get them done. After all the best part about list making is crossing stuff off of it! Get this stuff done ONE bite at a time.

The Right Time

This past week I asked you what you wanted me to write about and several of you said you want to know when the right time is to open a shop. I already answered this in part in a post called *Signing The Lease*[7]. (Stop reading this post and go read that post then come back. It's essential reading.) In that post, I talk about how you need to decide where you're going (that's in this post) and then make some hard core choices about moving that decision forward. I realise though that some of you are probably still hoping I'm going to give you some sort of checklist for how you will unequivocally just KNOW when it's time to open a shop. I can't do that (but secretly, I kinda want to.) I really want to be able to come down to your house and in a booming voice say, "NOW! NOW is the time!" and watch as you jump a mile and spill your iced tea all down your front because damn, that was loud.

Funny as that might be to watch, I can't actually do that.

This one thing needs to be 100% true BEFORE you decide to go and open a shop:

You need to be certain that what you want is, in fact, a shop at all.

We hold this romantic vision in our heads of owning our own little piece of bricks and mortar, something tangible we can point to and say, "This? This is MINE." Admittedly, it's pretty damn awesome to do that, but success is not hinged on opening an actual shop front (just ask Sharon Wee). Shops limit your life somewhat - in so far as there needs to be someone there during opening hours, someone to answer the phone, and someone to clean up the messes. It's not too dissimilar to having a child except this one does not talk back.

All those cooking shows on TV made everyone and his brother want to be a chef ... until those people went out and got cooking jobs and realised just how much damn hard work it actually is to be a chef.

So if a shop is **really** what you want - I want you to consider these two things before making the leap:

1. **Timing**. If you have very small kids, sick parents you're looking after, your finances are a mess, whatever ... maybe the shop idea needs to wait. Good ideas will keep, they really will. I'm not saying find excuses to delay opening. I'm saying take a look at your life and decide if you can handle the crazy (and the crazy awesome) which comes with a choice like this. Don't sit around waiting for the right time (because as I said earlier, that time will never come) but just think about timing in general. Maybe

---

7   See *Signing The Lease* in Chapter 3

the shop is the end goal but you really need another year - to get some experience in a commercial kitchen, to improve your baking skills, to learn more about what small business ownership is actually about. Maybe now is *exactly* the right time - I'm just saying, think about it.

2. **Money**. Shops are damn expensive to fit out, and then you have to keep them going until such time as you are turning a profit. You need to be able to get the finance from somewhere unless you are independently wealthy, and nothing kills a dream more than unpaid bills. Again, don't look at money as an excuse not to open your own place - just be realistic about it. How much have you got, how much can you get, how much do you need to be making in order not to sink within five minutes of opening.

We ALL want that glorious moment of walking into our boss's office and yelling, "I quit!" and then turning on our heel in a dramatic fashion (I had that moment, it's as awesome as you think). However, the number of people who get that moment is very, very small. Most of us have things to think about like families and mortgages and finding the money to finance the dream in the first place.

When do you know it's the right time to open a shop? Well, my lovely readers, I can't tell you that. I CAN tell you that a lot of people make a lot of excuses. Don't be one of them, but DO make the time to at least think about the reality versus the edible sparkles.

What Is A Business Plan?

Like many of you, my business started organically. One minute I was making cakes for my own kids, the next minute someone was giving me money to make cakes for their kids. As a result, I didn't have any sort of business plan per se ... hell, I had no idea what a business plan actually was! I only sat down to write one when I hired a business coach who suggested it was a good idea. By that time, I was already several years into business and I had heard of a business plan but didn't understand what it was and why I needed one.

Business Plans are a pretty vital part of business, so I'm going to talk about them for a few posts. In today's post, we'll go over what they are and why you need them.

Exactly what is a Business Plan?

Well, it's exactly what you might think it is - a plan for how your business runs and IS going to run into the future. At it's most basic, a Business Plan is a fancier version of a 'To Do' list for your business. It's not meant to be an iron clad document, it's meant to be something which evolves over time. It not only has goals in it, is also has plans for how you're going to achieve those goals. Some of it really does require a bit of crystal ball work, so that's why it should evolve - because reality might be better or worse than your original predictions.

I remember thinking that I didn't want to write up a document which was just random guessing - but it's not really about that. It's about deciding where you want your business to go and working out how you might get there, then putting some formality around that.

Your business plan is going to include a whole lot of stuff you may or may not have even considered at this stage. Things like your marketing plan, your timeline for achieving milestones, how much money you will need to start up or how much money you will need to continue to grow. It's going to have things like staffing plans (the good news is, you won't be doing every job yourself), things about your point of difference and so on. It's a big task to get done but at different stages it's a different thing - my first version was only a few pages long and pretty much said, "Within five years I will own a cake empire." (Needless to say, the current version is rather more detailed!)

I managed to avoid writing a business plan for a really, really long time. It just seemed like such a daunting task and it was filled with heaps of information I didn't know, words I wasn't familiar with, and it was asking me to answer questions I had not really spent much time thinking about. I was running a business, making money, and everything seemed to be going pretty well. So why did I even NEED a business plan in the first place?

Why do I need a Business Plan?

There are two reasons you need a business plan. One is entirely emotional, and the other entirely practical. Let's start with the emotional bit of it. When you've been in business a while without a plan, it's very easy to get burned out. You're making gorgeous cakes, your clients all love you, and you love the high you get from making someone's event just that little bit better. The following week, you're struggling to pay for ingredients, your competitor wins a big gig that you quoted for, you feel that if you ever look at another cake, it will be too soon. In both of those scenarios, the Business Plan is your safety net - it reminds you of why you're doing what you're doing, it gives you comfort, it gives you guidance. Just the act of sitting down and thinking about all the stuff you've got to put into that plan really spurs you into action. It makes you evaluate where you are at and think about where you would like to go. I'm not suggesting a Business Plan will help you avoid burnout entirely, but it does help in those moments when you feel like you're just treading buttercream.

From a more practical point of view, you're going to need a Business Plan if you need to seek finance anywhere. Private investors, banks, loan sharks, credit unions - anyone you might need to get money from is going to want to know how you're going to spend it. Having a business plan (even a basic one) tells that organization or person that this is a real business and that you're serious about it. A business plan is a communication tool. It's also a good thing to have if you are going into business with a friend or family member, as it shows (in black and white) what the plans are, and that you are all committed to that same plan. Someday if you're going to sell your business, the potential buyer needs to know what the future plans for the business are. They're going to want to know what the potential is for them - and the easiest way to do that is show them a timeline of past, current and future milestones.

In short, a Business Plan tells the story of your business.

In the next article I'm going to post about the topics which need to be included in your plan so that you can get started on this thing. It's not nearly as big a beast as it feels like, and the important thing at this point is just to get started. For those of you reading this for whom a business is still a far-away dream - create one for your dream business, even if you have to make stuff up. It's about starting to think as a businessperson - the more you practice getting that business hat on, the easier it will be once you're ready to start doing and stop dreaming.

Writing A Business Plan – Part 1

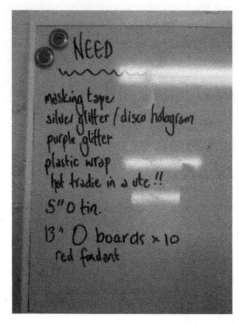

In the previous article we covered what a business plan actually is and why you might need one. This week, we're going to start going over what you should be covering in your plan. There are a plenty of different versions of business plans out there. I'm aiming to teach you the basics of creating this document, especially since you may never have done it before.

There are tons and tons of online resources for writing business plans, so don't feel like you need to do it entirely from scratch. You can find plenty of templates and examples to follow online and software you can buy. I did mine entirely from scratch, mostly because I'm insane and also because at that time the templates available were very basic. I didn't intend to use it to secure money for my business, but I still did it in a formal format so that I would not need to re-write it if I did need it for that purpose later on down the track.

At every stage of this process I suggest you approach it with a brutally honest eye. Absolutely sing your praises but also look for holes in your business which might need plugging. This isn't a "woe is me" thing, this is a "what do I need to REALLY do in order to kick business ass. " You're going to be a little overwhelmed by going through these topics. It's going to seem like a HUGE task - and I'm not going to lie, it IS a big one. You've got to just get started and then keep going! Tackle on section at a time, don't sit down and try to write the entire thing in one fell swoop. Full disclosure - writing the first draft was painful as hell but it got a LOTS easier once I realised how useful this thing actually is.

There are 7 sections, this article will look at the first three of them. The next article will look at the last four sections.

Section One: Summary

It might be helpful to actually write this section LAST since it's an overview of all the things contained in the document. Think about it like a cover page for a resume - this is the bit where you convince the men in the grey suits to give you some money, or on a more emotional level, it's where you get a quick bit of reassurance.

Introductory Paragraph: Briefly, what is the business and what does it do? When was it established? Who does it sell to, and what does it sell?

Key Success Factors: This lists all the things which make your business unique, or which are potential indicators of success. This could be anything from "we have a customer service focus" to "the popularity of macarons has increased 500% in the last five years". Essentially what does this business have which will make it likely to succeed in the current marketplace. This might be about product, about service, about opportunity, about innovation.

Key Risk Factors: What challenges might your business face? This might be anything from market factors "there are currently 20 macaron companies in a 2-mile radius" to distance, to "lack of cash to flow to support growth". I'm going to suggest that this section is really more for your own usage than the usage of the finance guys. I was brutally honest in this section and I suggest you should be too.

Finances: What is the current financial situation of the business and what are it's future needs? Is it self-funded, do you need start up money, what costs might you incur as you grow, what investment is require?

Section Two: Business Purpose

Note: this is a section that looks deceptively easy, so I'm going to talk about this in more detail further on, but it's good to at least start thinking about this stuff.

Mission: One or two sentences describing why your business exists. Big picture stuff!

Business Statement: One or two sentences describing HOW you go about fulfilling your mission.

Vision: One or two sentences about what you're planing on making this business into.

Milestones by year (3-5 years): This is a timeline by year of the goals you'd like to achieve. For a baking business, this can be anything from "hire a full-time decorator" or "open a second location" or "owner stops working in the kitchen" or "turnover of 1 million achieved". The last year might have "sell business" or "retire" in there - so you've really got to do some crystal ball work here, but within the parameters of what you know about yourself, your life, your business and your Final Cake Design[8]. You've got to do some realistic, long-term planning for this section. I actually printed this section out and I keep it in my desk and refer back to it. As life, money and other things got in the way, I've had to revise it a lot but it serves as a great reference of where my business is going and where it's been.

Section Three: Market Analysis

This section requires research, honesty, and a lot of legwork - but it's probably the most important section as it then influences your marketing and advertising decisions.

Market Overview: Who else is serving the same customer base you are? Is it a large chain bakery, is is home bakers? What else or who else is out there occupying the same market space that you are?

Market Changes: How do you find out about changes in the market, AND how are those seen in your area? For example, here in Australia, food trends become popular about 6-12 months after the US, so if you're reading lots of American food blogs all about salted caramel and your business is in Australia, it's a good idea to start planning for salted caramel products. In the US, how are food or baking fads born? Blogs? Climate? Television? How do you find out about trends and what do you do about them? [Sidenote: Three years ago my cupcake to cake ratio was about 3:1, these days it's gone the other way and I make WAY more cake than cupcakes. Why? The market changed!)

Market Segments: This is generally defined by events/purposes in which people buy from you. Let's say you own a custom cake bakery. Your market segments might be personal events (birthday etc.), corporate (product launches, etc.) as well as things like special dietary needs. In other words, to which types of people or for which types of events will you be able to sell things? What different parts of the market do you service?

---

8   See *The Final Cake Design* in the *Before You Begin* section.

Target Market and Customer Characteristics: Who buys your stuff and what are their characteristics? Are they female? How old are they? Do they care about status, do they have a high disposable income, are they time poor parents, are they health conscious? Get into the mind of your ideal client and in this section list everything you can think of which defines them and their buying choices. Where

do they live? Do they shop online? (and so on!) Build a picture of the person you're selling to.

Customer Needs: What is their problem and how are you going to solve it for them? Do they need convenience, do they need a cheaper price, do they need delivery, do they need to feel loved? In other words, how are you going to satisfy the characteristics you listed in the previous heading?

Customer Purchasing Decisions: What compels people in your target market to buy from you? This is again about getting into their head. Why would they choose your business over any other one? Is it about your location? Price? What you offer in terms of products?

Sales Process: This is a basic flow chart of the process from the customer needing something all the way to them purchasing from you. I did this with a paper and pencil to begin with - how would they hear about you, what do they need to do to get info, what happens after they have the quote, when do they pay you and so on. It's a visual representation of how a sale is made. Once you've done this, give it to a friend and ask them to go over it - this is definitely a case of two heads are better than one as you may have forgotten a step. This is a great little exercise to do external to the Business Plan because it shows you all the different opportunities you have to influence potential customers OR improve your customer's experience with you.

If you've read this far and you feel like you want to shove hot pokers in your eyes because that would somehow be less painful and more fun, I really want you to just hang in there. Even if you need to write one section then eat a sleeve of Oreos, or write a section and then not do anything for a week. The key is to get started. No, you don't HAVE to have this document to run a business, but it's a little like doing your taxes. You get all annoyed about it and avoid doing it, find a hundred activities to distract you, and then when you finally sit down and submit the damn thing you wondered why you waited so long!

Starting to write a business plan is boring, but important: and since it's not always rainbow sprinkles, by now you know it's the important parts which are going to keep you actually in business.

Writing A Business Plan – Part 2

Two articles ago we talked about what a business plan is and why you need one. The last article talked about the first three sections of a business plan.

This week, we're going to keep on truckin' and talk about the next four sections.

If you're still with me, I want you to bookmark these pages right now - because someday, you're going to find the time and energy to get this project done, and you're going to need some help. You might not be ready to do this right now, you might be halfway through it, you might have done it already - whatever your story is, YAY YOU for getting this far!

Section Four: Competitive Analysis

This section tells you which sharks to avoid swimming with.

Industry Overview: What is currently out there in your area or online? This doesn't have to be hugely detailed.

Competition: This is where it gets more specific. What types of companies are your competitors? Are they large scale bakers who can charge lower prices than you can? Home bakers? Already established companies? Bakeries who do the same thing as you do, but who offer more of a range than you do? Who is out there that you are competing with?

Industry Changes: This requires some crystal ball work. When I first wrote my plan, there were very few cupcake companies but I knew that more were coming - and on TV there were tons of cake shows. So just by looking around it became clear that the industry was going to change. I also noticed at that time that a whole lot of cake decorating supply companies were opening up, which made the trade much more accessible to home bakers.

Primary Competitors: Name them and name them by type - I had competitors for cake, for cupcakes, and for teaching classes.

Competitive Products/Services: This is where you get to list what makes your business uniquely your business. Given the nature of your competition, what about your product or services is actually competitive? Is it price? Level of service? Availability of the product?

Opportunities: What markets might you grow into? What things are currently not serviced by your competition? This is where things like offering vegan or allergen-friendly products might be considered an opportunity if nobody else does those kinds of things. How can you push your business even further?

Threats and Risks: These are the things you probably have no control over. Lack of skilled staff in your local area, increased cost of raw ingredients - things which present a problem to you (and probably the industry as a whole) which you're going to need to be aware of and potentially prepare yourself for.

Section Five: Our Products/Services

This section defines what the business actually does on a practical level - what does your business actually produce or provide to it's customers?

Product/Service Description: What are the different ways your business produces income? This is literally a list: cake, cupcakes, brownies, cupcake stand hire, candy buffet styling, classes. . . and so on.

Positioning of products/services: Where are your products and services going to sit in the marketplace? Very high end (and, therefore, exclusive) or more middle of the road? Perhaps you're aiming for volume, so your quality might be good but pricing will be cheap.

Competitive evaluation of products/services: Take a closer look at the other guys' products and how they compare to you. How are you better or different in comparison? What have you got going for you that the others don't?

Future products/services: Drag out the ol' crystal ball again and do some dreaming -but not massive amounts as it can get very easy to get stuck in dreamland! Just identify a few opportunities for growth within the business plan you are building.

Section Six: Marketing and Sales

This section is all about how you're going to go about telling people what you do and how you do it.

Marketing and Advertising strategy: You need one! This is where your marketing plan[9] is going to be, in a slightly abridged version.

Online/Social Media strategy: These days this is part of your marketing plan, but it's a pretty big part of it, which is why I kept it separate in my business plan. I had to think of it almost like an entirely separate marketing plan.

Promotions/Incentives/Publicity: How are you going to lure people to you? Referral bonuses? Facebook contests? This one is a part of your overall marketing plan, but

---

9   See *Five Steps To Writing a Marketing Plan* in Chapter 8.

it's nice to keep it separate as it reminds you to think about it in more detail.

Section Seven: Operations

This is about Human Resources - who runs this thing anyway?

Key Personnel: Who is currently employed by the business, and what to do they do? In the beginning, it might be three people - namely me, myself, and I - but that's okay!

Organisational Structure: Given the milestones you set out for yourself, what does the future organisational structure of the business? Is there an admin person, a 'head' baker, an apprentice?

Human Resources Plan: How are you going to go about finding, hiring, and keeping those staff members? Will you aim to promote from within, or hire a new? How do you train current staff? Is there an employee handbook?

Product/Service Delivery: Literally how does anything actually happen in your business? Who creates the product, who can deliver the services? Do you need to develop some procedures so that more than one staff member can create the product or service?

Customer Service/Support: How do you and how will you look after the people who matter the most to your business? How will you follow up? What's your plan for giving good service?

Facilities: Where do you operate from and where might you operate from if your business grows.

Financials: What's the current situation, and what do you need to achieve the goals you set out for yourself?

That's it! You did it! You took on this massive monster and conquered it! Woooot!

There are plenty of businesses who operate for a long time without a business plan (mine included) but just doing the work of creating one really forced me to shove the businesswoman hat on my head. Previously I was a kick-ass cake decorator with a good idea and some happy thoughts about my overall awesomeness compared to everyone else. After the fact, I had a much better idea of where I was at, and (most importantly) where I was going. I'm in this for the long haul, and I really needed to put some thought and effort into what "being in it for the long haul" actually meant.

If in reading all of this, you find it daunting, don't attempt to do the entire thing.

Pick one section (the one you know the least about or which makes you the most uncomfortable is the best one to go for) and work on it! Start the research, do the dreaming, make the choices, think about the future and just DO that one section.

CHAPTER 2
HOME BASED BUSINESS

The majority of us who go into the business of food (sweet or otherwise) will start out from home. It's just the nature of the thing, because we start out making things for our loved ones and soon enough we find ourselves making things for other people's loved ones! For some people, having a home based business is their ultimate goal because it allows for a lot of flexibility (hey, nobody will see you working in your pyjamas) and the overheads will remain relatively low. For other people (myself included), working from home is only the first step in a much bigger plan, a plan which might include a studio, shopfront or several shopfronts. If you fall into that second camp, your time spent running your business at home can be rather short or rather long, depending on factors such as your finances and family needs. Some people manage a mix of the two, where they convert a garage or build a structure of some sort on their properties. Whichever path you take, chances are good that you'll spend at least some time building your business up in the comfort and mess of your own home.

I should mention that there are positives and negatives to owning a home-based business – most of which I'll cover in the coming articles in this chapter. Sometimes people ask me if I think a home based business can ever be as successful as a store based one, and my thoughts on that are: 1) it all depends on how you define success in the first place, and 2) all things are possible.

Ultimately, I don't believe the success of your business is limited by the size of your kitchen. I've seen some incredibly amazing things come out of some very teeny, tiny spaces. Challenging situations can often inspire very creative solutions.

Work Versus Effort

We've all heard the expressions, "marriage takes work, " and "if you really love what you do for a living, it won't ever feel like work".

WHAT UTTER BULLSHIT.

The implication in both of those is that work is a bad thing to do. Both also imply that if it takes work then something about that relationship or that job is broken and you must fix it.

Again - bullshit.

So let's start with that first one - when did working become a bad thing? In my mind, work serves a whole lot of positive purposes. It gives me somewhere to be. I can meet other people from whom I can learn and who I can teach. It enables me to make friends. It allows me to contribute positively to society. It allows me to bring home money, which in turn helps to feed and educate my kids, pay rent, and purchase things which helps the economy at large. Work allows me to feel useful and needed (which I like feeling). In short, I can't find much which is BAD about work. Are there details which sometimes suck? (long hours, crappy bosses, ugly surrounds, boring, etc.). Sure. But am I damn grateful to HAVE a job when many are without? You bet I am. Just because you might not totally love what you do or have some challenging circumstances around it, **this in no way devalues your work or makes work "bad"**.

I don't think it's at all unfortunate that most of us have to work. By the way, I think of "work" as stuff you do for money, so this could either be a job or self-employment. I like working. **I have not always liked my jobs**, but I've always liked working. You know what's interesting? Lots of people who never need to work another day in their lives STILL WORK (Richard Branson. Taylor Swift. Bill Gates. Sheryl Sandberg. Oprah) because work isn't that terrible. it serves many purposes. Closer to home, plenty of mothers **choose to go back to work** after the birth of their kids not because they need to but because they want to.

As for that second bit - that if you don't love it every single second, it must be broken. . . yeah, and in my backyard I have a sprinkle-eating unicorn that serenades me every morning with "You Are My Sunshine. " **Seriously?** Every moment of your work should be wonderful? How BORING would that be if it were true and how entirely unrealistic that is to achieve. **It's almost as bad as saying that we all need that work/life balance**.

I won't talk about the ins and outs of marriage or love but I will say that a marriage and a business are not so dissimilar. Both are relationships. Relationships grow, change, shift and alter a lot depending on the people involved and the circumstances surrounding them. Businesses are much the same in that as time passes they too grow, change and shift - and sometimes you "divorce" by choice and sometimes not. To imply that your business or your relationship is somehow broken or not okay because it sometimes requires effort which is neither fun nor joyful - pppffftttt! When it comes to business, so much of it is fun and exciting ... but you know, I've yet to find someone who loves the part of their business which is filling out paperwork, firing wayward employees or doing their taxes. I personally don't **hate** any of those (because to me they mean better stuff is on the way) but nor would I say I embrace the crappier sides of business with a "WOOOOHOOO! I freaking LOVE THIS!" kind of outlook either. They're just part of the deal. A boring-but-important part, but part of the deal.

Every day I see people giving up on their businesses because "it's just not fun any more", or declaring "I'm giving up!" because the damn fondant won't cooperate or they've not had a Saturday off recently. I see people encouraging other people to stop trying to be in business because, "If it's all so hard, why are you doing it?" Are you for SERIOUS right now? Who the hell told you that every moment you're in business is going to be glitter and Oreos? Do I think business HAS to be "**hard** work"? Nope. I think sometimes it's positively glorious, and other times you've got to put in a bit more effort than is either comfortable, nice or affordable. **Sometimes it's going to feel like a hell of a lot of hard work (physically and emotionally) and other times it's going to be downright brilliant. Just like work/**

life balance is bullshit, so too is expecting or assuming that business is fun all the time.

Is your business ALWAYS going to feel like work? Probably - because it's a mix of fun and not-so-fun, just like a normal job is. Is that a problem? Not at all. I think it's wonderful when you can **marry your happy place with your work place** and my mission with this blog is to teach people how to do exactly that. If however you think that marriage will all be wine and roses ... then dear heart, you've been reading too many of those inspirational memes that say stupid things like, "Your calling should never feel like hard work". Yes, and Oreos will never make me fat.

All relationships - if that's the relationship between you and your partner and you and your business - require effort and love and for some people, effort IS work. It's **because the relationships are worth it** that you need to endure the times when it feels like your capacity for effort and love are being tested - and they WILL be tested. No relationship worth having is entirely effortless or without work of some kind.

If you don't believe me, I've got a sprinkle-eating unicorn I can sell you.

Planning Your Home Based Cake Business

When we start out making cakes as a hobby, most of us find ourselves magically in business without really meaning to be. One day we make a cake for our son, the next day someone asks us what we might charge to make one for their daughter and bim-bam-boom, we're in business! It's usually only months down the line that you start to even think about being "in business", and by then you're really and truly in the thick of it. At some point in your baking business, you're going to need to make the decision about staying home versus opening an actual store.

Many people (including myself) started out running their businesses from home and then moved into a shop front when they were ready to. Me, I never wanted to run a home-based business, so I always knew I would be heading out the door and into a commercial kitchen sooner rather than later. Others always wanted to stay home based and just altered their space to make it fit, or adjusted the parameters of their business in order to do so. Neither way is right or wrong, it's just what works for you and your future.

The decision to stay at home or move into commercial premises is based on many different factors - money, lifestyle, the kind of product you make, who your target market is and so on. There is a lot more to it than this list, but here are some things to think about if you're going to consider having a home based cake business:

- The overheads for running a home based business are generally lower. Some (not all) of your costs simply won't apply in a home environment, for example, there is no need for a trade waste agreement with the local water company. The bonus to having fewer overheads is potentially having more profit.

- It can be a great way to try out having a business. I'm not suggesting you go in and out of business overnight, but the outlay to starting from home is small enough that if you decide that business is not for you, it's a lot simpler and faster to close down. Sure, you'll still lose whatever time and money you put into starting it, but you're not needing to break leases and sell off big equipment if you decide it's not your thing.

- Kids and pets touch stuff. It can be a challenge to keep your work space as your work space without invaders of the 2 legged or 4 legged kind - but similarly, kids learn a lot by watching you work and are happier to have you around making flowers than not have you around because you're at your store.

- Space, or rather a lack of space, will either drive you up a wall or teach you how to work very efficiently. I used to do every cake on a bench that was literally 1 yard (1 metre) wide and deep ... until I got one which was 3 times the size and then I never seemed to have enough room!

- There is a perception (an unfair one) that prices from home-based businesses should be less than those at a store front, so you'll need to consider that when doing your marketing and branding.

- Perfect strangers will know where you live. This isn't a big deal, and there are ways to manage it (don't put your whole address on your website) but it's something to think about it. Your privacy becomes, well, less private than you might like!

- Working from home IS a lot more flexible, but that also means it potentially eats into your personal time as well. Working from home requires a fair amount of self-discipline because it's so much easier to "just answer this last email", or take that call at 5 pm on a Sunday night.

- Clients will expect that you are more available because you work from home, so they will be really late or really early to pick ups, will expect that you work to *their* timetable of when it's convenient for them to pick up or meet. They assume because you work from home you sit around all day waiting for them. You're going to be firm and discipline them about your availability, which is sometimes hard to do.

Setting Boundaries For Your Home Based Business

When you work from home, you've actually got TWO sets of boundaries you need to set up. The first is boundaries for yourself, things like being disciplined about not answering the phone at odd hours, not letting cake making take forever and keeping your business expenses separate. The second set of boundaries you need to set up is with your clients: the times they can come and pick up when you're available for consults and so on. Quite honestly each set of boundaries can be hard to maintain, but the second one is the more difficult because you just can't force people to be on time or respectful about your space.

Here are some ideas for how to keep customer boundaries when you're working from home:

- **TREAT YOUR BUSINESS AS A BUSINESS AND THEY WILL TOO.**

  Be professional across the board (no taking orders via text, no answering the phone when someone is screaming in the background, no giving people quotes on random scraps of paper) and people will take your lead on how to behave. It's when you start to be casual about things that they start to be casual as well - so if you're always bending the rules for people, not communicating properly or professionally ... guess what, they will do that too. You set the tone for your business. Set a friendly, professional one that has boundaries in it.

- **HAVE SET OPENING HOURS AND ADVERTISE THOSE WIDELY.**

  If you have set opening hours clearly listed on your website, social media profiles and in your emails people are much more inclined to follow and respect those rules. The opening hours tell them what to expect from you in terms of availability. Your opening hours are whatever you want them to be as they fit into your life - mine were 10am-4pm M-F and 9am-12:30 pm

Saturday (closed Sunday) because that's what fit around my kids. If anyone questioned this, I just said, "That's when I'm open, " and left it at that - if I felt pressured to justify it, I'd say, "**As much as I'd might like to work 24/7, my family doesn't appreciate it**, so having set business hours is how I make time for both. " Did I work more than my advertised hours? Of course, I did ... but my clients didn't need to know that. I also found that having a "range" of time that I was open on a Saturday worked a LOT better than having set pick up appointments, so if you can do it that way, I recommend it.

- **DON'T "ADVERTISE" THAT YOUR BUSINESS IS HOME BASED.**

 It's sad but true, people will naturally take liberties with your time if they know you are at home. Your website should have your suburb or area listed, but not an actual address unless you need to give it to them. People see the words "home based business" and for some reason they think this is a reason to behave as though you have nothing to do all damn day but sit perfectly still at home in your perfectly clean house waiting for their arrival as though they are the Queen.

- **REMIND THEM OF YOUR AVAILABILITY AT THE TIME OF CONFIRMATION AND *GIVE THEM A REASON* NOT TO BE LATE.**

When you email them a final payment invoice or call to confirm the details of pick up address, gently remind them what the rules are and INCLUDE A CLEAR DEADLINE. "So I'm here until 3 pm for your pick-up, straight after that I'm heading out to do several deliveries." They do not need to know that the truth is that at exactly 3:01 pm you will be on the couch in your pajamas eating Pringles and watching 'Grey's Anatomy'. **They only need to know that there is a damn good reason for them to be on time**.

- **IF IT LOOKS LIKE TIME IS RUNNING SHORT, CALL THEM.**

    If the time for pick up has passed, don't wait an hour to call and see where they are at then yell at them for making you wait. Do the polite thing and call them within 10-15 minutes of their being late. Sometimes they forgot to come, got lost or there was traffic, or any number of things happened to make them late. Make sure you remind them of your deadline. Be nice but firm. "Hi Jane, just checking where you are, because I need to head out for those deliveries in about ten minutes."

Lastly, even when you do all of that, **there are some people who are just chronically whiney or chronically late**. For the whiney ones, I find it's best not to enter into a long discussion about it. Your hours are your hours, that's when you can help them, and you have other clients/family which mean that pick ups at 9 pm on Saturday night are not an option. If you struggle with this because you are by nature a people pleaser (as many of us are), then in that moment I want you to remember that you're being in business is not only about your client's happiness - your happiness counts for something too! For the chronically late, make their pick up time earlier than you really need to. Want them there by noon? Make them pick up at 11. Better yet, offer to deliver - which solves their problem AND yours.

I highly, highly recommend having boundaries around your home based business. The major difference between home and store based boundaries is in how YOU behave around those boundaries. If you know that clients are more inclined to take liberties because you are a home based business, then you've got to be just that touch more firm and professional about your boundaries. Be polite, loving, and accommodating where you can - but also make the rules clear and it's win/win - they know what to expect and you can crack open the can of Pringles a little bit sooner.

CHAPTER 3
DAY TO DAY RUNNING OF YOUR BUSINESS

The delicious fluffy swirls of buttercream, the glossy romantic darkness of a bowl of freshly made ganache, the smell of vanilla that always fills the air … there is much to love about getting to make cake for a living. How many people get to say they play with icing and sprinkles all day? How many of us are in careers where our customers are always happy and excited to see us coming? We're pretty lucky to get to do what we do for a living, but as anyone who has done it for a while knows, there is much more to it than the vanilla and the icing. If nothing else there's also a heck of a lot of dishes (and please don't talk to me about washing piping bags or lining cake pans.)

When I teach my live classes, I often point out that the irony of small business is this: you got into it because you love making something. The more of that something you make and the more you sell of it, the more your business grows. The more the business grows, the less you have the time to be the person making the something, because the other demands of the business need your attention more. Pretty soon you find yourself in a situation where you're no longer the person making something...but isn't the making of something why you got into this in the first place? That being said, I do think you can still run a business and be part of the making process, it's just that over time where you are involved in that process changes a bit. As an example, perhaps at the start you did it all – design, bake, decorate, deliver. As time goes on, your role evolves so that you only do the designing and decorating and leave the baking and delivering tasks to others. I don't think being in business means you give up the joy of the making. I think it means you simply have to get more realistic about the demands of being in business and find more creative ways to conduct your business in the first place.

Most of you will find this chapter answers most of the questions you've ever asked me about your daily working lives. This is the stuff we really NEED to know about - deliveries, client complaints, terms and conditions. Just like they don't give you a handbook on how to parent day-to-day, there is no cake business owners handbook (although perhaps I should create one?). This is important stuff to know -how exactly does one get a toddler to stop having a tantrum in the middle of a supermarket? Does I really need a business phone number? On a bigger scale – how do I know when it's time to move my business out of home? In this chapter I'm going to give you some nitty-gritty tips to help you get it all done without sacrificing too much of the fun.

Boring But Important

There are a number of business-related jobs which fall into the category of "boring but important. " All the things which if they don't happen will probably mean someday you're going to waste a whole lot of time looking for some scrap of paper which you are SURE is in your blue folder. Well, it was there last week. Or possibly last month? Anyway, it's there somewhere ... if only you could find it!

This post also falls into that category - it might be boring, but it's important - so listen up.

Exactly how do you control all that paperwork which builds up around businesses (and man oh man is there a LOT of it! *Paperless office*, yeah right). First I think we need to realise that the world is full of people who are GREAT at paperwork and people who are crap at it. Me, I'm somewhere in the middle - which means I have yet to lose an order form, but there are definitely a few piles of things which could use some attention.

Here are some handy tips for keeping all that infernal paperwork under control:

1. Don't print it unless you really, really have to. If you're printing it out to DO something with it (attach it to an order, mail it to someone, keep records of a transaction) then go ahead and print. If it's going to get printed and then just ... hang around ... don't bother. In my email folders I have one which is titled, "Needs doing" and into it, I put articles of interest, blog posts of interest, new product announcements, whatever. All the stuff I'm keen to know more about but isn't essential for me to have a hard copy of. Every few weeks, when I've got a spare few minutes, I'll scan through that folder (and usually delete most of it). If I printed all that stuff, it would just hang around.

2. Designate certain days of the week (or time of day) for dealing with boring but important stuff and be specific about it. Really train yourself into a routine around this. Scheduling time for tasks like this works really well at keeping you focused and not distracted -and since you know you only have to do that task for a set amount of time (and then you're FREEEEEEEEEEEEEEEEEE!!!) it's much more tolerable. For example, every Tuesday is when you pay bills. Every Wednesday morning, for 20 minutes, you file paperwork. It's easy to remember weekly commitments like personal training sessions, reading this blog (ha) or book club - so make commitments to getting stuff done to a schedule.

3. Keep a small lined notebook (or lined post-it notes, or whatever) on

your work desk. Start *every* day with a short focused list of "must do" activities and always have one on there which is boring but important. Do that task FIRST if at all possible. You might find you add things to the list as the day progresses, but the "must do" will always take priority.

4.   "Chunk" tasks as much as you can - set aside chunks of time for doing the *same* kind of activity and do it all at once. One of the problems with modern living is that we're always distracted by something, so we rarely just sit and DO any one task with focus (other than play Candy Crush). Set aside a chunk of time in which to complete the SAME type of task and even save them up if you have to. For example, every time an order comes in over the phone, I'll put it aside - so at the end of the day, I've got a bunch of them to process the payments for all at once. That works a whole lot better than constantly stopping to process payments all day. Another example is voicemails and calls - I'll set aside a chunk of time in which the ONLY task is to reply to voicemails and make phone calls to people who are waiting for me to call.

5.   JUST DO SOMETHING. The problem with paperwork is that it very quickly snowballs. One minute you have it under control and the next nobody can see you behind the stacks of paper. It's so easy to ignore it, but that just creates more mess! Pick a paperwork (or boring) task, set yourself a fairly short time limit to be committed (and even set a timer if you need to), and just START. The starting is much harder than the continuing. I've been known to say out loud, "Right. For the next ten minutes, I'm doing the stupid filing." It's the starting, not the doing. So as Nike would say - Just. Do. It.

6.   Turn off the distractions, or don't turn them on in the first place. Don't open your email client until after you've done the task you've set yourself. Don't open facebook. Don't even turn the computer on unless the task itself demands it, and then only open the relevant programs to the task. In my case, it takes ages for my computer to boot - so I'll push the button to turn my computer on but spend the next few minutes writing my daily list (which does not require a computer.)

7.   Everything needs a place to be other than in limbo. Invest some time and money in decent stationary (folders, files, etc.) and dedicated work shelving in order to keep things in their rightful place, so that when you DO go to file something, it has somewhere to go. All those giant stationary stores are like crack cocaine to a business owner - so I invite you to go there, get your fix, then go back to work and actually use those useful

things. However - DO NOT buy an "inbox" or tray of any sort to put on your desk, because that's where good intentions go to die.

8. While you're shopping for decent folders and shelves, also buy a stand-alone plastic drawer and fill it with really useful stationary stuff: post it notes, stapler, staples, paper clips, 'paid' stamp, invoice/receipt books, envelopes, calculator, decent pens and a pencil, eraser, black marker, book of stamps and a ruler. Keep this drawer handy and that way you have the tools with which to be organised. This is your work drawer, not to be used at home or for the kids to go shopping in when they do their homework. There is nothing more annoying than sitting down to get organised and then spending ten minutes looking for a paperclip. If you are prepared, you have no excuse but to make progress. You would not start decorating a cake without having your piping tips washed and ready - so don't build a business without these small but essential tools either.

9. Seriously consider outsourcing. I used to do all my own bookkeeping. Not only was I bad at it, but I hated doing it so much I'd procrastinate in some very creative ways (did you know you can roll Oreos quite a long way across a desk?). Just thinking about it would irritate me. I swear I'd spend more time hating the idea of it than the doing of it! Eventually, I realised that even at the crazy rates bookkeepers demand, I'd save time and money by outsourcing it to the professionals. In the early stages of business it's hard to justify those expenses - but if you can spend that same time growing and developing your business (rather than rolling Oreos), then it's money well spent. Same goes for web design, social media content, etc. - and there is an entire industry of Virtual Assistants whose entire existence rests on your hatred of paperwork. I'd suggest that if there is an important office job you really hate, check out what it would cost you to outsource it. You might be pleasantly surprised.

10. Educate yourself. Just because you are good at cake, this does not make you good at administration. Take a short class in Excel, find out what the rules are about keeping financial paperwork, do a class in touch typing, do a seminar with the Professional Organizers Association (no I did not make that up) - whatever. Get yourself some business administration skills because without them, you'll just constantly feel frustrated by it. This is especially true of someone who is not naturally inclined towards organisation.

And

11. Realise NOW that the bigger your business gets, the bigger the paperwork gets, so it's best to set up some systems (however small) NOW. Yes, I started my business because I loved cake decorating - but the bigger the business got, the less I was a cake maker and the more I was a paper pusher. I spend many more hours on business administration now than I do on cake making, and I'm happy with that ... but plenty of people aren't. I recently spoke to a colleague who told me she is almost a year behind on her invoicing, and there is a company who owes her close to five THOUSAND dollars as a result. Not because they won't or can't pay it, but because she has yet to bill them. This is someone who needs to outsource, AND someone who needs to take a very hard look at whether she even wants to be in business or not.

Just like the formula for ganache is 1:1, so too is this formula necessary for a baking business:

More product = more success = more boring but important jobs which need your attention.

Commit to being a business owner, not just a baker or decorator and get this stuff under control.

Have you got any handy hints to share for climbing the paperwork mountain?

Confused In Cakeland - Your Telephone Number

Confused in Cakeland

Dear Michelle,

How important is it for my business to have a local phone number? Since I don't have a storefront, I use my cell phone for both personal and business calls. I previously lived in a different state, so I have an out-of-state phone number. Recently, someone suggested that I get a local number as it looks better to local clients, and not like I'm taking business (or money) out of state. Is he right?

Sincerely,

Locally Confused

Hi Locally Confused,

I definitely think you need a local number, and here's why: although YOU know you're local if they see an out of state area code, that might make them doubt that you are actually local. Basically, we don't want to confuse them and we want to gain their trust, too. Trust is really important with potential clients, so we don't want to give them any reason to doubt that you are where you say you are and where they want you to be. Plus if for some reason they pay a higher rate for out of state calls, that's a reason for them not to even try to call you, too. Definitely, get a local number if you can afford to.

I also usually suggest having a second, separate phone number for your business - so an easy way to solve this might be just that, to keep your personal number personal and get a new local one for the business. Change your voicemail to say, "Thanks for calling me, our business number is now ####" and don't forget to change your phone number everywhere it appears - online listings, your business card, your email signature and so on.

Locally Yours,

Michelle

Sign On The Dotted Line

Have you ever heard the expression, "Once burnt, twice shy"? That expression is pretty much the reason why my business has disclaimers on its website as well as pages of 'policies' as they relate to how the business operates. I knew from the beginning that I needed to have insurance for the business to protect not only me but the business itself AND its customers. I even knew that I needed to have policies in place in terms of what I would and would not allow people to do - e.g. cake stands had to be returned within a certain time frame, that I would not be responsible for cake disasters if they happened after delivery and so on. Then and even now, I didn't want my website to be filled with pages and pages of rules, so I kept it pretty basic and all in one easily accessible place.

Nice and naive, isn't it?

It only takes ONE jerk to make you think that perhaps "pretty basic" isn't going to cut it, right? In my case it was a jerk who- on a hot summer's day - picked up a 2 tier cake, put it on the front seat of his car (not a level surface), drove it around for several hours making several stops, and then drove it to a mountain top venue - only to call me and tell me that the top tier had slid to one side and the chocolate underneath was melting. His claim was that I'd sold him a faulty product. I've also heard plenty of stories from my colleagues of people wanting full refunds several days AFTER a cake has been eaten, of people claiming cake they ordered had gone bad (but the claim was made weeks after delivery), that cakes "suddenly" fell apart, and so on. How can we as cake makers protect ourselves from these sometimes truly outrageous claims? How can we as cake makers protect ourselves from the smaller things - like people cancelling orders at the last minute or failing to pay deposits and then coming to collect a cake we didn't bake?

Some people arm themselves and their businesses with loads of paperwork. They make people sign all manner of contracts, agreements, liability statements and so on at various stages of their order. I've heard of people asking their clients to sign a form when they pick up their cake, which says they were happy with it and the maker is not liable for any damage occurring after pick up. I've heard of brides being asked to sign non-disclosure agreements when a cake designer draws them a cake design. I've heard of cake companies whose signature at their end of email goes on for paragraphs and paragraphs of rules and regulations. I've heard of companies which have clients sign at design stage, deposit stage, AND pick up stage.

In my case, while I think protecting yourself is really important, I also think it's not a great experience for the customer if getting a birthday cake means they are signing five documents along the way. I really can't imagine a customer coming in to pick up a cake and me saying, "Ah. . . not so fast! Before you take that cake, I need you to sign on the dotted line, please." To me, that kind of thing takes something away from the personal touch experience, which for me is a definite unique selling point.

How do you strike a balance between protecting yourself but not having a lawyer on retainer every month?

1. Educate yourself. Find out what your rights as a small business owner are - does your liability really end even if they've signed something? What are the rules (if there are any) and what are the grey areas (and there are some)? This will vary widely so it's worth educating yourself as to the local and state laws as they apply to your business and your product.

2. Insure the business and it's customers (public liability) - I believe it's a non-negotiable business expense so don't skimp on it now and regret it later.

3. Think about the legal experience from a customer's point of view - if you really do want them to sign something, what's the nicest way to get this to happen without offending or taking away from the personal experience?

4. Think about this from the customer's point of view in terms of what might go wrong - and build your policies, disclaimers, and forms around those potential problems. This is where having bad experiences can force you to have good business practices.

5. Review your policies when things go wrong - so if you do get caught out, you can ensure that it never happens again.

6. Once you've written your legal stuff, get a real lawyer to look it over for you. Not some high powered old man in a suit in a 50 story glass building, but a lawyer with an interest in and experience of helping small business - and if possible, small food businesses.

7. Make your policies easy to understand and easily accessible. Publish them (or a link to them) on the bottom of your quote form, publish them on your website, remind clients in email or over the phone if you have to. Basically don't bombard them, but don't give them any reason to say, "I didn't know that." When a client hires a cupcake stand from us, I hand it over and I always nicely remind them of the returns policy. "The stand needs to be back by 4 pm Tuesday, but if you can't make it by then, please just let me know so the late fee doesn't start getting charged."

8. Accept that some people are just jerks and will find their way around any papers they signed or policies you published. In this day and age, there is very little which is truly iron-clad - and consumers have a voice called the Internet in which they can create plenty of trouble for you regardless of signed agreements.

9. If you truly screwed up, own up to it (and resolve it) as quickly and quietly as you can and take it as a lesson learned. Change how you do things, tighten your policies, take stock of how you currently do things - but don't let this be a reason to turn your business into a legal fortress!

10. Perhaps the hardest thing of all: don't let the one jerk ruin it for everyone else. You can be well protected without needing to make the experience painful and frustrating for everyone who comes after the jerk. There are nice ways to say, "This is how we do things, your cooperation is appreciated." There are some CRAZY stories out there about cake clients gone rogue - some of them are so truly unbelievable that they can only be true because you just can't make this stuff up even if you tried.

Bottom (dotted) line is this: don't be afraid to give people the benefit of the doubt, and don't be afraid to look after yourself. Both are important.

Signing The Lease

This topic is one which has probably crossed your mind: how do you know when it's time to quit your full-time day job for your full-time cake business? Last week we talked about the end design for your cake business. Today we're going to talk about when you know it's time to bring that design to life and sign the lease (so to speak.)

As people who have been reading this blog for a while know, I am qualified as a chef and I worked in that capacity for many years. The bit I haven't told you is that I worked as a chef even when I had rented a commercial kitchen for my cake business. Yup. I was chefing Sunday-Tuesday, and working on cake Wednesday-Saturday (hmm, no spare days in there, are there?). I answered the phone when I could and replied to emails after hours. The fact of the matter is, I was terrified of letting go of my 'real' job. We needed the money. My husband's work situation was a little unstable, we had three small kids, we had a mortgage. I wasn't making much money from cake and certainly not enough to replace the income I was making.

The very idea of leaving my stable chefing job to go into a very fickle niche business on a full-time basis was TERRIFYING. It shouldn't have been that scary - I did the same thing several years earlier when I left my stable, well-paying administrative job to go to culinary school. I'd already taken the plunge once. Why was doing it this time so scary? What was different?

The difference was this: leaving one industry to go to another is scary but ultimately I'd be relying on other people to help me pay the bills. Someone else was in charge, as long as I showed up and did what they asked of me. This time, leaving my steady job to go into business meant I'd be relying on ME. Just ME. Nobody else.

If the orders did not come?	My problem.
Bills didn't get paid?	My problem.
Orders got mixed up?	My problem.
Money ran out?	My problem.
I got sick and could not decorate?	My problem.

I'm sure you can see where I am going with this. Making the clean break from working for someone else to working entirely for yourself is scary because it feels as though there is no safety net. My world was black and white - either I would succeed, or I'd fail- but, either way, it was me who had that responsibility on her shoulders. To me, failure was almost worse than not trying because it was somehow safer. I kept thinking, "If I don't try, I can't fail."

What an utter load of bullshit that was.

The entire time I'm thinking that I shouldn't try too hard because failure will be too devastating, I'm taking orders. I'm designing cakes. I'm writing website content, ordering business cards, reading cake blogs, and taking out ads. You really want to tell me that's not trying?

Well, it IS trying. In a half-baked sort of way (I couldn't resist the pun. Sorry.).

So that crap about "might as well not try, if I'm going to fail" ... ? Yeah. A nice little lie I was telling myself. Still, I was too scared to take the plunge in a full-time sort of way.

Eventually, I decided to ease my way out of working as a chef and into being a full-time cake maker. I cut my hours down at the other job, slowly but surely - until I was working as a chef only two days a week, and working on cake 5 days a week. I still didn't make nearly enough money. I still wasn't sure how this was all going to work. I still did not commit fully to the business.

Why? Nothing had changed, not really anyway.

I still had a family, a mortgage, financial responsibilities, I still loved cake but was not brave enough to commit to it, and I still didn't have the money I felt I needed in order to feel secure. Not earning enough in either job, feeling like I wasn't giving 100% to either job, feeling pulled in too many directions. I was just ... stuck in limbo. As it happens, right around then the Universe conspired to make things happen. I lost my lease on my tiny commercial kitchen, and I had two weeks to get out. I had reached the biggest of all business crossroads: GROW ... or STOP. The option of continuing to tread water was gone. Even if I'd not lost my lease, I would have come to that crossroads. Many businesses (cake or otherwise) are faced with the "grow or stop" conundrum. The lease just pushed me down the path a little quicker. A friend of mine then said to me, "Why are you dithering about this? The decision has already been made." I argued with him, "No it isn't! I don't know what I'm going to do, I've got endless pros and cons lists, I'm just not sure if it'll work, what if I fail, I don't know what to do! Do I give up? Find a shop? Quit cheffing? I'm just not sure." I went back and forth on this issue for many sleepless nights. But ... when I took his words to heart and looked into my deepest thoughts, I had to admit: *the decision to work at this full time had already been made.*

In truth, the decision to commit myself full time to this business had already been made several times. When I bought business cards. When I got a dedicated business phone number. When I rented that first kitchen. When I registered my business name. When I started to reduce my cheffing hours. When I talked about the business as though it was bigger than it already was. The EMOTIONAL decision had been made a very long time <u>before</u> I reached that crossroads. Allowing that decision to see the light of day was the scary part.

This brings me back to the original question - *exactly how DO you know* when it's time to quit your stable, full-time, paying job and take the plunge into owning a cake business full time?

You don't.

There is no "right" time.

The sign you are waiting for may never come. The 'right time' might never happen exactly as you want it to. The planets may never align. If you spend your time waiting for things to happen (waiting for your kids to grow up, your finances to settle, the magical signs to appear) you may find yourself not moving forward from where you are this very minute. If you spend your time worrying about details like the size of the oven you want to buy, what you will do if you get an order for 10,000 macarons and can't make that many, and what will you do if the sky falls ... you'll just get paralysed by worry and find excuses not to move forward.

Today, I want you to think about this post and your business. Soul search a little bit (or maybe a lot) about what stage you are at in your business in terms of commitment and decisions you've made so far. By the way, it's TOTALLY okay to admit to yourself that you are not fully committed and that you may never be - that for you, it's a great sideline but that's the limit of it. I also want you to remember last week's homework: the decision I had you make about the overarching purpose of being in business in the first place.

So, when should you quit your day job?

When you realise that if it's important enough to you, you'll make it happen.

If it isn't, you'll *make excuses*.

Let's be honest here.

The decision has ALREADY been made, hasn't it?

(Spoiler Alert: you made it when you decided to think about where you were headed.)

Well Equipped

At some point, all of us are going to need to buy equipment of some sort. Commercial food equipment is seriously expensive - and I mean seriously, ridiculously expensive. I paid more for the flooring in my commercial kitchen than I did for my first car! I've never truly understood why a commercial food processor is thousands of dollars when I can pick one up for $200 at the local department store but that's just the way it is. Equipment is a big investment for any business, so it's no wonder that some of the questions I've had from you recently are around what types of ovens to buy, what things to invest in, and what sizes of baking sheets you need.

I can't answer this question in specific without seeing the space you have, the money you've got available and knowing what the bigger plan is for your business. However, I can give you several pieces of advice about equipment and what works or doesn't work when deciding what to invest in.

My first commercial kitchen came fully kitted out with a stove top, oven, massive cool room and one shelf of shared freezer space. When I did my costing for moving into that space, I didn't include any of those things because they were already in place. I DID, however, include a broom, a mop, a set of scales and myriad other small things on my list and I thought I was the smartest business owner that ever lived.

Exactly one week after moving in, I found myself writing a check for $6, 600 for a new commercial oven. So ... there went the money I'd reserved for rent for the next two months. Damn.

It turns out that the oven under the stove top was useless to me because it could literally bake no more than a domestic oven could and it was very uneven. And ... it turns out that since I only ever used one pot on the stove to melt chocolate or boil cream, I really didn't need the full 4 burner commercial stove top. It also turned out I had no need for a fridge the size of a ballroom but I did need much more than one shelf of freezer space. Hmmm. Who knew?! (Clearly, not me.)

When it comes to buying equipment for your business (home based or commercially based), here are my top ten tips:

1. Remember that ovens (or mixers, or anything at all) are not meant to be kept forever and that you can (and will) replace them as your business grows. You're not stuck with it even if it cost you a bomb. You can replace it, upgrade, downgrade, whatever you need. Nothing is forever even if making the decision feels enormous because the cost is enormous.

2. Heating up an empty oven costs WAY more to run than a full one. Don't buy equipment you can't justify actually using. If you're only baking 5-6 cakes a week, don't buy something which can bake 50 cakes at a time. It's a waste of money and resources. Invest in things big enough to cover what you need plus a small amount more.

3. Don't buy the big stuff brand new if you don't have to. Commercial cooking equipment can often be found second hand for much cheaper and remember that you can get rid of it if it does not suit your needs (my oven was a floor model used for display at food expos. I got it for that price because it was 'second hand' although it had never been used. Original price was $14k.)

4. Decide on which items are truly non-negotiable and invest the money there. So for me, that was an oven, a planetary mixer, and baking tins and trays. I spent more on getting good quality essentials and bought cheaper versions of the not-so-essentials (microwaves, food processors, pots, knives and so on).

5. Keep small stuff on hand because it will come in handy more often than you realise. In my kitchen, I've got plenty of "big batch" items but I also have a small, domestic, hand-held beater - which is perfect for making small batches of royal icing.

6. Resist the urge to buy toys. The baking industry has ridiculous amounts of fabulous toys to play with - cool cutters, shaped tins, fancy rolling pins, impression mats, special chocolate melting pots, edible image printers, Cricuts ... the list of ways to spend money on baking and decorating toys is endless. I bought tons of that stuff (who can resist it?). Most of it was a colossal waste of money. I can count on one hand the number of times I've used the tin shaped like Pooh Bear or the special pot for melting isomalt. If it's trendy, expensive, or can't be honestly used for more than several different designs or products - don't buy it. How many times are you going to get asked for a cake in the shape of a frog, really?

7. Buy up big on consumable stuff - consumables being anything you use only once and then get rid of. I'm talking about tin foil, baking paper, white cupcake papers, paper towels, plastic wrap, take out containers, thin cake boards. Anything which is "throw away" is much cheaper when purchased in bulk (assuming you have somewhere to store it). Invest in a good stash of this stuff. You're going to use tons of it and it's not the stuff you want to run out of and then need to pay a premium for.

8. Be resourceful and look and ask around. Look for a solution among what you already own and who you already know than immediately running out and buying something. One of the best tools in my commercial kitchen is my dehydrator - I happened to mention to my Mother In Law that I wanted one but they were very expensive. The next day she brought me one she had bought back in the 70's when dehydrating stuff was apparently all the rage. It was sitting in a cupboard gathering dust. Five years later and it is in use almost every day in my kitchen (and I'm not making homemade fruit leather or semi-dried tomatoes). Essential item for FREE. Win!

9. Everyone wants a Kitchen Aid because they are cool and sexy, right? Don't buy a product because everyone has one - check out what the options are and make a choice based on need and usability not just cool factor. You need your equipment to be useful, efficient, easy to use and robust. if not, it wasn't worth buying in the first place. (All of you who bought a Cricut would be feeling this pain right about now.) (By the way, I'd buy a Kenwood.)

10. Recognise that good equipment is an investment in your business and it, therefore, is worth taking care of. We are all bad at maintenance but it's one of those things which bites you on the backside when you least expect it. I recently paid $1700 to repair my fridge because I didn't clean the filter and so the compressor died in the middle of summer. Who knew the damn thing even had a filter?

Good equipment becomes the backbone of our business. It makes us more efficient, it allows us to have a business in the first place (can't sell cake without an oven to bake it in) and it can make or break our sanity sometimes. We've all been in that place when the cake you're expecting to be done at midnight is still liquid in the middle because the oven died and you didn't realise it - and you don't have time to re-bake it as the cake is due tomorrow night.

All that being said - equipment needs to be paid for over the length of its life, not just when you first purchase it. Buy the item which best meets your current needs and which you can best afford, always remember that it's replaceable or upgradeable - and you can't go wrong. By the way - best purchase I ever made? A local cake maker decided to retire. Sight unseen I bought the entire contents of her garage for $200. I'm still using those 20+ cake tins, flower stamens, stands, and have some of the cake boards - nearly 7 years later. Worst purchase I ever made? Any shaped tin made by Wilton (and I mean no offence to Wilton, but those pans are flimsy, too low, and I never got asked for a cake shaped like a hot air balloon again.)

Have you bought anything you can't live without - or anything you're embarrassed to admit you own?

Confused In Cakeland - Buying Cake Tools

Confused in Cakeland

Hi Michelle,

I recently got asked to do an order for a wedding cake that requires some tools I don't currently own, and they are pretty expensive tools. Should I buy them? If I do buy them, should I charge the customer for them?

Thanks,

Tina

Hi Tina,

If you get asked to make a cake with tools you do not have, then you basically have two choices:

1. *buy the tools; or*

2. *improvise using what you already have.*

Some tools you can improvise pretty easily - cookie cutters can be used in more than one way, you can hand-cut templates for some things, you can borrow tools from friends and you can modify designs slightly to use the tools you already have. I personally think cake decorators these days rely on fancy gadgets WAY too much rather than look at what they have and find new uses for them.

If you decide to buy them, then you absorb that cost and you cannot hand the client a bill for the tools. That's just not cool. Chances are you're going to be using those tools again for another client - and a smart business owner would make sure of it! I would buy the tools, make the cake that was ordered AND make at least one or more dummy cakes using that same tool. Take some good pictures of those cakes and share them with your audience, print them out for your portfolio and have the dummy cakes on display. People love to order what they can see. It's up to you to recoup the costs of those tools, not up to the client to be 'penalised' for picking a cake which requires specialist tools. If you're investing in it, make it work for you!

The same thing applies when it's tools you just want to try out but nobody has placed an order for that style. Personally, I won't buy any tool unless I can immediately see more than one use for it - because I consider tools to be an investment into my business, and that investment needs to pay off sooner rather than later. In the back of the cupboard we all have crazy shaped Wilton pans and weird flower cutters we bought and never used again, so my aim is always to reduce the amount of "seems like a good idea" tools and only really buy the stuff which is going to become invaluable to me.

Yours in investment,

Michelle

Like A Cake Boss

FOLLOW YOUR HEART BUT TAKE YOUR BRAIN WITH YOU.

Today, I want to talk about the realities of owning your own cake business. We often see people in business and they make it look so easy, don't they? Their pictures are all beautiful and basically, it appears like they love every single minute of it. The good news is, that's exactly what they should be portraying - because you as their customer don't need or want to know that they struggle to pay rent, suck down anti-inflammatories by the bucket load, or that last week's cake fell over in a blaze of glory or butter cream. The bad news is, we're comparing ourselves to a carefully curated image of what we think it is to own a cake business. I owned a cake business for ten years and I can tell you that while there are plenty of perfect pictures and I maintained a very happy-go-lucky exterior, the reality of it was that there were times I struggled to pay rent (in the beginning certainly), and I downed a lot of anti-inflammatories (thank you, dodgy back spasms) and that I had plenty of cakes that fell over (it feels as awful as you might think.) Every one of those things, from the perfect pictures to the cakes that fell over, were my responsibility to deal with. Why? Because I was the boss.

Anyone who has had a child knows that the biggest secret women share is that parenting is way way way way way harder than you think it will be. Anyone who has "birthed" a business knows that the biggest secret business owners share is that it's way way way way way harder than you think it will be. I can say (having done both of those) that the joy and pride is also way way way way way better than you might think, too. Basically, you're choosing to take a much bigger risk in the hope it leads to a much bigger reward. Kids or business, the idea is the same.

In both situations, you're the boss - and so it's your role to take the good with the bad.

Do you know what I find most interesting about the cake industry at the moment? That there are so many people going into business (for any number of reasons) and not realising that it's not enough to be able to decorate "like a boss" ... you've got to actually BE the boss in the first place. Every day I see posts from people asking, "Do you think it's okay if I ... use inedible glitter / use a copyright image / fire an employee / take time off (etc.)?" Every time I see those I want to reply with, "Who cares if we think it's okay? YOU ARE THE BOSS HERE."

So what does being the cake boss actually mean?

It means that you make ALL the rules.
It means you get to (and have to) do the fun stuff, but also the not-so-fun stuff.
It also means that you get ALL the risk ... and ALL the reward.

All of you who watch the TV show Cake Boss can see that Buddy is there making cake ... but he's also disciplining staff, taking care of equipment, planning for growth, investing money in renovations and looking after his cake empire. I can guarantee he is spending more time doing boss stuff than he is piping anything. Do they show that on TV? Well, maybe a teeny tiny bit, if the staff problems make for a good story. Most of his being the "cake boss" actually doesn't happen on TV at all, because it does not make for good TV. It's not exciting or edge-of-your-seat ... and while it might involve a lot of drama, it's not the sort of drama people tune in to watch because business drama isn't as spectacular as a cake falling down a flight of stairs.

The year is drawing to a close and it's now that we start to think about goals and what we might like to achieve next year. For some, you'll start to take action towards opening a store. For others, you'll register your home kitchens. Some of you will get the excitement of getting your first business card. Others of you will start teaching classes. Some of you will just start to play around with that idea of owning a business, while others of you will choose to wind down your existing businesses. We are all at different stages of the experience - and we all have different stories - but the important thing to remember is that no matter what stage you're at, you're the BOSS of the place, not the employee. The mindset is entirely different.

Remember what I said earlier? Bosses take all the risk - and get all the reward. To put this in cake terms: bosses get the biggest slice of the cake AND they decided what flavour it's going to be.

This year, no matter where you are in your cake business, it's time for you to start thinking - and acting - like a boss. Make your decisions and choose your path from that mindset and you'll already be miles ahead of your competitors.

Like. A. Boss.

Make More Money, Spend Less Time

Does any of this sound like you?

- You seem to spend hours and hours each week answering enquiries, but ...
- You aren't getting enough orders to make a living or make it worth the hassle, and ...
- You're sick and tired of having to explain to people why you charge what you charge ...
- You're exhausted from the constant emailing back and forth and back and forth before the client either doesn't order from you, or changes their mind about what they want ...
- You are losing track of enquiries because they are coming from multiple sources (Facebook messaging, emails, texts on your phone, comments on Instagram) ...
- You feel like you say the same thing to the same people over and over (you've answered that question about your flavours about a million times by now) ...
- It feels like people only care about price ...
- You feel like you rush through orders (or do them at crazy hours) because you're struggling to keep up with the administration of the business ...
- You really just want or need to make more money and spend less time chasing orders ...

If any one of those sound even remotely familiar, then this blog post is for you.

All of the above are things which most of us have felt or experienced at one point or another in our businesses. We DO spend a lot of time communicating with prospective clients, and it eats up quite a lot of our working hours. So how do we cope when we're just had enough of it?

STEP ONE: Adjust your attitude.

Answering emails and messages about orders gets you more orders. It's what you need to do in order to get to the fun stuff of playing with cake lace and steaming wafer paper ruffles. It's not optional. A bit later on in this post I'm going to give you some strategies for how to make the communication process a little more efficient, but in the interim we need to work on your attitude. If you're feeling like answering those messages is a boring, frustrating, time-sucking chore, or if you're feeling like people only care about price or if you're feeling like you've explained your prices countless times and you're just damn sick of it all ... I want you to stop for a second and think about your own behaviour as a consumer.

The last time you needed new tires, needed some painting done, needed to get your car repaired, bought a big ticket item like a washing machine - didn't you call or email more than one supplier and ask for a quote? Were you concerned about price? Did you send emails to several suppliers? Did that salesperson answer your questions about why one brand of dishwasher was better than another? Did the tiling guy send you a written, detailed quote about the work you needed done? Did you look at the 3 quotes you got and consider what they were offering for the money? Did you look at the most expensive quote and wonder why it was so expensive? Did the saleslady who answered the phone give you some prices and information? Did you buy something, only to return it because you just changed your mind or found one you liked better? Did you search online to see if you could get it faster or cheaper elsewhere? Did you look at more than one company's options and compare the two products? Did you reply to the two guys whose quotes you didn't go with?

If you as a consumer have done any of those things, then it should come as no surprise that your potential customers are doing and expecting the EXACT SAME THINGS.

They're just being consumers. They buy stuff ... but they also compare stuff, think about stuff, shop around, ask a lot of questions, change their minds and make decisions based on many factors. Their behaviours are not any different just because one day they are shopping for cake and one day they are shopping for washing machines.

I'm not going to lie to you. The endless emails, messages and explaining over and over can get tiring, frustrating and it's not even one tiny percent as fun as playing with cake or chocolate is going to be. Let me remind you, though, that cake is not always fun either. It melts, it falls over, it stresses you out, it brings you to tears, it robs you of sleep and sanity and money. . . but ultimately we still get up and do it again. . . Every. Single. Week. Why? Because we love it.

Here's my BFO (Blindingly Freakin' Obvious) point: if you don't send quotes and answer emails <u>every single week</u>, you do NOT GET ORDERS to have fun with <u>every single week</u>. It's a non-negotiable part of the deal. You're not special in this regard. The plumbers, electricians, wedding dress makers and tire companies all have to do that as well. *You've got to quote (a lot) if you want to get a gig. (Or as Disney might put it, you've got to kiss a lot of frogs to find your prince.)*

So: adjust your attitude and be grateful that you've marketed well enough to get people to your door in the first place. There are plenty of people out there who would kill to get half as many emails as you get. Also - remember that part of growing your business is investing time in it. You can't say you want to grow your business and then turn around and tell me how annoying it is to answer emails all the time.

deep breath

Okay so now that I've gently told you to stop complaining about it, I'm going to teach you how to deal with it. Here are a few strategies to help make quoting easier:

- **Redirect enquiries to ONE place**. You can actually disable messages on your Facebook business page and I suggest you do so. It's too easy to read then totally forget about Facebook messages - both for you and for the person who sent it. If you want to keep that function on, just reply to every email with a STANDARD and friendly reply (so you can cut and paste): "Thanks so much for your message. We don't take orders via Facebook, so please email the details of your order to cakes@cakes.com or call me on 123 456. Thanks." The same message can be used for people who PM you on Instagram (or comment on pictures) and so on. REDIRECT people to where you want them to go and so you can keep track of correspondence in a single place. (Also: Don't forget to make your website address and phone number easy to find in the first place.)

- **Turn email notifications off on your phone**. Every time my phone pings, I look at the emails, then forget I saw them, or mentally reply to them but don't actually do it. Eventually, I get to a PC and see them, and vaguely recall having read them the first time. The problem here is that I'm double handling those emails, and wasting countless minutes every day re-reading something I already read. If it's an actual emergency (of the truly important sort, not of the "I need six cupcakes" sort), then your phone will RING and not DING. Turn off the dinging so you're not looking and re-looking at those emails.

- **Answer correspondence at a set time, for a set time**. So for example, every night after the kids go to bed, between 8-9 is when you reply to correspondence, then you work on orders from 9. Why does this work? Because it means from 8-9, you're working on building your business, and from 9, you're working on getting the orders done. You won't have one without the other, so set aside some time to do it. You'll be FAR more efficient if you're doing it that way rather than in dribs and drabs all day long.

- **Here's a whole new concept: pick up the damn phone!** If emails with a client or potential client are getting any further than 2 replies each, CALL THEM. It's much faster and better to have all your questions answered at once, and most of the time when you're on the phone with them you'll close the deal. It's much easier for them to say no over email than over the phone talking to a live person. Over the phone, you can also gently lead them to make a final decision and pay that deposit already! If you do all your work at night, either get out of the house earlier or make phone calls on your lunch break or SOMETHING, just please call people rather than endlessly email them. They'll appreciate the personal touch, and you'll get more sales (or END conversations which were not leading anywhere regardless) and above all you'll save a lot of time.

- **Ask people what they DON'T want**. Some of the most frustrating clients are those who really have no idea what they want, and run you around in circles showing you tons of pictures and asking you to quote and re-quote, only to never order anything (or at least, not order anything from you). You need to take control of this situation and FAST. If you can feel it getting out of hand, you need to lead them in the direction you want, which is towards making a decision. Ask them, "Is there anything you really would not want on your cake? Colours you do not like? Do you love stripes or hate them?" and so on and so forth. Narrow them down by forcing them to answer very pointed questions. If they've sent you 10 photos to look at, see if you can't find the unifying thing in all of them. Chances are they will all be round, or all be 3 tier, or all be buttercream - there will be some element that links them because they've chosen all of them, so those photos are a reflection of their aesthetic and taste.

- **Make your website really easy to use**. Also, whatever people ask you about often, make that information really easy to find. If you answer a lot of emails about your flavours - put that somewhere obvious. If people ask you about your availability, put a calendar on there which clearly shows the dates you still have free (and please don't forget to update it). People keep emailing you about price? Have at least a basic pricing guide on there - one-tier cakes from $100, two tier cakes from $300 (and so on). Having a clear, informative website will do two things: 1) weed out the people you do not want as clients anyway or who you cannot help, and 2) encourage the people who are still interested to either call or email you. It isn't foolproof but it certainly weeds out a heck of a lot of tire kickers, and thus saves you a heck of a lot of time.

- **Develop an email formula**. No, not a form email you sent to every single person, but a method for how you're going to answer emails so that you're not trying to re-write a novel every single time you reply. So every email looks something like this:

  ➢ Greeting (Dear Samantha,)

  ➢ Acknowledgement (Thanks so much for your email.)

  ➢ Answer their question with a reasonable amount of detail (We'd love to make you a Thomas the Tank Engine cake for your son's birthday.

You can choose from any of our 6 flavours, and it's no problem to make it gluten free for you, the one you saw on our website is $xyz and it feeds 20 kids.)

➢ Give them a call to action (We'll just need a deposit in order to reserve that date for you, so I'll give you a call tomorrow to discuss the final details.) (more on how to do this further in this post.)

➢ Sign off (Yours in sweetness,)

➢ Name (Michelle)

(And don't forget to have a signature file at the bottom with all your contact details.)

Okay, so now we've cut down on the correspondence (or made it a little easier to deal with), how do we close the actual sale? Here's some tips to convert those enquiries into sales:

- **Give them <u>a clear call to action</u>**. You need to end your email or call with a sentence that makes them DO something. Closing with something like, "I look forward to hearing from you," is just way too open-ended. Closing with something like, "I'll confirm your order after I receive the deposit, deposits are accepted via credit card," makes it seem like the deal is already done. These days people want their problems solved quickly and easily so you need to make that happen for them. "I'll call you tomorrow morning and we can finalise the details", "If you need more information, please call me tomorrow on 123 456", "To finalise this order, please pay the deposit of $X to this account number", "I'd love to cater your wedding and I think you'll love our flavours, why don't I reserve you a spot at our next tasting session? It's at 2 pm this coming Saturday, I look forward to meeting you then", and so on and so forth. Figure out a few carefully worded sentences which you are comfortable with, but the key is to basically convert them into a sale by telling them EXACTLY what and how to do the next part (place the order or take it closer to that goal).

- **Here's a whole new concept: pick up the damn phone!** Yep, I'm repeating this one again - emails have a tendency to just go on, and on, and on, and on. I guarantee you that you're probably not the only company they emailed for a quote, but if you're the one that calls them back and actually solves their problem, you're going to get the deal. Good customer service is often about following up - so follow up! People are very time poor (we're all busy sending emails apparently) and nobody more so than parents and brides ... so if you can fulfil their needs quickly, save them time and hassle, you're going to get the gig. Everyone else is still emailing them ... and emailing them ... and emailing them.

- **If your website has an enquiry form, have a few required fields in it.**
  Name, email address, phone number, date and type of event, and where they heard about you. Why does this help you close the deal? Because: a) you can contact them by phone, and b) you have enough information to direct the conversation. (Bonus: you'll immediately know which of your marketing channels is getting you the most traffic.) Knowing where your business is coming from potentially tells you the demographic of the person calling. For example, the price conscious would probably not be calling you from an ad you placed in an ultra high end mega expensive bridal magazine. If that's where they found you, chances are they care a lot about design and exclusivity so that's what your conversation with them should focus on.

There is an entire art form to sales - highly trained and skilled salespeople will never be out of a job - and what I've given you here is really only the tip of the iceberg. As an industry generalisation, we don't like to talk about money, we don't like to be forward with closing sales, and we don't like to actually call people. We like to send a lot of emails and make a lot of beautiful things and post a lot of pretty pictures, all of which is lovely, sweet rainbow sprinkles but also MASSIVELY TIME CONSUMING.

Guess what?

It isn't always rainbow sprinkles in here.

I like to eat, as do my children. In order for that to happen, I have to answer all those emails, make those phone calls, send quotes, answer questions over and over, tell people my price and then get them to pay for what I make. Last I checked those things are true of EVERY OTHER INDUSTRY, which sells products. We are not special in that regard.

If you read this far, I'm impressed. Thanks.

If you skipped to the bottom, here's the gist of it: Adjust your attitude, and help people quickly decide to buy your stuff. It's either that or go back to complaining you have no orders and you're sick of answering emails.

Personally, I'd rather make more money doing what I love and spend less time complaining about not having enough orders to do so.

Friends With Benefits

Your friends and family are probably the people who got you into this whole cake thing in the first place. They're the ones who gave you the shove in the cake business direction. The ones who praised you until you blushed, who told their friends about you, who asked you to make them cakes, who made that fateful comment - "You should totally sell these!" - which moved you along the path to where you are now.

Your friends and family are probably also the people who will be your initial "clients". I used the term in quotes because I don't know about you, but I don't really want clients who call me at home after hours, who expect to pay very little for their cakes, and who will then fail to call you to appropriately gush about how awesome the cake was. Nor do I want clients who refer to me condescendingly as, "this woman I know who makes cakes from home", and I definitely don't want clients who think 24 hours is long enough for me to create them a 5 tier extravaganza and then somehow make you feel guilty about it if you baulk at the idea.

However.

You NEED your friends and family, at least initially. They are the people who will order because at first, they are the only people who know what you're doing in your kitchen in the first place. They'll be much more forgiving of the wobbly top tier, the misspelling of the word "birthday" and the not-quite-right shade of blue. They'll give you the work because they know you want it. They'll tell everyone they know that you're making cakes because they love you and want to support you. In the first flush of business, your friends and family are absolutely vital to get the ball rolling.

Here's the funny thing about friends and family. They (while extremely special and important human beings) only have birthdays once a year. Anniversaries once a year. Christenings every few years. Unless they're the Twitter-loving Ashton Kutcher of the cake world and your friends actually have 10 million friends, they just won't have enough orders to keep you in business. Here's the other funny thing about friends and family - you rarely feel right about charging them what your work is worth, because they've seen you when your roots needing re-touching and they've seen you in your dodgiest pair of yoga pants (the ones with the bleach stain). There's just something wrong about charging your sister $200 for a cake, isn't there? (Ignoring that it cost you $187. 66 in fancy cake tools and ingredients to make it.) It's just somehow ... not cool.

While it is true that some of your friends and family may fall into the category of your target market - based on their age, stage of life or financial situation - they simply cannot be the only clients you rely on if this is going to grow into a real business. Here's another thing about family and friends - they can easily turn into your business's numero uno frenemy. Another cake maker I know (who makes cakes as a sideline to her normal job) recently made a birthday cake for a neighbour. She'd made cakes for her before and charged a ridiculously low price. She decided it was no longer worth doing it that way and tried to decline the request, but the neighbour was insistent (another type of client you don't want: the bullying sort). Against her better judgement, my friend agreed to make her neighbour a cake, but for a bit more money than last time.

She busted her butt to make her a gorgeous cake. The neighbour loved it. The neighbour was appreciative. The guests loved it.

The following week the neighbour told all the other women in the street (potential clients!) that she'd gotten a great cake from my friend. How nice of her, right? Sure, except then she bragged about what a FANTASTIC BARGAIN she got. Suddenly the glowing recommendation is not so glowing, is it?

What lesson was learnt by my friend's potential clients?

If you bully her into making you a cake, she'll make it for you at a bargain price.

Would you still call this neighbour a friend? Nope. Frenemy #1.

Still not convinced that your friends are not your clients, at least not in the long term?

Let me tell you a story from my own archives of embarrassment. Early in my cake making days (when I was still operating from home, in an unregistered kitchen, and impressed as hell that I was actually making cold, hard cash from what I considered to be just a fun hobby) a friend invited my kids to her daughter's birthday party. I made the stupid mistake of *offering to make the cake instead of bringing a gift*.

Let me stop for a second. If at least one of you did not groan out loud in understanding sympathy at that one, I'd be shocked. We've ALL made that mistake, haven't we? (And some of us more than once ...)

She was thrilled with my offer. She wanted a "simple cake" for about 20 kids, in a Wiggles theme. Okay, that seems easy, right?

Nope.

Over the next few weeks, the brief on the cake grew ... and grew ... and grew. It needed to be egg free. Feed 40 kids plus a handful of adults. Had to include the colours green and pink. Needed to be High 5 instead of the Wiggles. Needed to also have Thomas on there somewhere. Needed to be delivered. Needed to have a few dozen matching cupcakes. Couldn't be chocolate. Needed to feed 60 kids and 20 adults. Needed to be 2 tiers. Needed to be a Tinkerbell theme with all of those damn fairy friends on it.

Do you see where I'm going with this?

I couldn't go back on the offer now, could I? But this was WAY more than I had anticipated. So I sucked it up, and I made her a seriously kick-ass cake. I spent something like five squillion dollars more on making that cake than I would have spent on a gift. I know there was sweat and tears involved and I'm pretty certain there was blood, too. I put my heart and soul into that thing.

That was 8 years ago. I'm still waiting on the actual thank you.

I delivered the cake, and waited a week for her to call me. She didn't. I ashamed to say that I could not help myself, I called her and pointedly asked, "SO HOW WAS THE CAKE?"

"Oh! Yeah! The cake. It was good, thanks".

Wait. WHAT? It was ... good? That's IT? It was just ... good?

Technically speaking, I got my thank you. But it was a bit like squeezing the last scrap of buttercream out of the piping bag when you've still got 3 cupcakes left to ice. In other words, a valiant effort but one which ultimately fails.

Your friends and family are wonderful people. They really, really are. You love them, they love you, it's all great, yadda yadda. Don't rely on them to be your customers in the long term. Don't rely on them to be your marketing plan. Don't give your work away for free (and definitely not in lieu of presents) and above all, *don't expect your friends to be anything but your friends.*

Small business ownership is a crazy, busy, insane, fabulous, chaotic life. You need your friends and family - as babysitters, dinner makers, coffee drinkers, shoulders to cry on, back up delivery drivers, therapists, errand runners ... in fact, they'll fulfil almost every support role in your business you need them to fill. EXCEPT being your clients. Leave that role - to your clients.

Your Business, Your Rules

A few weeks ago, I talked to you about not relying on friends and family to be your long term clientele. The fact is, they're going to be your clients - at least in the beginning. What happens when you have friends and family who genuinely want to order from you over an extended period of time ... but you still just don't feel right charging your bestie real money for a cake? What if the same bestie insists on paying you real money for your effort (congrats, you've got a good bestie. Hang onto her!)? What if the same bestie wants to order from you all the time, but constantly expects a really good deal? (Oh, that sucks, what a bad choice of bestie. Dump and run I say.)

This is one business conundrum which has a very simple solution.

Very early on in the establishment of the business, work out what your official Mates Rates Policy (or in the US, what your "Friends and Family Plan" 🙂 *) is going to be.*

First, work out who are the ONLY people you will work for free for (because there might just be some.) Make sure that is a *very* small group of people and for heaven's sake do not let anyone know, not even them until they actually order something. There may be nobody at all on this list. Not a single soul. That's okay. <u>This is your business, these are your rules.</u>

Then, think long and hard about who you are willing to call your friend or family for the purposes of this policy. Your sister, the woman you see in the playground twice a day but hardly know, your long lost cousin Antonia, your friend from mother's group, your old work mate. You would be amazed at the people who will ask for a discount and you do not want to be caught out when they ask. Some people deserve this deal. Some don't. *Be very clear about who those people might be.*

Then think about what you're willing to offer to the people you've decided fall into this category.

You want to give them something truly of value (because in essence what you're valuing is their relationship to you, more than the actual product in question) but not something so over the top that you're losing money every time they order. A discount of some sort. A dozen free somethings if they order a big something. Free delivery. Wholesale pricing. Extra special flavours of something. Free cake stand hire. Whatever. Work out what you can do for them without causing yourself any real financial or emotional dramas.

Decide what your policy is for these people and be very specific. Write it down somewhere. Don't advertise it to anyone. Ever. Then be open, honest, and fair about it by actually sticking to the policy. In fact, offer it to (very good or close) friends before they've even asked for it AND use the language of "the Official Mates Rates Policy" (or whatever you're choosing to call it.)

Here's how the conversation goes with someone you've pre-decided is eligible for the discount:

"I need a cake for Ava's party. What do you charge for a princess cake to feed forty kids?"

"Normally I'd charge $300, but the Official Mates Rates Policy is a 50% discount, so for you it will be $150. Does she like chocolate or vanilla?"

This is a win-win on both sides. Win for you as you're doing the right thing by offering a friend a sweet deal but not busting your chops, and a win for her because she knows she's going to get seriously awesome cake but for a good price. Between you and me, my friends and family know I'm highly likely to exceed their expectations anyway just because I love them, but making them a concrete offer like this manages their expectations (from a cost point of view) from the very beginning.

Here's how the conversation goes with someone who you've pre-decided is NOT eligible for the discount (and yeah, you might know them pretty well. Makes no difference to how you handle it.)

"I need a cake for Ava's party. What do you charge for a princess cake to feed forty kids?"

"I charge $300 for a princess cake, with all the sparkle she can handle! Does she like chocolate or vanilla?"

"Oh, but we're cousins! Can't you do any better on that price?"

"No. That's the best I can do. "

(Allow the silence to settle as they decide what to do next.) Either they will order, or they won't. Makes no difference to you. You are not in the business of freebies or cheapies, remember?

There are a few key points to making this Mates Rates work for you:

1. Be confident about your decision. You already know who you're willing to offer the deal to and who you're not. You've already done the hard work

of thinking about the WHO and the WHY of this deal. By the time, they get around to asking, you already know the answer. You're simply educating them.

2.   Don't be bullied. You're in the *business* of cake (not the hobby of cake), and you are most certainly not in the business of freebies or cheapies.

3.   Don't be rude. It's totally legitimate for them to ask for a discount - but it's legitimate to be nice when you turn them down.

4.   Don't advertise that you even have this deal in the first place. Nobody needs to know. And since it's a CLEAR and DEFINED policy, chances are the very few people you offer it to are unlikely to brag about it to their friends because they already know you're unlikely to offer it to anyone else. It makes them feel special because they ARE special. By using the actual words "official policy," you are drawing a very clear, permanent line. They know it. You know it.

Let's be clear about something. You're not making cakes all night just because it's fun (although it is.) You're making cakes (and reading this book) because you are serious about making an actual living from this.

This is YOUR JOB (or one of them at least.) This is how you PAY YOUR BILLS (or some of them at least.) Treat it as such.

If your friends and family truly want to become your long term clients, they'll understand this.

<u>You are in the business of cake, NOT in the business of freebies or cheapies.*</u>

Mates Rates Policies are important to small businesses, they really are. So - go. Figure it out this week. Let me know if you've developed your policy, and if you've had the chance to try it out on anyone yet.

* If you are actually in the business of freebies or cheapies, please stop reading this book. This book is not for you.

Delivery Etiquette

At some point in your business, you're going to need to deliver your products somewhere. Assuming you survive the ordeal, here are a few Dos and Don'ts to make your delivery experience that much better:

DO:

- Take a repair kit in the car with you. A little plastic box which has spare dowels, a piping bag, a few piping tips, a small spatula, a spare sugar flower or two, glue stick, small container of egg white powder (so you can make royal icing on the run), scissors (to cut ribbon or flowers), baby wipes (for cleaning fondant). Basically, a little box of tricks you can have on hand in case everything goes to hell on the way there.

- Wear your company clothes to deliver - either your (clean) company apron, a t-shirt with your logo, a hat. Something which makes you look more professional and is company branded. If you don't yet have those, at the very least ALWAYS be neat and clean and have your hair pulled back.

- Take extra business cards and samples (if you have some) with you. Delivering is a great opportunity to network with venues. Even if you're delivering to a person's house, it's nice to bring them a little extra treat or a spare business card for them to share with a friend.

- Bring along: a printed cutting guide (I like the Cake Slicer app for this purpose: https://www.bakingit.com/app/#stacker), instructions for disassembling the cake if it's complicated, a picture of whatever internal structure it's got, and any storage instructions. When you give this to the venue, take a note of who you gave it to (get their name) and write that down somewhere.

- Take a picture of the cake where you left it. This might save your butt later and you can use it as a social media post later (and tag the venue, it's good networking.)

- Invest in a little flat trolley on wheels that lives in your car along with the emergency repair kit. Sometimes you've got to walk a LONG WAY and it's easier to put a cake on a platform and wheel it in. (Here's an example of what I mean: http://amzn.to/1Ga3oAo)

DON'T:

- Use bad language or be anything other than polite and accommodating.

- Talk smack about your clients, no matter how freaking annoying they are.

- Show up looking like you just rolled out of bed.

- Show up in some sort of manky looking car. I'm not saying go and buy a Ferrari to deliver in. I'm saying showing up in a flea infested hunk o' junk that drops its carburettor in the driveway of the venue is not really a good look.

- Show up late.

- Drink any alcohol to calm your nerves before you go. Save it for AFTER you've delivered it safely.

- Assume they will understand anything about the care of cakes, and don't assume they will have a table already set up for you. CALL AHEAD a few hours or the day before to introduce yourself, check if there is a cake table, and ask what time they need you to arrive. A little bit of kindness to the venue will get you very far when you show up and need a hand.

- Assume that everything that's supposed to be there will be there. SO MANY TIMES brides told me they organised flowers for their cakes, and then I get there and it's a random pile of half-dead blooms that are not arranged at all and suddenly I was a florist as well as a cake maker.

- Run off like a bat out of hell. Sometimes we're just so damn relieved to get rid of the thing that we drop it and run. Take a second to make sure you're happy with it, say a polite goodbye to the venue people, and walk away calmly. When you get in your car, scream at the top of your lungs to relieve the pressure and THEN you can run like hell.

- Do as I did and leave a delivery. And, then reverse into a parked car and smash it, especially when the parked car belongs to the son of the groom. Also don't do that on the day you take your employee with you so you can teach her how to do deliveries. Trust me on this one. It's horribly embarrassing.

Of all the parts of my business I hated, deliveries ranked as #1 on that list. I'm not a drinker but if I WAS, I'd have gone through a heck of a lot of bottles of vodka. I actually had my husband do a lot of my deliveries for me, as he was much calmer and far more sane than I was about it - not to mention he was stronger physically AND emotionally to deal with it all! Inevitably you're going to have to do some deliveries yourself - so hang on this post for when the time comes so that it all goes a little calmer and smoother for you.

If all else fails, pre-purchase the vodka.

Hiring Versus Outsourcing

When your business starts to feel like it's getting out of hand, or you're just feeling overwhelmed by how much you've got to do, the first thing we often think we should do is hired an employee. There is a lot to consider when hiring your first employee (and I will get to that), but in today's post, I want to chat about the differences between hiring an employee and outsourcing, and when to use each of those methods.

Firstly, let's define the difference between them. <u>Hiring an employee</u> is when you have another person in your business who you need to look after - pay them, train them, manage them, keep track of them, pay all the associated costs. Usually, they work in your actual premises, even if your premises is your home kitchen. <u>Outsourcing</u> is when you don't hire anyone, instead, you give a task (or several tasks) to another company or person external to your business. You pay them based on the specific job they do, you are not responsible for any of the infrastructure involved in having them as an employee (insurance, etc.). Usually, their work is done at their own premises rather than yours.

<u>The first thing I suggest you do is to identify the jobs which need doing</u>, and then define which are your weaknesses and strengths. What are you good at? What do you absolutely hate doing? What kinds of activities are essential to the business's long-term success? Are there any activities which you might enjoy, but can be easily done by someone else, thus freeing you up to do the more important tasks? What's currently eating up your time? As a business owner, your time is both more

in demand and also more expensive than an employee's will be, so there would be no value in (for example) paying you to make ganache when someone else can be doing that. Think about your strengths and weaknesses from a business sense. Are you great at the numbers and spreadsheets, or do you hate them? Are you great at marketing and social media, or is that a chore? Does baking the naked cakes take days and days of your time, when you could be answering quote requests?

Once you've developed that list, you can start to determine which of those things you could reasonably hand off to someone else. Determine which of those tasks are directly impacting both your business growth and the use of your time. Then, decide if those jobs need to be done in-house or not. When I was growing my business, I found that initially outsourcing jobs was of more use to me than hiring. At that time, the biggest 'boring but important' job I had (and hated with a deep passion) was bookkeeping. I was handling all the cake stuff just fine, but I was making a mess of my bookkeeping and it stressed me out a lot. Money, taxes and financial paperwork are vitally important to a business and there I was screwing it up and hating it - so I outsourced it to a bookkeeper. Sure, it wasn't cheap, but what it cost me in money it more than made up for it in time, effort, and stress reduction. If I had been good at that paperwork stuff, but terrible at (or hated) 'basic' cake tasks like making buttercream or cutting our hundreds of flowers each week, I probably would have hired a staff member rather than outsource.

Basically, the decision to hire or outsource will depend on what jobs actually need doing. In the first instance, I usually recommend outsourcing the speciality tasks and/or the very time-consuming ones- because you'll get the most immediate value out of those tasks being done efficiently and professionally. If you can get all your financial paperwork sorted out or if you can save three days a week in baking time, that's doing you a whole lot of good. Remember too that as your business grows, you can always 'take back' the tasks you previously outsourced. Suppose you get to the stage where you hire an admin assistant - that person might have finance skills and could do your book work for you. Or if you've outsourced your flowers, you might find that one of your employees is then happy to get trained in flower making and you can bring those back in the house again. Outsourcing can apply to a number of tasks. There are plenty of virtual assistants, social media companies, bookkeepers, flower makers, naked cake bakeries and so on which can help you get a handle on your business. You don't have to be everything to everybody all of the time. You may also just need to outsource for a short period of time, perhaps during peak wedding season when your time is shorter than usual. Outsourcing is great for small businesses because can fill an immediate gap and the risk is generally a lot lower than hiring an employee but it's also potentially more expensive.

Many of you have asked me when you know it's the right time to hire an employee. You can't know the answer to that until you've worked out what you need help with the most. Knowing what needs doing and why is the first part of working out if you should outsource or hire. Remember that when you make the list of tasks which need doing, it's not just about what you love or hate doing, it's also about what jobs (when done by someone else) are going to free up your time to work <u>on</u> your business and not just <u>in</u> it.

Dealing With The Cow Down The Road

Oh boy. This is a HUGE issue for so many people. We work our butts off to create amazing products, we actually sit down and do our pricing, we register our kitchens, we do our marketing and we do ALL the right things ... and yet some cow down the road doesn't register her kitchen, charges close to nothing, and then STEALS all our clients from us.

Seriously. The nerve of some people.

Even worse is that lady down the road who not only steals our clients, but she steals our IDEAS too. We post a cute picture of a bunny cake ... and the next day, she posts a bunny cake. We offer a winter special on cupcakes ... and she offers a winter special on cupcakes. I mean it's flattering and all - but COME ON LADY.

So the question is ... what should you do in this situation?

Should you:

a.   Call her up and give her a piece of your mind?

b.   Call the local food compliance authorities and tell on her?

c.   Email her and suggest that she might want to read this blog or let her know about food laws (because maybe she has no idea that what she's doing is illegal)?

d.   Submit fake reviews on social media which mention her unregistered kitchen, rude manner and her very large and hairy dog that wanders into her kitchen while she's decorating?

e.   Do a LOT of complaining about her on social media?

f.   Ignore her. You've got better things to do?

Truth is, it's probably REALLY tempting to do ALL of those things to a degree. It's seriously freaking annoying when you've gone to the trouble and effort to do things the right way and others haven't. It's even more annoying when they copy you and what you're doing.

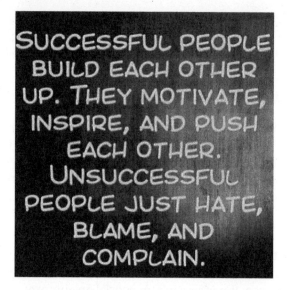

SUCCESSFUL PEOPLE BUILD EACH OTHER UP. THEY MOTIVATE, INSPIRE, AND PUSH EACH OTHER. UNSUCCESSFUL PEOPLE JUST HATE, BLAME, AND COMPLAIN.

Of the above choices, don't ever do a, b, d or e. Honestly, those are just plain pointless things to do and a complete waste of your already precious time. As for c - I'd LOVE it if I could convince you to extend the hand of friendship to one another, but I know that's not always possible or reasonable to expect.

Sometimes you know for sure that other person KNOWS they are in the wrong, sometimes you've had previous run-ins, sometimes you're just not comfortable with reaching out. If however you are willing to reach out, I would recommend that if you do it by PHONE not by email, since email has no tone of voice and can easily be misconstrued.

Mostly, though, I'd suggest going with option f. Sure, the under cutters and copycats can be really, really frustrating and annoying - so step one is just to get them out of your life. Unfollow their business page, block them from your page, stop looking at their website and just pretend they don't exist. Truth is, they are not your problem and if they are charging so little and doing it all so wrong, they are unlikely to last terribly long anyway. **I want you to have a long-term business, and surviving in business long-term means you are going to outwit, outlast, and outplay the others who will come along that are just dabbling in it.**

Step two is to keep on being your amazing self. Keep marketing. Keep innovating. Keep pushing yourself to try new things, extend your skills, do more marketing and carry on with creating the business that you want to have. Let's be honest, for a little while there we were no different to that lady down the road. We too did stuff illegally for a while, and we too charged too little for a while. It's no big deal that the lady down the road is still doing it - what matters it that **you were brave enough and smart enough to grow from that point to where you are now.** As for our friend the copycat ... you know, the thing about copycats is that no matter how hard or fast they run, they will ALWAYS be behind you, eating your dust.

I don't know about you, but I think it's more important to be building the road ahead of me than worrying about who is in the dust behind me.

Taming The Email Beast

I don't know about you, but I get a heap of emails. Not just enquiries from potential clients but also thank you emails, a whole lot of newsletters I've signed up for, various adverts from various companies, emails from suppliers, statements and bills ... you name it, I seem to get it (via email). I find that with a smartphone, emails are even crazier because my phone pings and dings all day long, and I stop to read them (skim them) and don't action them right then. This then means I come back to my desk on a Monday morning feeling like I only really vaguely know what's going on and I've got a brain full of mush.

Here's a few ways that I tame the email beast:

- Spend a bit of time UNsubscribing from stuff. I sign up for things all enthusiastically, read them like mad for a few weeks (okay, days) and then I lose interest and become efficient at deleting them daily. There are some that I think "I'll come back to reading that someday" and those ones I will filter into their own folders. Everything else - BUH BYE! I also get rid of any newsletter that is more frequent than weekly - for me, it's just too much to read a daily digest. Seriously, go into your email today and unsubscribe from a bunch of stuff and you'll be amazed at how much crap you didn't even realise you have signed up for (hello, emails from Oprah and Ellen!)

- I lloovvee using the "auto response" feature in email and I use this for the end of the week, when I am busy with making cake. I set up an automatic email which says something like, "The end of the week is a busy one for us as we prepare for all our weekend orders. Emails sent Wed-Fri will take a bit longer to get to, so if your matter is urgent or time sensitive, please call us on (phone number)."

- I END email conversations before they start - especially with clients who want to get a quote or schedule a time to meet. Those email conversations can go on for days and days when a simple phone call will do the job. So a vast majority of the time, I will answer a "how much is this cake" email with a phone call. It gives me the chance to save time in answering emails, gives them the opportunity to get to know me and my products a bit better, and best of all: I almost always make the sale because it's a lot harder for them to say no over the phone.

- I also END email conversations which have gotten out of control. You know, the ones where they want to change the colour and then get a new quote, then change the number of servings and then get a new quote, then ask if you deliver and then get a new quote, then ask if they have Elmo instead if that changes the quote ... and so on. If a conversation over email has surpassed 4-5 replies, I just pick up the phone and call them!

- I do not give in to email Nazis who try to make me feel crappy because I did not reply in 0.4 seconds to their request. This are the people who complain that I did not answer them quick enough, or who need something URGENTLY for tonight or tomorrow but who emailed rather than called, OR the people who tell me that my delayed reply means that I did not get the sale. Yeah, no. I'm not getting sucked into your vortex of evil. You've got a phone, please use it (and this is why *I* use a phone with clients, too - because I'm educating people that it's a much, much faster way to communicate. Let these people go. Do not reply and apologise.

- I have a defined time of day when I will answer email, usually the same as my office hours. I don't reply to emails outside of business hours unless they are personal. The problem with replying to customers at odd hours is that they then learn to expect replies at odd hours, and get frustrated when you're not at their beck and call. Train your clients not to expect a reply unless you are actually at work.

- Ruthlessly delete stuff. Seriously. If you really and truly want it later, create an "Action Later" folder where you move all the stuff you would like to get to eventually. Once a month go and clear that out - by reading them, deleting them, forwarding them, whatever.

- Do not allow your inbox to have more than 10 emails in it (I'm an overachiever, so I aim for 8). It just ends up being overwhelming to look (and scroll past) all that stuff every day, and you end up just cherry picking stuff instead of actually moving it out of your life or doing something about it. I love the expression "messy desk, messy mind" and I think you can apply it to email - "messy inbox, messy mind". Clean that stuff up and I promise you will breathe easier the next time you log in.

- Don't allow personal emails to clutter your work in-box. You should have a business email address, and your friends shouldn't be using that address. Similarly don't sign up to horoscope newsletters and daily joke emails with your business email address (even if I think a bit of humour is essential to running a business).

One of the hardest tasks as a small business owner is keeping all the paperwork (virtual or otherwise!) under control. One minute you seem on top of it, the next minute you're overwhelmed by it - and email is one of those places where overwhelm happens in the blink of an eye (almost literally). Being disciplined about it - even just a little bit - can make the world of difference to how you're feeling about running the business, especially in those weeks when it seems like the sky is falling.

I Have No Life. Only Cake.

When I started out, I used my own mobile phone number and personal email address as the contact points for the business. There is nothing wrong with that as a starting point and it worked really well for a while. Pretty soon I found that my business life was creeping into my personal life more and more. The end result was that I was accessible to my clients 24/7 and I was resentful of how little down time I seemed to have for myself.

This is in the days before smartphones, so my mobile phone would ring at 10 pm on a Sunday night and since it was my personal phone, I'd answer it - only to find myself having a 10-minute discussion about the available flavours for a pink fairy cake. I would obsessively check email at all hours of the night and day and because I didn't want to miss out on orders, I'd reply to people at midnight. I'd stand at the school gate picking up my kids and be having phone conversations with potential clients where I could not hear a word they said over the din of shouting children. In short my business was creeping into my real life like cancer and I could not work out how to stop its growth. In those early days, you don't (or can't) invest in much, so you use your existing resources to run your business, which is totally fine until one day it's not so fine anymore. (For me that moment was when I realised my kids used to have to actually say, "I NEED YOU TO FOCUS ON ME!" before starting every conversation - because I'd hear them talking but not absorb any of it.)

From an administrative point of view, being available 24/7 might seem kinda reasonable but from the point of view of having a life, it's totally unsustainable. I don't know about you, but it irritates my family if I have to leave the dinner table to answer the phone, or I'm not watching my son play basketball because the thud-thud of the ball means I'm needing to be outside straining to hear someone asking if I make gluten free cakes.

There have got to be boundaries for your work and your life even if you think your work IS your life.

To help you claw back a bit of your life, here are some tips for getting some of that elusive work/life balance when it comes to running a baking business. The first of these is the MOST important of all.

1. Set boundaries and then educate your customers about those boundaries. So- start by deciding what your official, published working hours are going to be and then **actually stick to them**. You do not work at 10 pm on Sunday night, so don't answer your phone at that time. If it's not a

number you recognise, don't answer it. If it's something or someone truly important calling, chances are they will leave a message. If they know you personally, they will call back or call you at home. Your efficiency will increase enormously if you have dedicated, focussed business time as opposed to snatching five minutes every couple of hours. Educate your customers about your availability, and then train yourself to work within those time frames. If they see you replied to an email at midnight, they will email you at 11 pm and wonder why they did not get a response.

2. It's baked goods. Not rocket science. Not brain surgery. Not life or death. There is not one single cake "emergency" which requires your immediate attention and that means you do not need to answer a call or email within 10 seconds of receiving it and especially if that call or email comes outside of your defined working hours. I promise. These days, I do have an 'emergency' phone number which people can call outside of work hours, but when they call it they immediately get voice mail. I keep that phone on over the weekend, but I don't answer it - and if a message comes in, I listen to it and action it if needed. Number of times it's rung since I've had it (in the past several years): twice. (Neither time was an actual emergency.)

3. Accept that you might lose orders because you didn't reply fast enough. Believe me, you don't want clients who are so demanding and impatient anyway.

4. Absolutely nobody calls or emails a place of business at 9 pm and truly expects somebody to answer, unless that place of business is a restaurant, strip club or other evening-based industry. Generally speaking, bakeries are not night-based businesses and just because they are Googling cakes at midnight, *this does not mean you need to be awake to get their call*. Half the battle is teaching your customers what they can get from you. If they already know that you always answer at stupid hours of the night, they will call at stupid hours of the night. (See #1 for a reminder on this.)

5. Keep a pad of paper and pen (or smartphone) handy and write down the business stuff you suddenly remember needs doing. Don't stop and action it right then, wait until your official business hours - but keep track because you WILL forget and the best ideas come at the strangest times.

6. Don't ever - and I mean EVER - feel bad or guilty about choosing yourself and your family/friends over your business. You deserve to have a life even if you run a small business. You really, really do.

7. Always be honest with your clients, even if that means you can't immediately give them what they want. I have NO problem telling a client that I can't meet with them after 4pm because I am on the school pick up run. It not only teaches them what my boundaries are, but it makes them respect me all the more because they realise that I am a real person with real commitments - and that includes a commitment to giving them the best experience possible, because I *actually commit to things*! Honesty will get you very far when it comes to customer service. By saying "this is when I am available", you're also saying, "this is when YOU are the most important person to me and I won't be distracted".

8. You are a business owner. Not a slave. Not even if it sometimes feels like it ... and the people who feel that way probably set it up that way without even realising it. Since you're not a slave, it's entirely within your rights to decide how and when you will reply to calls and emails - and you should do so in a timely, respectable manner but sometimes there are better ways to spend your time. So if that means you put the phone onto voice mail for a few business hours while you develop a new product or work on a customer's order - that's okay. It really is. Effective multi-tasking is a myth - you can't possibly be 100% involved in one thing if you are doing another.

9. Technology rocks. Voice mail, email 'away' messages and the like work very well and you should use them. Use your voicemail to educate your clients, "Thanks for your call. We answer this phone between the hours of 10am-12pm. If you're hearing this during those hours, it simply means we are on another call. Please leave us a message and we will reply as soon as possible." Several cake companies I know have a permanent 'away' message set up in email, so that every time you send them an email you get, "Thank you for your email. Please note we are often in the kitchen creating amazing cakes, so emails cannot always be answered immediately. Please allow up to 24 hours for a reply." In other words - make the boundaries very clear and educate the people who are going to order from you and manage their expectations using the tools available to you (there goes #1 again!) Use technology to your advantage. By the way, this also applies to turning technology OFF when you need to.

10. Everyone wants to know what to expect. We all love certainty and we all love time frames - so it's not just about educating your customers, it's also about delivering what you said you would in the time you said you would ... but here's the thing about having a life. It's messy. Things don't

go to plan. Things get in the way. If that happens - don't waste time feeling crappy about it. CALL your customer (not email, not text, not Facebook) and sincerely *explain* the delay and *what you are doing to do* about it. Your customer is FAR more likely to understand if you call and say, "I need to cancel our appointment because my Dad is in the hospital", than if you either don't show up, or cancel with no reason, or pretend not to be there when they call. Deliver what you said you would when you would - but own up if something keeps that from happening. Will you irritate them? Maybe. But far better to treat them with respect and courtesy than to hide under a rock. Also - the opposite is true. If they call to cancel or change things, thank them for their courtesy. If they took the time to be nice, be nice back by acknowledging it. Give them the personal touch and remember that email is not always appropriate as it has no tone of voice to it. Also - calling is often a much faster method of getting things actually done!

It's SO VERY EASY to get caught in the 24/7 business trap (I know because I lived there for a very long time), but there are other parts of your life which need and want your time and attention. With smartphones and tablets and the infernal bling-beep-ding of technology demanding our attention all the time, we are all in a rush to do things and race around like crazy people.

We might be crazy people, but we're *human crazy* people.

Make the choice to give your business the focused time it deserves but also make the choice to give the rest of your life the time it deserves, too. Your business will not succeed or fail just because you're not answering questions about cake while you're on the toilet (I know. I've done that. More than I care to admit.)

How To Make Friends

When you consider how we all talk about how crowded this industry is, isn't it a bit funny how lonely of a place it can be, too? Sometimes it feels like those endless Facebook groups[10] are only filled with keyboard warriors, that everyone only wants to complain, and that when you're stuck in the middle of a bad moment (either emotional or the "oh shit it's 3am and my cake is raw!" type) there is nobody to turn to other than your partner who could care less if that pink flower is more fuchsia or magenta. Here's a business skill I think is essential to success: building a tribe. A wolf pack. Your cake peeps. Your sisters in arms, your buttercream babes, your crisis management team. The thing is, if you're sitting home all day making cake and reading stuff online, how the heck do you find NICE people to hang out with in real life?! Never fear, Michelle the friendship fairy is here to help with some fabulous ways to meet fabulous people IN REAL LIFE. Note - there is a small amount of bravery required here, but then I never promised this would be easy, but I can promise it will be worth it.

Here are some ways to gather a posse:

- Next time you go to a real life cake class or small business class, introduce yourself to someone who looks nice. Start up a conversation with them, even if it's just to say, "I'm so nervous about this class!" Be vulnerable - chances are the other person is nervous too. The key here is also to GO TO LIVE EVENTS. (This is how I met Faye Cahill - I did a class at her studio and told her I was peeing my pants with nerves. She doesn't remember that moment, but the next time we met I told her about it so we had an instant point of reference.)

- If you're in a local online cake group, and there is someone whose posts always make you laugh or you find yourself nodding along to what they say, send them a PM and say, "Your posts always make me laugh, we should have a coffee sometime," and then (and this is key!) if they seem even vaguely interested, MAKE A TIME AND DATE and actually make it happen. The follow through is super important and I promise you that you are NOT bothering them if you do it. They'll be glad you were the brave one.

- BEFORE you refer a client to a local cake maker, CALL them up, introduce yourself, and say, "I've got a request for an order I can't fulfil. Is it okay if I pass this person onto you?" They won't say no and you've got the perfect excuse to start a conversation with them. Or if someone has referred a

---

10   See *Breaking Up Is Hard To Do* in Chapter 9.

bunch of people to you, call and thank them (that's how I know Rudy from Man Bakes Cake - he shared my stuff and I wrote him a PM to thank him, so when we met in real life it was not awkward.)

- If another cake person randomly comes into your life for some reason and after bumping into them a couple of times you think you'd like to get to know them better, swallow your shyness for as long as it takes to say, "XYZ shop is having a massive sale on next week, do you want to come with me to check it out? We can make an outing of it!" (This is how I got to know lots of different people on a more personal level.)

- If you like someone, chances are you will also like the people they associate with, so take the time to say hello to THEIR friends as well. Friends of friends are wonderful people and worth getting to know, so next time you see someone standing awkwardly next to someone you know, lean over and say hello. I promise they will be grateful and you already have someone in common. (This is how I met Sheryl Bito, who is friends with Sharon Wee.)

- Reach out online to people but not in a "tell me ALL YOUR DECORATING SECRETS!!" way. Send a PM saying, "I loved that bunny cake you made, it's really amazing!" Leave a comment on their blog if they write one, send an email introducing yourself and thanking them for whatever beauty they bring into the world (cake or otherwise), send an email asking an intelligent question (not something you can just YouTube or Google yourself please). Some of my closest friends are not in my local neighbourhood at all but they are only a text or phone call away because I reached out and told them I admired or respected them. (This is how I met Shawna McGreevy ... I told her that if I ever met her, I'd fangirl all over the place, and I did exactly that.)

- Be the planner and the do-er - we are ALL BUSY, but what we really are is WASTING a lot of time doing not much. So be the person who plans the monthly local cakers get together, and even if only one other person shows up, it was worth the time and effort. You need to be the one to MAKE IT HAPPEN because other people are the type who will sit around waiting for it to happen.

- Make friends with people who are super connectors. A super connector is someone who is really great at making connections between people. She's your really nice friend who always "knows someone who knows someone", who just seems to know a lot of people. We all know someone like that - and likely we wonder how she does it so effortlessly - but the beauty of knowing someone like that is that they will either naturally introduce you to more people, or not mind at all if you ask them to introduce you to a specific person they may know. (This is how I know a bunch of cool people through Raewyn Read, because Raewyn is a super connector, as is obvious because she's in almost every one of these pictures.)

Of course, this post would not be complete unless I mentioned that sometimes, you're going to make friends (cake or otherwise) who turn out to <u>not really be great friends</u> to you. Maybe business got in the way, maybe they were not as nice as you were led to believe, maybe a small misunderstanding blew up into a giant

mess. This happens in normal friendships, not just in cake friendships, so please don't let it stop you from forming new bonds with people. My tip on finding a tribe you're going to love and cherish is this: you have to share the same core values. What does that mean? It means that at the very heart of it, you share the same belief systems (and I'm not talking religion). As an example, perhaps you really value honesty and education. Perhaps you both believe that you're in business not just for the love but also to make a shed load of money and neither is ashamed to say it. Perhaps you both come from similar cultural backgrounds. In other words, there have to be things about you which connect on a soul level, not just on a cake level. Cake might be the reason you met, but it won't be the reason you remain friends.

We're all in this together, only sometimes, YOU'VE got to be the person who BRINGS US together.

p.s. I reference plenty of well-known cakers in here (and they're in those photos) but the truth is, famous or not, we're all just people who need one another to lean on.

CHAPTER 4
PRODUCTS

The reason most of us went into business is because we were good at making cake, cookies, or cake pops – well, either that or someone else convinced us we were good at it. The PRODUCT was the main reason we started this whole craziness. Like you, I learned that cake decorating was my happy place, and then I realised just how addicting the world of sweet art can be. When we're making things for our own enjoyment, or for the enjoyment of our family and friends, there are very few rules to follow. If something isn't quite level, or you had to use box mix or you made way too much cake for the number of guests, it wasn't a big deal. As soon as money started changing hands, and people started asking more complex questions, the details of the product became ever more important. Those simple questions about our products, like, "How many people will an 8 inch cake feed?" got more complex over time, with questions about copyright and design popping up more often.

When I teach people about marketing, I make a point of mentioning the importance of your product and knowing which details of it matter to your clients. It's all good and well to use fancy vanilla beans, but not if the client can't taste that flavour in the end product. Funnily enough, so many of the cake makers I meet don't enjoy (reality: hate) the baking process. While I understand that it's not nearly as fun as decorating is, it's still a vital part of what we do. My philosophy about this is simple. People will buy things like look good at least once. People will buy things that look good AND taste good more than once – and for my business to survive, I've got to sell it over and over again. Don't underestimate the importance of your products both on the inside and the out.

Why Be Standard When You Can Be Generous

It is the common belief in the baking industry that a 'coffee' serve of cake is 1" by 1", and a 'dessert' serving of cake is 1" by 2", assuming that most decorated cakes are also 4" high. Apparently nobody knows exactly where the standard started, but it's been perpetuated by the Wilton cake serving guides.

I'm going to call bullshit on that industry standard.

There is nothing standard about it and here's why:

First, for many years, I worked as a pastry chef in a number of different capacities - in cafes, bakeries, for catering companies and in special event venues. Across those jobs, I've had the opportunity to see (and cut) a whole lot of cakes. I have yet to meet any chef (and I've met some incredibly skilled ones) who can consistently cut pieces that small. Have you ever tried it? Bake or buy a square cake (just to make it easy on yourself) and then cut 1" x 1" pieces out of it (don't cheat and use a ruler, there are no rulers in function venues). Then take a few pieces, measure them and see how many are exactly that size. It's virtually impossible to do consistently, and yet we're asking very busy chefs doing catering functions (or Mums catering for sugared up kids at a party) to be able to do it. Plus - can you really cut 1 x 1 squares out of a 3D cake which is the shape of a fire truck?

Second, I think giving someone a piece of cake which is basically the size of an index finger is ridiculous. It's like, thanks for the sample, now where is my real dessert? As a chef, I can't imagine putting that slice on a plate and feeling like I'd given my customer something worth having. It just looks cheap. Imagine if you went into a cafe and ordered a coffee and a slice of cake and got given something which was 1" x 2". You'd be looking at the plate wondering where the rest of your cake disappeared to.

Call me crazy, but the berry coulis artfully pooled around the cake should not actually be BIGGER THAN the cake.

Third, I get a whole lot of feedback from clients and nobody has ever complained that they had too much cake left over. *More cake is not an actual problem*. NOT ENOUGH CAKE, on the other hand, IS a problem. It reflects poorly on the person hosting the event. That's a problem because a big part of your job as a cake maker is to make your client look like the most amazing hostess in the entire Universe (because, if nothing else, she was clever enough to order from you.) If there isn't enough cake, your client looks like she cheaped out. It makes her look bad. The last thing you want is for your client to be made to look bad - because it's highly likely, she'll turn that around to you. Not enough cake = embarrassing. Too much cake = not embarrassing (and therefore not a problem).

I promise that nobody calls and chews you out, sends you a nastygram email or asks for a refund because they had cake left over.

This does not just apply to cake servings, though. What's the industry standard on the number of pieces you should allow per person for a dessert buffet? What's the industry standard on the number of bread rolls you should allow per person for a meal? The number of sugared almonds in a bonbonniere box? The size of a custom cookie? The width of a petite four?

Most of all, how are you as a baker supposed to know how many people your cake serves when the client asks? Or how do you decide how big of a cake to make when they let you know the number of guests they are expecting? What if your product is way more generous - or way skimpier - than your immediate competition? How to you explain this to your customers when they are comparing prices if they cannot compare with the industry standard?

Remember my rule about this stuff? *Educate*, don't justify.

The simplest way to do this is as follows:

1. Cut yourself a piece of your own cake. The kind of piece you would like to see presented to you on a plate. The kind of cake serving which looks nice and yummy but does not use up a month's worth of Weight Watchers points in one shot. The kind of cake serving you think gives the recipient something to look forward to, showcases your layers and your flavours,

and which looks like more than just a sample.

2. Measure it. Draw that rectangle on a piece of paper or take a picture of it next to a ruler to demonstrate the size in a visual way.

3. Use that measurement as YOUR standard, and then use that as a way of differentiating yourself from your competition. Your cake serving size should be a selling point. Not, "We go by the industry standard" but, "Our cake servings are generous because we'd rather you had some left over than not - more cake for you to enjoy the next day!"

You may decide that the slice of cake you cut yourself is too big for a 'coffee' serving, especially at a wedding where cake is often only eaten as a few bites worth. That's okay - just cut yourself a coffee serve, measure it, and then use that as your coffee serving standard. This applies for dessert buffets as well - decide on how many pieces YOU think should be served and go with that. Petite fours, macarons, whatever - work out for yourself what your serving is going to be and then go *with that*.

We are operating in a crowded industry. There is NO reason for you to be 'standard' at anything particularly when the current environment demands that you innovate, stand out, and differentiate. Let your rules about servings be one of the ways in which you not only stand out among your competitors but also a way you demonstrate your generous spirit to your clients.

Generosity will always be rewarded. You want your clients to tell their friends that the cake was delicious, there was plenty of it, and you were nice to them. You don't want them telling their friends that it was expensive and there wasn't enough of it.

The industry standard is ridiculous (please go try and cut those slices to experience just how ridiculous it is ...) - but more than that, it's just a standard. You don't make standard products, do you?

You make a custom product. You get to make the custom rules.

Confused In Cakeland – Allergen Free Baking

Confused in Cakeland

Hey Michelle,

Here's one for you. . . allergies and anaphylaxis, I get enquiries all the time. Should it be a flat no? Would you be covered if you sold something as dairy/ gluten/egg/nut free? How do you guarantee no contamination? Thought it might be interesting with allergies on the rise ...

Signed,

Confused in Cakeland

Hey there Confused in Cakeland,

Whether it's a flat "no way" depends on the level of risk you as a business owner are willing to take on. Food allergies and intolerances are on the rise, and it seems like people ask for 'no egg, no dairy, not gluten, no nut, etc.' products more and more these days. My business offers these sorts of products, but we only do so because:

1.   There is a big fat disclaimer on our website, which I had checked over by a lawyer before I published it, and

2.   When I take the order from the customer, I remind them that they are ordering at their own risk, and I ask them to go and read the disclaimer before confirming the order with me.

Basically, I think it's great if you can offer this kind of service to your customer (especially if other companies around you do not), but it's vital that you protect your business as best you can and also protect the consumer. You don't want to make anyone sick, nor do you want to be held responsible should something go wrong that you may not have had any control over.

It is basically <u>impossible to guarantee</u> no contamination, especially if your business makes other products which contain those ingredients. Different people have different levels of sensitivity, so you may take every precaution in the world but there might still be a reaction of some kind.

In short - only take this kind of order on if:

1. You're willing to accept that it might be a bit risky to do so,

2. You're well protected (legally), and

3. You are very clear and very honest with your clients about everything you do with their products (be willing to tell them brand names, provide ingredient lists, etc.). It's a great service to offer, but you can't create your products in a vacuum so you've got to exercise a bit of caution.

Yours in being healthy, wealthy and wise,

Michelle

Cakes And Copyright

Since starting this blog, I've gotten literally dozens of emails and messages from people asking me to address the topic of copyright and cakes. I've avoided doing so until now because I wanted to spend some time doing some more in-depth research, asking my colleagues their thoughts, chatting to copyright lawyers and also forming my own coherent thoughts about it. Let's be real, I also avoided writing it because I did not feel like ducking the rotten tomatoes which might have gotten thrown at me. Something about this topic turns mild-mannered cake makers into rabid, hysterical lunatics.

However, since I believe in having the hard conversations and being brave, I'm writing about this topic today. This is not a post where I tell you exactly what you should and should not do, or how to best stay out of trouble. This is not a post about whether using copyrighted characters or images is morally right or wrong, whether the 'big boys' should be damn grateful we're all making 'Frozen' themed cakes, or whether those that choose to make Chanel cupcakes are going to be slapped with a big ol' lawsuit. I'm also not going to talk about those big companies needing common sense, or how children all over the world will be bitterly disappointed if they cannot have that Lightening McQueen cake or how damn unfair all this is because your business survives entirely on Dora cakes. This post is also entirely devoid of judgement because I have made, sold, eaten and otherwise been surrounded by character and logo cakes for a very, very long time now.

This post is going to be about the ONLY two things you really need to be concerned with when it comes to copyright and cakes (or cupcakes, cake pops, macarons or whatever it is you make.)

Issue Number One: Understand what copyright actually is.

Copyright at its most basic protects the rights of person or organisation who owns or generated the work to use, distribute and profit from it as they see fit. If you're using or reproducing someone else's stuff without their permission (and then making money off of it), you're basically stealing it. Let me put this another way: all us cake decorators complain bitterly when people 'borrow' our designs, or are 'inspired by' our ideas, use our photos to copy our work and then claim those designs as their own. We put our logos on our work, watermark our pictures, and insist that we want to be credited. In other words, we wanted to be recognised and respected for our original effort and creative skill and acknowledged as the creators of these things.

Guess what? Disney, Pixar, Burberry, Chanel, Jack Daniels, etc. etc. etc ... want the EXACT SAME THING. They paid some artists a bunch of money to come up with those concepts and artwork, they want to protect those images by copyrighting them. Someone, please explain why we think it's okay to just take their stuff, profit off them ... and then complain that it's unfair when they ask us not to. *We complain about this <u>happening to us all the time</u> and yet the vast majority of us <u>are doing it all the time</u>*.

Reminder: This is not a post about whether or not Disney should appreciate us making all those damn Olaf cakes.

Issue Number Two: There are a million and one sides to this debate, but all that really matters is what you as a business owner are going to choose to do with your business.

Just like it's your choice to use ganache or buttercream, box mix or scratch bake, couverture or compound, you are the only person who can decide on a definitive company policy.

The excuses of, "everyone else does it", or "If I refuse to do it the woman down the road will get the order instead", or "Why should Disney care if I'm really just promoting their brand?" will not hold up in a court of law anywhere in the world. They own this stuff, you choose to use it without asking, so they have the right to come after you in whatever way they like.

I've heard plenty of companies getting "cease and desist" emails and letters asking them to take down their creations which include copyrighted logos and images. I also know the vast majority of cake companies will never, ever get caught. Lastly, I know some companies actually LOVE giving you permission to use their stuff and I've heard of plenty of companies then asking for pictures of - and then showing off - creations made using their logos and images. The issue is not really with people making cakes for their kids and cousins just for fun, the issue is really about people using these things for commercial use. I don't care if what you're getting for it is five bucks and a bucket of chicken wings. If you're getting money, goods or services in exchange for that Minecraft cake, you're using it for commercial purposes and that places you at risk.

The decision about using copyrighted characters, logos or images is entirely yours to make. The risk, however, is also yours to own and yours to manage as you see fit.

Like most business decisions, all it really comes down to is those two things:

1. What the issue actually is, and
2. How you're going to deal with it.

Inspired By

Many of you have asked for my thoughts on the very common practice of businesses 'borrowing' ideas from one another but not crediting the ideas to their original owners. It's an issue which is endemic to the industry and an issue which starts endless dramas among 'friends' ... and it very quickly gets very ugly, doesn't it?

Here's my two cents:

Remember my post about how I divorced all my Facebook groups[11]? I feel much the same way about chasing down copy cats as I do about Facebook groups - basically: my time as a business owner is better spent elsewhere.

The reality of it is, you can spend countless hours chasing people who 'are inspired by' your ideas but who fail to be inspired enough to credit back to you. You can do lots of reverse Google image searching, chase them down on Facebook, 'name and shame' them on your own FB page, email them directly, hire lawyers to send them 'cease and desist' letters and basically create an entire job out of hunting these people and demanding the credit you deserve. On the flip side, you can also do things like spending a lot of time emailing the people who may (or may not) be the original designer of something and ask their permission to re-create it. Both are a total waste of time. Why? Because who says the watermarked picture you're looking at is an original of that maker anyway? Maybe that cake maker copied it from another picture which wasn't watermarked, or maybe it was watermarked, only the cake maker before them copied it from another one that wasn't ... you get the idea. Last I checked I don't know a single cake maker who got royalties for something they designed. Nor have I ever seen copyright on cake design actually enforced by any legal organisation. Following the trail of creativity is a very time-consuming process and in my opinion, a total waste of time.

Me? *I'd much rather be making fabulous products for paying clients. That's where my time is better spent.*

 In the digital age of sharing, pinning, posting, Tumblr-ing, tweeting, Instagramming, hash tagging. . . is *anything* in the creative, edible realm really able to **remain** "owned" solely by the person who created the first one? In my opinion - no, or at least not for very long. As speciality bakers, we WANT and NEED to share our work with *as wide an audience as possible*. Sharing publicly is how we build our reputation, get new clientele, and showcase our ability. We work in a very visual medium, ergo, we need to publish photos of our work. I would even go

---

11   See *Breaking Up Is Hard To Do* in Chapter 9.

so far as to say we have *no choice but to share freely and widely*. Many people do this on their business's sites but I bet ALL OF YOU also do this on cake

forums of one sort or another, thus freely and widely sharing your work *with your competition* (hello, "Sharing Monday" ...). The problem with this of course is that people **steal** freely and widely too. Or "borrow", or are "inspired by", or "put their own twist on, " or whatever words you put around it - the end result is pretty much the same. Suddenly the things we spent hours on are being recreated by others, whose clients now think **they** are incredibly clever to have thought of this concept in the first place when it's **you** who thought of it.

You know what?

It's not very nice to be stolen from. *But ... I'd much rather be making fabulous products for paying clients. That's where my time is better spent.*

Let me be very clear about the point I'm making here: when someone uses your ideas and credits you, it's flattering. When someone uses your ideas, but doesn't credit you, it's incredibly irritating but ultimately probably isn't going to harm your brand in the long run. Don't waste what little precious time you have available to you on becoming some sort of Internet cake-identifying vigilante. You can't stop the digital chain growing no matter how hard you try. If your photo has been shared 6000 times that you know of, it's probably been shared 6000 times that you DON'T know of and for cripes' sake that's a lot of gnashing of teeth you're doing AND a hell of a lot of emailing you are going to need to do. I ask you: who really has time for that?

Let me be real here and give you some guidelines:

To the bakers here who are just starting out: if you choose to recreate then share a cake you copied from someone else, and you can credit it, do so. It's the right thing to do. Can't find any identifying info? Either don't post the cake anywhere, or post it with something like, "The client gave me this unmarked photo to work from, so I'm not sure of its design origins. Please let me know if you do know where it's from", and then go back and credit it if it ever gets identified. *Then go back to making fabulous products for paying clients. That's where your time is better spent.*

To those of you who have been at this for a while: if you see unauthorised "borrowing" of your photos or designs (and they're claiming that it's their original concept or picture), send a polite email to that person asking them to credit you. Educate them if you can but be prepared that not everyone is educable and some people are just jerks. For those, you cannot chase (and there will be thousands), do yourself a favour and get over it. Accept that by posting anywhere online, you're also *inevitably* going to be copied. *Consider* it a compliment. *Then go back to making fabulous products for paying clients. That's where your time is better spent.*

All of you: it's really pretty simple. Be kind to one another and treat other cake makers and their work with the same level of politeness and respect you expect of them in return. Accept that while not everyone will behave respectfully, YOU certainly can. Give credit where credit is due if you are able to. Yes. It's really that simple.

And ... I don't bother to watermark my photos. I honestly don't care if people create those cakes again. I'm never going to get royalties and I don't have time to chase people down just to feed my ego. Clients bring me watermarked photos ALL THE TIME to work from. Watermarking is by no means a guarantee of any kind. By all means watermark your photos to provide yourself with some protection if you like - just don't think that watermarking necessarily means you're protected very much at all. I have yet to meet a client who saw a watermark and then bothered to find the cake maker whose watermark it is (some might. Most won't.) Watermarking just means you (probably) made that version, not necessarily that it's your original design. . . and thank you, Mr. Photoshop, watermarks can be put on photos of cakes you never made in the first place, too. A long time ago I decided that ultimately, I cared a lot more about pleasing my clients than I did having my ego stroked by people crediting me because of a watermark. In other words, I focus on the GIVING more than the GETTING.

So ... and you knew this already, didn't you? ... I don't spend time watermarking because *I'd much rather be making fabulous products for paying clients. That's where my time is better spent.*

Ultimately, I'm in business to fulfil my higher purpose and please my clients.

I can't really see where chasing copycats is meeting either of those goals.

Here's the gist of it:
Spend your time JUST BEING AWESOME. (For YOU, and for your CLIENTS.)
(Stop caring so much what everyone else is doing.)

I'm So Clever, I Bought It All By Myself

One of the earliest dilemmas home bakers come across is, "Do I make it, or do I buy it?"

Inevitably you're going to get a client who wants something you've never done before - usually a figurine or a sugar flower. Something which requires specialist skills or resources you - as a beginner - just don't have. Should you even have taken the order in the first place, if you can't actually deliver what your customer wants?

There are a couple of ways you can deal with this situation. I pride myself on operating my business with integrity and never promising a client something that I cannot deliver. However, if the only barrier to my delivering it is my skill level, that's not a good enough reason to refuse the work. If the reason I can't do it is because they've asked for the impossible ("Hi, I'd like a 400-foot tall replica of Macchu Picchu and I want it made out of edible fairy wings!"), that's a different story altogether.

So what do you do when someone wants something you've never done before? (Other than panic. Panicking helps nobody.)

As I see it, you've got two solutions here:

1) Learn how to do it. Pretty damn quickly.

   In some cases, you've got a bit of time up your sleeve and can acquire education in a short time frame by signing up for a course which runs before the cake is due, or watching endless YouTube or Craftsy videos until you've worked out how to do it. Talk to cake friends who might have this skill. Research and practice until you actually get the hang of it. You didn't realise it at the time because you were panicking about it all, but your client did you a massive favour. They forced you to up-level your skills, and, in turn, made you that much more able to help the next client that comes along. They also forced you to realise just how much time it takes to master hand-made oversized David Austin roses in five colours - so that next time, you're not undercharging for a cake which has those flowers on it.

   I'm extremely grateful to my clients who ask for things I've never done before, because there are major benefits do being forced to learn a new skill in a short amount of time. I love the constant challenge, I love that they have faith in me, I love that I will end up with a new (sugar) feather in my cap. The bad part about this method is that you've got to have balls of steel in order to do it, and probably need to take some blood pressure medication to handle your elevated stress levels. This is definitely NOT for the wusses among us, especially if you're working to a short time frame.

As a human being, being challenged is how we learn. As a cake maker, being challenged is how we EARN.

But.

Let's be real here. You're a good cake decorator - but are you good enough to risk this with a paying client? In my case, the answer was always - depends on the client. If it was my Mum, sure. If it was a complete stranger. . . depends on the personality of the client. Some are completely over the top anal retentive, some will give you some wiggle room. Figure out if YOU can handle it, and if THEY can handle it. At the very least, be honest. "It's not something I've done before, but I'm willing to give it a go!" Worst case, they go to someone else and you breathe easier. Best case, they appreciate your honesty so much they let you do your thing, and you get a client who will grow with you as your business grows. Guess which kind of client I'd rather have?

2) Buy one. Or several.

For many years, I was utterly petrified of making figurines of brides and grooms. I realised my local cake decorating supply shop sold them (and even customised them) so I used to order ALL my figurines from them. Why? I was too scared to learn, so I made every excuse under the sun to not bother. No time (yeah, right). Nobody would ever order them again anyway because I'm not known for being a wedding cake maker (yeah, right). Bride and groom figurines are going out of fashion (all together not: YEAH, right!) I came up with millions of excuses to keep ordering them instead of just learning how to make the damn things. (Yeah. Embarrassing. But this blog is all about the truth of running a cake business, right?)

I eventually went and did a course on figurine making. I was pretty proud of the little Bridezilla I made and her adorable but slightly shorter groom. It wasn't nearly as hard as I thought it would be. I left that course thinking I'd just made a brilliant investment in my education and that I was going to be the MOST awesome figurine maker that ever lived.

Guess what? Shortly thereafter, I got another order for a bride and groom figurine.

I ordered it in.

Why? Because I realised a few things. Firstly, although now I had the knowledge and skills, I didn't really enjoy making them. Second, it cost me LESS to buy them in then it would to make them myself - and that's even if I included the time to both order them and pick them up (which had to be included for my costing to be correct). Sure, if I was mass producing these things and had some sort of efficient system going, that wouldn't be the case. I was only making one every few months and it was taking me the better part of 4 hours to do them (excluding drying time). In other words, by choosing to do it myself, I was losing money on the deal. No client is going to pay for 4 hours worth of my time for 2 figurines.

The exact same scenario played out for me with flowers. I can make roses with the best of them ... but I find nothing so mind-numbingly boring as sitting there and making 1, 000 rose petals. There are way better ways I can spend my time. I know plenty of cake makers who love the flower making process. Yay for them, but for me it's just not my thing at all. I enjoy it sometimes. Other times, sticking pins in my eyes is way more interesting.

The world is full of extremely talented sugar flower makers and figurine makers who do beautiful work. Me, I'm capable but hate it. So these days - I tend to do a bit of both. Buy the things from people I trust who I know will do work to my standard, and make the things which interest me and which I'm good at. I see no shame in outsourcing some of my work. That's just good business.

If your time can be better spent elsewhere, on something you're actually good at and which will make you money - DO IT. Don't waste your time doing something you don't like and aren't very good at when there are capable people who can do it better, faster, and cheaper.

This rule applies to everything about your cake business - it's why there are companies which make everything from undecorated cakes to coloured fondant.

So - is there any shame in buying a few bits in? Are you cheating your clients by not personally making every single item on that cake?

Nope. I'm pretty sure Dolce and Gabbana themselves do not actually hand sew the fabric which is used to make their gorgeous clothing. And Hermes does not breed the cows which makes the leather for their Birkin bags.

Repeat after me: there is no shame in outsourcing.

However ... (oh you knew that was coming, didn't you?) ... you can't entirely rely on it, either. This wouldn't be a post by me if it didn't include an embarrassing story about how choosing to buy it in blew up in my face.

A client ordered a cake with a figurine of Sophie the giraffe on top (a very expensive, well-known baby chew toy. So it wasn't just any old giraffe. She has a name, for god's sake. Posh and Beck's kids had one!) At that point, I knew how to make PEOPLE, not animals! So I ordered it in. I made the cake. Late the night before the client picked up her cake, I opened the box with the figurine in it, and ... well ... Sophie wasn't so much a giraffe as she was some unidentifiable animal with a very strange angle to her neck. She looked AWFUL. Literally just nothing like Sophie at all. Who am I kidding, it hardly looked like ANY giraffe, let alone one well loved by the Hollywood glitterati. I felt sick. Really, truly sick (and I know you all know that feeling, right? Same feeling as when a cake falls over.) I had no time to learn to make one, and my attempt at buying one in was an epic fail.

I'd never made this client a cake before, so I didn't really know her well enough to know if she would rip me to shreds or laugh it off.

There was nothing for it. I had to suck it up. I called the client and I was honest about what happened. Honesty is something we'll talk about later in more detail - but remember I said I only ever operate with integrity? For me, honesty was the ONLY option here since I couldn't re-make Sophie in time. I called and fessed up. I told her that because I didn't think I had the skill level to make Sophie, I'd ordered it in, but it looked too terrible for words.

I got really, really lucky on this one. She laughed, thanked me for my honesty, and said we'd put a real Sophie on top and it would be fine. She could have just as easily told me off, demanded a refund, and basically given me a hard time - and I would have probably deserved it. I was telling her that I couldn't give her what I want . . with only a few hours notice. I'm in the business of making people happy, and there I was having to disappoint someone. SO. NOT. COOL.

The next day when she came to pick up her cake, I spent about 10 minutes apologising and offering refunds and basically making a complete moron of myself in front of this poor woman. She spent about 10 minutes calming me down. It all worked out fine, and I am very proud to say that, five years later, she's still a regular client of mine who orders several times a year from me.

What's the final word on this one? Is it better to do it yourself, or is it better to order it in? Well, I'm afraid only you can answer that one ... but here's what I think. Order it in, or make it yourself** - but ALWAYS, ALWAYS have a Plan B. (Even if that Plan B is begging your client for forgiveness and learning to grovel effectively.) Learn the skill AND have the resources to order it in - which choice you make will depend on the client, the details of the item, and your time.

** But never try to outsource Sophie. She's just not worth it

No Bake Cake

A few months back I wrote an article about there being no shame in outsourcing (see previous article). I was referring to times when you need to buy something in like a figurine or a flower because you do not have those skills, not when you need to buy in something bigger like cake. I've recently read a few people get torn to shreds on social media because they - gasp! - admitted to buying in their cakes. There are several reasons why you may not bake your own cakes - lack of time, your oven has broken down, you don't enjoy it, or you cannot get Council approval to bake in your home kitchen but they will allow decorating. I think we should establish first that the reason for doing it doesn't really matter - it's actually more about managing your client's expectations and your reputation than anything else. The question here really should be what the best way is to tell your clients that you do not bake your own cakes, or even if you should tell them at all. You are in business FOR YOUR CLIENTS, *so they are the people that matter.*

As I see it, there are a few different ways to handle this situation:

Option 1: Lie about it.
Don't do this. Ever. Seriously. It's not worth it.

Option 2: Say nothing about it until they ask.

I actually don't have a problem with this option and I'd recommend it. You don't need to put out a big sign which says, "I don't bake my own cakes!" because there would be no point at all in doing that. If you are using a good quality, tastes great, purchased product which you are happy with and you know your customer will be too, then I really don't see a need to announce it.

I don't announce that I buy in my fondant, do I? I'd consider that a pretty essential part of the cake making process, but I still don't announce it. (By the way, I DO buy in my fondant. I made it from scratch once, and that was really more than enough for me.) I also don't announce what brand scraper I use, the brand of cream I use for my ganache, or anything else which ultimately is not really a selling point.

If a customer asks you outright (and it's inevitable that some will), be honest about it, but remember there are a few different ways to go about answering them. You can use your circumstances as the reason, e.g., "my local Council won't approve my kitchen for baking, only for decorating", or "my oven is just too small to fit in the larger cakes". Alternatively (and I prefer this one), don't talk DOWN the fact that you are buying in your cakes, talk UP the benefits!" I actually prefer buying in my cakes as it gives me more time to decorate, which is what I really love doing", or "It's win-win because I get to decorate more and I'm also supporting another local business", or "This way I get a consistent product every time, rather than depend on my domestic oven which can be a little temperamental", and so on. I really don't think you need to justify it much further than that. Acknowledge that you don't bake, give a positive reason why that is, and move on to all the reasons why they should order from you.

There are plenty of very talented cake decorators who are either buying in their cakes OR baking them at home from a box mix. *Does this make them any less talented?* It really makes no difference as long as your customer is getting the product they want AND are happy with. If you're buying in your cake, and it's a good quality, nice tasting cake, then you're giving your customer both LOOKS AND FLAVOUR ... and it's the combination of those two things which will bring them back to you a second time.

I always aim to give customers products which both taste great AND look great, and frankly if in order to achieve that I've got to buy in my cakes or my fondant (or anything else), well, so be it.

I think as a community we have become so hung up on people who bake versus those who don't, and people who use box mix versus those who don't, couverture chocolate versus compound, marshmallow fondant versus traditional, swiss meringue buttercream versus American buttercream and so on and so forth. It's honestly a little ridiculous. Let us ALL remember who we are in business for: our clients and ourselves. That's it. Those are the ONLY people we need to please with our choices of ingredients or methods.

Oh, and if you're one of those cake makers who needs to talk down your competitors to either other competitors or your clients, "Oh my Gawd, did you know she uses BOX MIX?! And plain old Cadbury chocolate!?" - I invite you to leave this blog. Your time is better spent somewhere else. Here, we *work on our businesses*. We work on *lifting ourselves and others up*, not on bringing them down. If you bake your own cakes, from ingredients imported from mysterious far-flung lands, and your chocolate comes from virginal cacao trees looked after by fairies - by all means, talk that up to your clients because they are definite selling points. Just don't talk shit about the woman down the road because she has not chosen to do the same.

Different strokes for different folks, yes?

Confused In Cakeland – Choosing Ingredients

Confused in Cakeland

Dear Michelle,

Until recently I was using really good quality European chocolate in all my cakes, but it's really expensive. I did some experimenting and realised that I can use a different (but still good quality) product and it doesn't make the cake taste any different but saves me a lot of money. I'm going to change my recipes. Do I need to tell my clients?

Signed,

Confused in Cakeland

Dear Confused in Cakeland,

You only need to tell your clients if you have been using the expensive stuff as a specific, advertised selling point. Even then, I wouldn't go making a big announcement about it. New clients won't know, old clients probably won't notice - but if you feel that's being dishonest somehow you can always say to them, "I'm using a different brand of chocolate in my cakes now - I'd love to know what you think!" It shows you're always striving to be better and that really you want their feedback - both of which you should ACTUALLY be doing anyway.

I think most consumers (unless they are mega foodies) aren't all that fussed by brand names of raw ingredients as much as they care about the end product. A lot of people are quite happy as long as their product looks and tastes brilliant - they're not bothered by the 'behind the scenes' bit of it. However, if you are using your "100% organic, European, imported, exclusively exclusive, made by small protégé children, travelled by extinct ferret along the tops of the Andes, translated into 16 languages" chocolate and you talk it up as your point of difference ... you should probably come clean if you're not doing that anymore. There are ways about this, though - don't talk down the old ingredient, talk UP the new one..... and in my opinion, expensive chocolate is wasted when baked into a cake. Save it for eating by itself or for using in ganache's and fillings where it can actually be tasted.

Yours in cocoa dusted love,

Michelle

CHAPTER 5

MONEY

By far the most difficult topic I tackle on the blog is money. Not the pricing of products (after all, that can be reduced to a formula) but the actual value behind money and our feelings about it. Our industry is overwhelmingly female and generally women find talking about money rather difficult. That's why we can do all the calculations in the world which tell us how much to charge for something, but the minute a client calls we just blurt something out in a panic. For the purposes of this book I left this chapter about the mindset behind money matters and kept the pricing chapter separate. In truth I think this one is more important – because how you feel about money is what makes you less likely to blurt out a number.

In the online resources of this book (http://www.thebizofbaking.com/BestofBoB) , there are some (non cake related) links to money mindset books and courses I've personally found quite useful. I find it interesting that overwhelmingly, those resources are by women, for women, and about women – which makes one wonder if the ABBA song is true: "Money, money, money, it's a rich man's world!" My firm belief is that this attitude is changing, and I welcome a world where there is no longer a gender pay gap and where I can leave this chapter out of my next book.

Working For Free

Is it ever okay to work for free?

Truth is I really want to say, "NO, it isn't okay," and leave it at that ... but it hardly tells the whole story, does it? In this article, I'm talking about the times when either you do not charge at all for your labour (and we all know how I feel about that[12]) or the times you do something for no money and it might even COST you in time or money to do it. You really should have a proper Family and Friends Discount Policy[13], but even if you do, you will probably still get asked to do things for free.

A few examples might be - making a wedding cake for your brother in lieu of a present, giving a presentation to a group of people in your target market, creating a tutorial in a magazine, providing a cake for a photo shoot, doing some demonstrations at an event, making products for a charity event, giving a testimonial for a product, participating in a webinar, promoting someone else's product ... etc. You get the idea. We get asked to do stuff for free in this industry all the time (often by other cake people), and then we complain when our customers want us to work for free, too. What the what?! How does that work exactly?

As I see it, there are only ever TWO instances where you should be willing to work for free:

---

12   See *In It For The Love AND Money* in Chapter 11.
13   See *Your Business Your Rules* in Chapter 3.

Firstly. LOVE. When I say 'love, ' I mean that you love it or them enough not to feel resentful that you spent your precious time or money on this project. If you

find yourself MORE than happy to do this free thing, because it's for someone you love dearly or for a cause/project/product you really love and want to support - then go ahead and do it. I would still put some rules around it, though - because you want to agree to something for love but then you don't want to be taken advantage of and then be running around in Resentment Land. I'm not saying you LIKE this product or this person a lot, I'm saying that you really and truly love love love love LOVE it or them. Enough that you don't really think of it as doing it for free in the first place, because you probably would have done it ANYWAY.

I'll give you an example. My first formal cake decorating class was a Wilton Level One buttercream class. I met a woman in that class named Grace, and she and I got along really well. I jokingly said to her that if she ever got married, I'd make her a kick-ass wedding cake (which was rich considering I only just learned how to pipe with a star tip, and she was already working as a pastry chef). About a year later, totally randomly, I ended up working for Grace at a patisserie and she taught me a hell of a lot about the pastry arts. She became my friend and mentored me and even though I left that job, we remained in touch. Fast forward 10 years, and Grace was getting married - and by then, I had a successful, busy cake shop and I literally hadn't made a free cake in maybe 5-6 years.

She got her free cake. All 5 tiers of it, delivered to the ends of the earth, with a whole bunch of different flavours and work which was WELL outside of my comfort zone. I did it for the love, entirely for the love - and I have zero regrets or resentment about it.

So. If you're doing it for free, you had best be loving the hell out of that person, OR if it's a product or service or event you're helping out with ... love the heck out of those too. Ask yourself two questions, "Am I going to get irritated about this if it starts to suck up too much of my time or money? Is there something I would rather be doing, or which will serve me better?" If the answer is NO and NO, then go right ahead and do it. Guilt free.

Secondly: You are _**100% satisfied with the ROI**_. ROI stands for "return on investment" and basically that means you are getting OUT of it the same if not MORE than you put IN to it. Unless there is something in it for you which you are totally SATISFIED will meet or exceed your OWN INVESTMENT in it, just don't do it.

If you're being asked to demo at an event at your expense but it's not really going to do much for you in the way of either sales or profile raising - don't do it. If you're being asked to create a cake for a magazine, but their readership is not your ideal clientele - don't do it. If you've been asked to write a tutorial for a magazine, but you would really rather not share that skill because you can teach it elsewhere for money - don't do it. Magazines, online schools, cake events, should have a budget for talent (because they make money from advertising and ticket sales) so why then do you need to work for them for free? I'm sorry, but if a magazine can't afford to pay you, but they take money from advertisers ... something is wrong with that business model. They would not HAVE a magazine to sell ads in unless it had good quality content, and that content is what you are creating for free for them. So let me get this straight, you create brilliant content so they can sell ad space, and then they keep all the money and you see none? Someone explain to me how that's fair? Why on earth would you spend time and money to _improve someone else's business_ when you could be spending time or money on i_mproving your own business_?

I hear a lot of cake makers tell me that they do things for free just because if they don't, someone else will. I can't even wrap my head around that one. So someone else is going to pimp themselves out for free, and you should do it just to keep them from doing it. Ummmm ... okay. Right. Wait. WHAT?

If nobody else will say it, I will: All of us out there agreeing to do stuff for free (with no decent return) are hurting the industry as a whole. _We want to be taken seriously as artists, we want to be paid appropriately for our time and skill, and yet over and over and over we're working for free. It makes no sense to me._ WE are the ones killing ourselves here, not the magazines or the events who ask us to do it. WE are the ones saying "Yes, I'll do that for free," when we should be saying, "I'd love to do that for you, here's what I charge for it or what I'd like in return." It makes me crazy that we all get so frustrated with clients not paying what we're worth and yet within the industry, among our peers, we either don't ask for our worth or we do it for free because we are afraid someone else will come along who will. How is this different to undercharging, exactly? The reasons for doing it seem to be the same.

<u>We created this culture. It's time to change it.</u>

Before you all jump up and down at me, let me explain what a "decent return" is. When it comes to money, <u>only you</u> can decide what you're needing to make in order to make that activity worth it. You need to work out what you would charge for these kinds of activities and that's going to depend on a whole lot of factors. Of course, there are instances where the return to you is not in dollars at all. Perhaps you're really wanting to grow a global audience and the opportunity you've been given is to do a video tutorial (for free) which is going to be seen by millions of people, and the video will link back to your business and social media pages (worth it). Perhaps you have a product of some kind (a book, pdf tutorials, a physical product like a tool of some kind) and you've been asked to demonstrate it at a cake event (for free), where you can then sell a whole lot of product (worth it). Perhaps you've got a big event coming up and you've been asked to teach a workshop (for free), and the audience are all in the target market of people who are likely to attend your event (worth it).

Basically, you've got to be really satisfied that the ROI is WORTH the time and money it's going to cost you to do this thing. We all know that nothing is actually free. There is always a cost to you somewhere along the line. There sure as hell needs to be a BENEFIT to you along the line, and that benefit has got to be the same if not more than what it costs you.

Here's another example: suppose you've been asked to teach a class (for free) on a Saturday morning at a cake event, which is normally when you would be doing deliveries for your paying clients and doing wedding cake consultations. Honestly? Unless the people attending that class are a) new students for you to whom you can sell other classes, b) an entirely new market segment of people you're wanting to get in front of, or c) it fits some sort of 'dream' element ("I've always wanted to ...") then it's plain and simple not worth you doing it. Why? Because the entire thing is going to come at a cost. Someone else is going to have to do the deliveries (for money), and even if that's your husband (who works for free for you), that's still costing you in family time. Saturdays are also a big day for wedding appointments. Can you afford to take that Saturday off to work for free for someone else, when instead you might be booking in some new orders for yourself AND paying for the deliveries to get done? If so, go ahead. If not, say no or tell them what you charge for Saturday teaching.

I've also heard the, "but I'll get lots of exposure!" reason for doing work for free as well. This one is a lot harder to quantify but a lot easier to work out if you're willing to do it. Go back and think about the other people who did this thing last time. Six months later, can they really say if it built their brand up or not? Did that event, article or video really catapult them into the stratosphere of fame? Here's an idea - contact them and nicely ask. "I'm thinking about doing this event and I know you did it last time, did you find it was worth it? Did you really get as much exposure as they've promised me?" (Marketing tip: I also do this for advertising. I contact OTHER advertisers who are already doing it and ask them if they think it's worth it.)

Anyone who has ever done a celebrity cake for free knows this feeling ALL too well - that the exposure that comes out of it after the fact is entirely reliant on YOU telling everyone that you made that cake. The article in People magazine isn't about your cake, it's about that celebrity wedding ... so while your cake might appear in the pictures, chances are there is no mention of your business name or a link to it. The same principle is true of almost every 'you'll get sooo much exposure!' opportunity you're presented with. The exposure you get out of it and how long it lasts is about how much work you do to ensure you get it. What I'm saying is, the promise of 'exposure' almost never delivers - and you can often generate your OWN exposure in a whole lot of ways that won't take up quite as much time, money or effort.

I'm going to be straight up and tell you that I've never heard of the value of promised 'exposure' actually paying off for anyone. I've heard of lots of people doing things for exposure, but nearly nobody is actually satisfied with the exposure they got versus what they were promised. "Exposure" is marketing speak for, "Let me bully you into believing that you should be GRATEFUL that I'm asking you to work for free, because someone else will do it if you won't." They're playing on your FOMO (fear of missing out.)

I can hear you asking, "But what about for fun, Michelle? Can't I just do something because it's fun?" Yes, of course, you could choose to work for free for fun, but I'm pretty sure in that case it's not actually work. My idea of fun doesn't help someone else make money, nor does it keep me from making money in my own business, and usually fun is something I do other than cake. So if I'm going to do something cake-related which is "just for fun", I'll look for opportunities to make that fun work for me. I want to try out a new technique for fun? I might turn it into a business blog post, or make a dummy cake I can then use on my website. I want to create a tutorial for fun? I'll take plenty of pics so I've got stuff to put on Instagram. I want to do demos because I love talking in front of an audience?

I'll invite my best customers to come along and watch a class for free, as a way of thanking them for their support. There are lots and lots of ways you can have fun doing these kinds of things and yet still have a business mindset so you're not losing out. I never said don't have fun with what you do I'm telling you that if you're wanting to build a sustainable business, you've got to be thinking of your time as worth something. Here's the harsh bit: this isn't a blog about just having fun. It's a blog about having fun AND making a decent living. It's the people having fun but not thinking about making a living who are burning out really fast and who are living in Resentment Land. I don't want to be one of those people and I'm pretty sure you don't, either.

We need to change the culture of this industry. We cannot keep asking our clients to value us if we are not willing to value each other.

So ... do I think it's ever okay to work for free? Only if it's for a hell of a lot of love, or a hell of a lot of return. How much love and how much or what the return is made of is entirely up to you, but it's got to be one or the other. No such thing as a free lunch OR a free cake.

(Or a free demo.)

Being Charitable

Free cake is not free.

Almost as soon as I hung out my cake-making shingle, I started to get requests for donations. Everyone from the local school fair to PR agencies wanting wedding cakes for big-name celebrities wanted a piece of me (pun intended.) I also had requests from really wonderful local people who decided to hold charity events to honour their friends or family. I'm generally a nice person but I'm also a bleeding heart, so, in the beginning, I used to agree to pretty much every request. A lot of the time the people requesting finished product would promise me things in return - the company name on all the literature pertaining the event, exposure in magazines (especially if it was a celeb event), posts about us on Facebook, acknowledgement certificates ... you name it, they promised it. The savvy ones would even go out of their way to explain all the HUGE benefits I'd get from being involved - according to them this exposure was practically *priceless*. Funnily enough, the time and money I'd need to put into that product - not priceless! In fact - the time and money I was donating in 'free' cakes was in fact costing me a heck of a lot.

I did a bunch of cakes for charity events and here's what I learned: you never get the exposure they promise. Not because they didn't try, but because the people attending the event don't care who made the cake, they care that there IS cake. Your name might appear in the glossy brochure, but nobody is going to reference it later to find you. Your cake might appear in a magazine (if you're lucky), but it will be YOU telling everyone it's there because the PR agency is being paid to promote the celeb, not the cake. The MC might mention your name over the microphone to the crowd of 10, 000 people at the charity ball - but they won't stop to write down your name. The organiser might deliver on everything they promised, but you're probably not the only business which helped them out so the message will likely be diluted anyway. If you do get some sort of really great exposure, like all PR it's going to be short-lived and you're going to need to churn out another cake for another event to keep it going. There is simply no longevity in these sorts of donations or involvement.

Have you ever noticed that football stadiums, local sporting teams, various charities and the like often have a business associated with them as a sponsor? Insurance companies, car companies ... even on a local level the Little League team will have a sponsor name on their jerseys. Being a sponsor implies a LONG TERM involvement (and yes, often a long-term investment). I'm going to suggest that you take that same approach when it comes to charitable giving, and here's why:

1. Charities survive on support, but generally speaking, it costs them more to collect a whole lot of small donations than it does bigger or ongoing ones. Think about how many times you've gotten a letter from the Red Cross, or had a door knocker come by. All of that costs those charities time and money. If you can give to them without them having to chase you, you're costing them less and giving them more.

2. From the beginning, I've stressed the importance of having some rules around your business (remember the Family and Friends discount[14]?). The rules make it so that people know what to expect from you, AND so that you have the confidence of a defined answer when those conversations come up.

By choosing a smaller number of charities to support, you're doing a much better thing both for those charities and your business. They will appreciate the longer term support, and you will have an answer as to why you cannot make a cake for the Basket Weavers Association. I'm not suggesting you call up a charity and offer to be a formal sponsor of the name-on-a-jersey type (but if you can, by all means do). I'm suggesting you pick a charity and then support them over the period of the year (or more) in whatever way you can handle.

You might:

- give them a percentage of your profit one month
- bake something for one of their events
- keep a collection tin next to your register
- promote their events in your store or through your online presence
- ask clients to (voluntarily) make donations via your web store
- create a special charity-themed product (eg pink ribbon cookies) and donate the profits

... and so on. There are LOADS of ways that small businesses can support charities in a meaningful, ongoing way without having to pimp themselves out every time someone decides to sell cupcakes for cancer. I don't mean to sound crass or unloving. You ABSOLUTELY can be a business with a conscience - in fact, you should be. There are ways to be charitable which benefit both the giver and the receiver and as a business owner you've got to think about that. I also think charity is a very personal thing - and if I'm giving to everyone who asks, I'm diluting my own experience. I'd much prefer to give more to an organisation I feel strongly about than one I didn't. It means more to me, so I'll work harder to get them more support - as opposed to feeling a bit resentful that I'm making yet another 'free' cake because I didn't want to say no.

Here's how I do it:

At the start of each year - I decide which charity or organisation I'm going to support (it's often two.) I contact them and ASK how I can help. Some want just money, some have events they need cake for, some might ask you to provide some ideas. Believe me when I say they will be thrilled to hear you call and say, "I own a local business and your cause is dear to me. What's the best way I can get involved and help you?" I then PLAN to help them. So maybe I sell pink cupcakes during Breast Cancer Awareness week, or I donate 5% of my October profits because it's Autism Month, or whatever. I actually plan the events and make them part of our usual business activities - then talk about and promote them exactly as I would any other event. I feel strongly about the causes I picked, so it's a pleasure to both do those activities and promote them.

Let's be honest here - it also looks good for my business that I make the time and effort to support causes which are meaningful to me. It makes me FEEL good and it makes me LOOK good. Win-Win.

What do I do when people come knocking, as they inevitably will? I use the rules I developed to politely decline. "My company actively supports two charities every year. This year we chose X and Y charity, and we focus all our giving this year on supporting those. Thanks for the opportunity to be involved and best of luck." Sure, sometimes, even with the rules, I might contribute to their cause - but most often it will be some sort of door prize or voucher which doesn't cost me much in terms of time or money. Overall, it's the *commitment* I made to those two charities which I honour above all else.

Choosing to support only a few causes but saying no to many others does not make me greedy, unloving, or unsympathetic. It makes me a better business woman, and it makes me a better person.

... and as for the celebrities who want free wedding cakes? As a small business, you won't get much out of it other than perhaps requests from other PR companies. Leave those things to the bigger players. Do ANY of you remember who made Kim and Kris's wedding cake?

The take home message is this: give ... and give generously, but give wisely.

Your Dirty Little Secret

This is one of those posts where I'm going to lay my soul entirely bare, then hit post without editing it.

This morning I heard about a local cake company which is going out of business ... and it's the second one I've heard of this week, third one in the last fortnight. I'm not talking about the part-time businesses which people run for a bit of extra cash, I'm talking about the businesses which are the sole means of livelihood for people. These are businesses closing out of duress, owners needing to sell personal effects or the assets of the business, break leases and basically go through a whole lot of unpleasantness to wind things up.

I can't comment on WHY they went out of business (usually it's more complicated than just one thing anyway) but I can say that, even if they were my competition, I still find it heartbreaking. Heartbreaking because those businesses were a part of people's lives, were dreams they once had, things they built up from nothing, entities they put their heart and souls into. It would be so EASY to say they were jerks, their business model was crappy, they were dodgy operators from the get go, it's one less competitor I need to deal with ... and so on. Maybe all of those things are true, maybe they aren't, but it does not (for me) take away the sadness I feel about it all, competitors or not.

I really want to carry on judgementally about those closed businesses but I can't, and I won't - because I've flown as close to the sun as they have, and I've got the burnt wing tips to prove it. Being in small business at the moment is rough. Really rough. Not just in cake or baking or the makers' movement - small business is not an easy thing to be in (no matter how much they sell you the whole "make your own hours, be your own boss" lifestyle stuff.) We all know this, we all say it privately to our very close friends (who themselves are probably not in business) and at night, secretly, in our dark hours, we sometimes wonder what the HELL we were thinking when we got into this venture.

I've said this so many times, I probably sound like a broken record - it's very easy to get INTO business, hard to STAY IN business ... and yet, we don't like to admit that the business bit of it is actually the hard part. FAR harder than dealing with buttercream at the height of summer, far harder than dealing with the haters in the online communities, harder than figuring out what the heck is the difference between marketing and public relations and working out why you need either of those. And yet, when Sharon and I devised the **Business of Baking on Tour** program (http://bizbakeontour.com), we knew that the hardest thing to do would be to convince people of its value.

We all KNOW that business is the hard part, but we've got to convince you to come and learn about business with us? Wait ... WHAT?

We knew we'd need to convince you because there are lots of people out there who are embarrassed or ashamed to admit that they don't know enough about running a business. These are people who were never given those skills in the first place, have no formal education in it, and who just sort of fell into business organically. It's not their fault that they don't know this stuff.

But hold on just a second ... a few days, months, or years ago, did we know much about our craft either? Did we - back then - have much in the way of skills or formal education? Or did we just give fall into it by giving it a try?

As a community, we open ourselves up to feedback and criticism (and sometimes actually invite it) when we post a picture of a cake to our peers. We ask our heroes for advice on techniques, we eat up tutorials like they are Mn'Ms, we ask questions of others, we watch YouTube videos and we learn, learn, learn, learn about how to create beautiful things in the same crazed way as camels who have not had a drink in decades. We literally SUCK UP education.

As a community, we are avid learners and sharers ... so it begs the question, then: If we are a community that values education and learning, why do we not value it when it comes to the bigger, harder things we are challenged by every single day? Why do we only value it on the smaller stuff?

Here's why: On the outside, it looks like running a business is easy. Hell, people do it every single day, in all sorts of countries, in all sorts of economies. People you know that are far less clever than you seem to be succeeding at doing it all the time! But ... success or failure is easily hidden. You can be drowning in business messes and nobody will ever know. The very core of your business can be rotting away ... but it can be your dirty little secret.

Cake - or macarons, brownies or whoopie pies - are *not like that at all*.

On the outside, if you've done a crappy job at ganaching your cake, or you swapped salt for sugar, or you burned your brownies, there is NO WAY to hide that. Other people will see the bulges on the sides, other people will tell you the cake is inedible, other people will notice that your swiss meringue buttercream has split. You can't hide your cake mistakes the way you can hide your business mistakes. Your cake mistakes are out there for the world to see (usually because you posted them there).

And ... let's be real here ... at the end of the day, it's cake (or whatever). It's fixable, it's not going to affect anyone's life in the long term (unless you've poisoned them), it's disposable - eaten, enjoyed, GONE. Next year, you'll barely remember the cake disaster other than perhaps to laugh at it.

Business is not like that. Business - the experience of it - lasts a lot longer than the cake you served at a 21st birthday party. So because it's bigger, and scarier, and more important to us personally ... it's harder to ask for help, and easier to drown without anybody really noticing until we're really and truly with the water over our heads.

Other than so far seeming like just a really long rant, I do actually have a point here - this industry is changing dramatically: growing, shrinking, re-forming, being redefined and becoming something entirely different to what it was one, two, five years ago. We can no longer afford (quite literally) to only do the fun stuff if we've got any hope of surviving. We've got to do the hard stuff. Admit we need help, then go and get that help - to make us into *better* business owners, running *better* businesses. Is airing out your dirty little secret about your lack of business knowledge going to guarantee your success? Maybe not - but rotting away from the inside is surely not a great strategy for success either.

Honestly? I'm getting very tired of hearing stories of business dreams which fell apart because the ganache just wasn't strong enough to hold the business together.

Confused in Cakeland - Making A Living From Selling Cake

Confused in Cakeland

Hi Michelle,

It seems like there are a lot of cake and cupcake businesses going out of business. I've been researching my business model, making a lot of plans and saving up to open my dream store. I want to move forward but I have to admit I'm really scared because I see so many closed businesses and people who burn out. If all those people are failing, what chance have I got? I know you tell it like it is. Honestly, do you really think it's possible to make a living out of selling cake?

Thanks.

Worried Caker

Hey there Worried Caker,

Firstly, I don't blame you for being worried, it feels a little scary out there at the moment.

That being said, YES, I think that even in this crowded industry, you can make a real, decent living out of selling cake. I think you will work harder than you think you will, I think you MUST diversify your offerings from the very get-go, and I think the best investment you'll make in your business is in learning business skills.

No, I'm not just saying that because I teach a class like that (https://www.bizbakeontour.com), I'm saying that because it's been proven over and over again. Your ability to ganache can easily be copied by someone else and is easily learned via YouTube. Dealing with customers, marketing effectively, and having the right entrepreneurial mindset? THOSE are the things you'll need to succeed in the long term and which can't be learned in a video.

As for the diversifying part, I mean this on several levels - offer more than one product or service, have staff members with diverse skills but with some overlap, make sure your marketing plan is diverse.

To put this into baking terms: don't ever put all your eggs in one basket, in ANY aspect of your business.

You can do this, my Worried Friend. I still believe - actually, I KNOW, it's entirely possible - because I've both done it and seen it done.

Michelle

CHAPTER 6
PRICING

Entire books have been written about pricing handmade products. There are plenty of spreadsheets available online for pricing our products. I've personally created an online class and written dozens and dozens of articles about this very topic. Why then do we all find this so hard to figure out? The answer can actually be found in the chapter before this one about money mindset. It's not the numbers which are hard to figure out, it's the emotions around the numbers. Think about this: when you buy a small ticket item, you hardly think about it. When you go to buy something of significant dollar value to you, suddenly you are asking other people's opinions, trying to justify the item, price and feature checking it against other items, searching online for a better price, weighing up your options. The same is true if we are the seller. If we were selling things of a relatively small dollar value, the topic of price would not come up nearly as often as it does. We get a double emotional whammy on this topic, too – not only are we often selling things of much higher value (which would often be classified as luxury items), we are also selling art. Art is subjective – it's beauty is measured entirely by the person looking at it, and it's price is determined by what that observer is willing to pay for it. Add those two highly fraught emotional concepts into the equation, add our own questions about our self worth, add in the hundred other local cake makers who are charging very little ... and you end up realising that all the spreadsheets in the world won't help you figure out your pricing.

I teach whole classes about pricing, but in all those classes, I concentrate on the emotion behind the pricing as much as the solid numbers. Once you've been in business a while and you have balance sheets and bank statements to look at, you'll get a handle on working out how much to charge. Getting over that little cringe you get when a customer asks for a price over the phone is a much harder skill to learn.

You'll see me mention this later on in the chapter but it's worth repeating here: pricing is a process, not a project. It's not something you do once and never do again. It's a skill you learn and then as you go along, you recalculate and re-evaluate. Most people hate it when I say that, because they would much rather I told them to work out their pricing once, create a pretty little chart and be done with it forever more. They usually feel a lot better once I ask them, "In a year from now, when your decorating skills have improved, would you really like to be charging the same as you do now?" Pricing is a process, not a project.

Charge What You're Worth

COCA-COLA SOLD 25 BOTTLES IN THEIR FIRST YEAR SO WHATEVER BULLSH*T YOU'RE GOING through right now, GET OVER IT.

I'm willing to bet that the thing which stresses you out the most about pricing isn't the stuff like the cost of flour or butter, it's the more flexible things like your hourly rate. More than once you've wondered how much you're really worth. You've seen the memes and videos online where people seem to be constantly shouting at you, "You are an artist! You have to charge what you're worth! You deserve to get paid more!" but they give you no REAL idea of how to charge what you're supposedly worth. So you nod your head and agree with them, you know you should charge more ... but you really have no idea of your worth. I'm going to help you figure that out.

First, let's remember this:

Pricing is a PROCESS, not a PROJECT.

It's really easy to sit around and say, "Nobody will ever pay me what I'm worth," or "There is no way I can get paid for every hour I work," or "Everyone only wants something for nothing," and so on. Sitting around complaining is a hell of a lot easier than getting up and DOING something about it, isn't it? This is especially true for those of you reading this in small towns or countries, or places where highly decorative or speciality products are either non-existent or not yet fully appreciated. It's really hard! I totally get it. Let's also be real about the fact that nobody NEEDS cake or cookies in order to survive so it's not like you're high on their list of priorities. Newsflash: Part of owning a business is teaching them why they should want those products and specifically why they should want them from YOU. (See the next article which is about that very topic.)

Have you ever purposely low-balled a quote, or immediately offered a refund because we didn't like how the product turned out? Or secretly, would you rather lose the order than quote a proper price to someone? <u>We do those things because we lack confidence in ourselves</u>. Confidence isn't something that I can bottle up and give you. Confidence is something that comes with time and experience.

So we know that a big part of educating your customers about price is confidence ... but here's the thing: it's not YOUR confidence. IT'S THEIRS. They need to trust you and be confident that you are going to give them what they need, that their money was well invested. No, you can't just print up a bunch of business cards and think that someone is going to pay you the big bucks just because you're "an artist". You've got to build up a reputation over time - <u>that's why it's called "building" a reputation, not "magically making"</u> a reputation. You've got to build a reputation for producing great work, giving great service, and delivering to your clients' needs and expectations and that's not something which happens overnight.

Let me say that again: Customers are not going to "just get it, " and you are not going to "be worth it" without some long-term effort involved.

Let me put it to you this way: suppose I make a cake and Ron Ben Israel makes the EXACT same cake, down to the last petal and crumb. Want to guess which one of us will be able to charge more? Which one of us is WORTH more? <u>Your worth is something which increases over time</u>. You get better skills-wise, you get faster at making things, you put in place systems so your business runs more efficiently, you develop a reputation because word of mouth gets around and so on. <u>None of that comes in the mail with the business cards</u>.

Here are some ways you can **build your reputation and give your customers the confidence to order from you (which in turn, allows you to increase your worth and charge more)**:

1. **Evidence that you're good**: Did you get a great review from someone? Share it! Post a picture of the cake and the thank you note you got on your social media accounts. Sign up for external review websites (make sure it's a legitimate one please). Testimonials should be on your website and they should be updated regularly. If you've been told you're the bee's knees, please tell everyone so that new customers already feel confident because other people have said so. We like to shop by word of mouth, even if that word comes from a stranger. Often it's not what YOUsay that convinces people to buy, it's what OTHERS say.

2. **Visibility**: get involved in local charities, support local schools, find ways to be seen to your target market in and around your area. Join your local Chamber of Commerce or small business forum. Network with other business owners in the same industry as you are - the party planners, the photographers, the florists. Get your work into magazines, online newsletters or blogs. Offer to do some demonstrations for local events. The more places people see you or your work, the more your reputation will grow because you'll keep cropping up. Stop hiding your light under a bushel and BE SEEN in whatever ways you can.

3. **Branding**- Make sure if you want to be seen as "high-end" that EVERYTHING you put out there needs to be high-end, from the photos you take to the packaging you use. From a behavioural point of view, act in a way that is reflective of the brand. As an example, if you're aiming to be high-end, don't take orders by text message, don't rant on social media and don't show up to deliveries wearing a onesie. In other words, I'm pretty sure nobody orders Prada handbags by text message.

4. **Systems**- you need HAVE systems in the first place. You need proper terms and conditions, clearly written order forms, a dedicated business phone number, a website (not just a Facebook page) and so on. If you want to be considered legitimate, you've actually got to BE legitimate. You really don't want a client to come for a consult and you're there scrambling to find a scrap of paper to write their order on and all you've got is a crayon and supermarket receipt. And YES, all of this applies to home based businesses as much as shop based one. Nothing about being based at home means "operates in an unprofessional manner" unless you make it that way.

5. **Certificates**- If you won an award at a cake show, registered your business properly, appeared on a cake website, took some classes or in some way got an official "Yay You!" from a third party, say it loud and proud! Show those badges on your website, hang those certificates on your wall, say it in your marketing - "We got 4 stars at our recent Council review!", 'We won Cake of the Week!" Don't hide your accomplishments from people.

Your clients will pay what you're worth <u>once you've done the work to show them WHY you're worth it</u>. You've got to build the reputation that will make them confident to order from you. This past weekend in my business class, someone shared a story about how she screwed up a client's order. The client not only refused a refund, but came back to order from her time and time again. WHY? Because she'd already proven her worth. They had the confidence and trust in her to realise that the screw-up was a single, isolated event and not an indication of what they could or should expect from her. She also dealt with the situation calmly and professionally - again proving to them her worth. They paid her for that order and will continue to order because she's build the reputation <u>which PROVES to them that she's worth it</u>.

Today, ask yourself this -
What have I done lately to prove to my customers that I'm worth it?
(Hint: Just making amazing creations isn't good enough in the long run.)

Educating Customers About Pricing

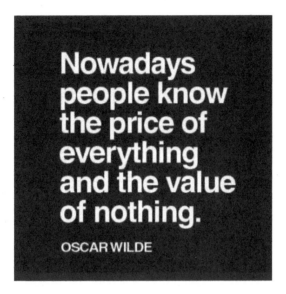

Nowadays people know the price of everything and the value of nothing.

OSCAR WILDE

When you get lots of phone calls or enquiries which all seem price based, or lots of rejections based on price alone, it can seem as though that's all people care about. To be fair, there is some portion of the population to whom price is the only deciding factor in purchasing decisions. However, I find most people are willing to get more than one quote, and willing to consider why those quotes differ. I recently saw some cake business advice online which said (I'm paraphrasing here), "Don't ever explain why you charge why you charge, people should just be paying you what the price is with no questions asked. Don't bother trying to communicate with people who only ask about price, you're wasting time. The clients you really want will just GET IT."

What? They'll just "get it"... ?

The thing about baked goods is (especially custom made items) that your potential clients are not actually IN this business, so they don't really have any idea of how much effort goes into creating those things. The cake TV shows have done a LOT to educate the general public about the amount of effort and artistry which goes into what we do, but not everyone watches those shows. Plus, there are a lot of perfectly reasonably decorated, mass produced baked goods out there which will do the job just as well. If all your client wants or needs is a cake that a five-year-old will be happy with and which will feed 10 kids at a backyard party ... you're going to have a hard time justifying why they should spend $100 with you when a $20 cake from the supermarket meets their needs. The challenge for us as business owners is working on the people who see a cake (no matter where it's from) as "just flour and butter" and get them to see why our version of cake is so much more than that.

They don't just "get it. " They really don't.

Part of our job as business owners (no matter what we are selling) is to convince our customers to buy what we're offering, and that means taking the time to explain why it's worth why it's worth. You don't need to look any further than McDonald's to find a great example of this - they market their speciality and seasonal burgers by telling us about the 100% Angus beef, the Swiss cheese, the sourdough bun it's on. Why? Because those special things are more expensive than your usual Big Mac and they want to convince you to spend that little bit more. They do not assume that consumers just "get" that the fancier stuff is worth the money, they explain why it is worth it.

Cakes - or whatever speciality item you make - are no different. You've got to market your products and your business precisely because not everyone understands what makes your product special. Are there some people who will not care one tiny bit that your product is better? Sure there are. If they say a flat out "no" based on price, that's okay ... but there are plenty of people who, with a bit of education, will be willing to spend a bit more to get something a bit better.

Instead of just getting annoyed that "all anyone seems to care about is price" and "I keep losing orders even though I've made my prices as cheap as possible" - why not try educating? Re-examine your marketing. Re-examine how you answered their email about the price. Did you say, "A Peppa Pig cake for 20 people costs $50", or did you say, "Thanks for your email! We'd love to make you a Peppa Pig cake for your son's upcoming 3rd birthday. Our cakes are all baked from scratch, and we've got an array of kid-friendly flavours to choose from - I've attached a list for you to pick from. We're also happy to customise the birthday message, and if you need delivery, we offer that service too. To feed 20 people, you're looking at a cost of $50. Please give me a call on 123-456-789 and we'll get the ball rolling. I look forward to helping make your celebration fantastic."

Does that second email require a little more thinking, a little more effort? Sure it does - but the investment in service and education are worth it if it means you've converted them into buying from you rather than just settling for the mass produced item. Every company, everywhere in the world, selling anything at all is going to come up against people who seem to only care about price. In every market (clothing, cars, food ...) there will be companies who service the very low end, companies that service the very high end, and a whole lot of companies right smack in the middle of that. Even the companies selling things for cheap have to market themselves and their products - because they are not the only ones in town claiming to be the cheapest. The companies at the top are no different - because they too are not the only one in town that sells a premium product.

Believing that your customers should just 'get it' and assuming that all anyone cares about is price is a fairly short-sighted view. If you're in this for the long term, you will aim to be the company that educates and then converts to the sale, accepts that some people just won't be won over ... but is clever enough to at least try.

Not everyone gets it, and not everyone needs to ... but you would be foolish to not even try because you have decided ahead of time that they can't be taught.

Getting More Sales

When you're first starting out in business, it can be a little disheartening to answer a whole bunch of enquiries but not get any orders. In business speak, we call this your 'conversion rate' - meaning the amount of people you manage to convert from prospects into paying clients. Effective converting and selling is a skill set all on its own. Some people are just born salespeople who have the gift of the gab and are naturally persuasive, while the rest of us really need to work at it. If you already find "putting it out there" uncomfortable, then me telling you that you've got to learn sales skills probably feels a little, well, yuck. It feels somehow dishonest or desperate, both of which are things nobody wants to be! Here are a few things which help you convert better (make more sales) but that don't require you to wear a bad suit or feel like you're begging for the order.

Make it really, really easy for people to order from you.

Don't make ordering a fifteen step process that exhausts people before they have begun. If people can order online from you (either product or classes), make sure the entire process, from selecting the item to checking out of your shopping cart is uncomplicated and easy to use. The "buy now" button, "shop here" and "online ordering" buttons and pages should be really easy to find. I've seen a lot of websites where I want to buy something from them, but it takes me so long to figure out HOW to buy something that I just give up! Don't make it hard for people to buy from you.

The same is true for off-line purchases. Make it VERY clear how they can pay their deposits, what the process is (and make it a short process.) Don't wait for them to ASK how to do it, tell them! This is another place where having clear, simple and defined business procedures will really help you out because there is no question for you or your customer how to proceed with the order.

Take control of the communication.

When you've reached the point in the email conversation where they clearly are interested and wanting to order from you, actually pick up the phone and call them. "Hi Jane, I thought it would be quicker if I just called you to confirm the details we spoke about in email and get the deposit organised." The longer you keep dragging out that email conversation, the more of your time you are wasting, and the less likely you are to get the sale done and over with. It's also a lot harder to say no over the phone to someone - so you're effectively closing the deal just by calling them. If this sounds scary to you, remember that you've already established their interest in you via email, so this isn't a cold sales call. (*How to get their phone number*: Make it a required field on your website "contact us" form so that they have to give it to you to submit their order question. If they didn't come through your website, ask for it at the very beginning - "What's the best number to reach you on in case I need to get in touch about your order?")

People always ask me if they should chase up quotes after they've sent them. My feeling on this is two-fold: if you've got the time and you really want to do that order from a creative point of view, a follow up is not a bad idea. If however it's not really an order you need or are interested in (or it's a small one that won't make much difference to you), I'd leave it alone and not bother. I DO think there is a lot to be said for following up, if only because your competitors won't bother - but nor do I want you wasting hours and hours on chasing up people who aren't the kind of client you want (e.g., a client that calls back).

Act as if you already have the order

This one works unbelievably well, so often in fact for me that it was far and away my secret weapon to converting enquiries into orders. From the very first time, someone contacted me, I would act as if I already had that order confirmed. This means that the language I used in emails or over the phone had an assumption in it that I'd be doing the order. You're not ASKING them to pay the deposit, you're telling them they're going to do it! No, not in a "pay now or I will cut you" kind of way, but in a gentle, natural way as though the deal has already been sealed and you're just helping them get there. So at the end of the email instead of saying, "The price is $100", my email would end by saying, "To create this for you is $100.

To secure the date, I ask for a 50% deposit which needs to be paid by Pay Pal (and include a link to PayPal) by April 20th. I'm really looking forward to making this for you, you picked a gorgeous design - the party is going to be amazing!" Nobody reading that would say it sounds slimy or desperate in the slightest. It's 1) friendly, 2) makes the sales process VERY easy for them by outlining the steps and gives them the chance to take the next steps, and 3) it openly assumes that I'm going to get the gig. If you're acting as if the deal is done, and confident that you're going to be the only person who can make this thing for them, they are going to feel that confidence and just go with it. Plus you're saving them a ton of time and effort here - you're making the process easy, simple and most of all you are meeting their needs right NOW, not ten emails from now.

So how do I know this stuff works? I used to ask ALL my clients for feedback and testimonials and the one sentence which got repeated over and over again was, "Thanks so much Michelle, you made the entire process so easy for me!" We live in an age where people are immensely time poor, reluctant to commit, and bombarded by sales requests all day long. If you can help them save time, help them commit to making a choice - you're already halfway to getting the order. You're flat out saying that you're going to make it happen for them. Don't we ALL just want that certainty, that confidence, that knowledge that a job is going to get done, get done right, and not require a bunch of flapping around to make it happen?

Here's the BFO (Big Fat Obvious) key to closing the deal and making more sales: Don't make the process all about you, <u>make it all about them.</u>

Pricing Cakes Is Not Just About You

If I had a dollar for every time someone told me "I feel bad about charging people" … I'd be a wealthy woman indeed. Today I'm talking directly to any of you who have ever struggled with pricing, felt bad about charging for your cakes (even if you know it's too little), anyone who cringes each time they send a quote, and anyone who has ever felt angry when a customer has asked, "Why is it so expensive?" I'm talking to you because I want to address your money mindset as it pertains to pricing your work. A 'money mindset' is just a fancy way of saying "how we feel about money". Your money mindset is all the voices that run through your head every time you think about money. "I'm not good enough to charge as much as she does", "People who are in it for the money are greedy", "I don't want to make millions from my business", "She's sooooo business oriented!", "Of course she can afford it, she's Oprah", and so on. I know you're all nodding in agreement because we've ALL felt those things from time to time (me too.)

You've all heard me talk (and talk, and talk, and talk) about how there is no shame in wanting to make a living from your craft and be able to pay your bills. You know that how I feel about working for free[15], and doing stuff for "exposure"[16] and that it has to be about the love AND the money[17]. (if you don't, take a minute to go read those articles).

Here's a really BIG FAT IMPORTANT THING about why you must charge correctly and not feel even vaguely bad about it. Something I'm willing to bet will blow your

---

15   See *Working For Free* in Chapter 5.
16   See *The Promise of Future Work* in Chapter 6.
17   See *In It For The Love AND Money* in Chapter 11.

mind because it never occurred to you before.

PRICING IS NOT JUST ABOUT YOU
IT'S ALSO ABOUT THEM

Wait, what? Didn't you just say that I've got to earn a living? That it's about paying MY bills?

Yes. Yes, I did. Let me explain what I mean by that statement.

The more money you make, the more you can create and give. TO OTHERS.

*The more money you're making in your business, the BETTER your business can become **FOR YOUR CLIENTS**.*

The more money you're making, the more you can invest in your business in ways which will **directly benefit your clientele**. Think about it like a staircase. Every step up is a step closer. You can afford to take more classes and upskill yourself - so you're going to be giving your clients better products using modern, more interesting techniques. You can afford to hire staff, which frees your time up to develop products - that your clients will then enjoy. You can afford to source better ingredients - which means your clients are getting a much higher quality product.

If you choose to, you could afford to find a bigger premises for your business, and therefore not be "booked out" as often - and, therefore, serve more people and make more lives better and more parties happier. Maybe it's simpler than that - perhaps earning more means you can afford to get nicer boxes for your products, thus giving your clients a much nicer experience overall. Maybe earning more means you can afford to get a website, making it easier for them to find out what they need and get what they want. Do you see where I'm going here? The more you earn, the more you can do - FOR YOUR CLIENTS! Proper pricing isn't just about you, it's also about them. You're in business to solve your client's problems and meet their needs. Earning more just allows you to do more of that and do it better than you currently are. If you earn more, you can spend more ON THE PEOPLE who deserve to get brilliant things from you.

Aren't we all here to serve our clients AND ourselves? Isn't that one of the reasons we're all in business - to make beautiful things for other people? If our businesses were only about ourselves, would we be in business? Nope. We'd be in a hobby that did not need to make a single dime. We go into business because we want to share our gifts with other people. Imagine if you could do that in a better, faster, more wonderful way than you're doing it now. Isn't that reason enough to be charging for your work? *Earning more allows you to give your clients more and in better ways. THEY actually **benefit** from you doing it.*

Let's look at this on a personal level too - earning more means you can give your family and friends more if you choose too. Maybe it means you can afford to take your kids out to dinner once a month. Maybe it means you can get your child tutoring help in maths. Maybe it means you can buy your child a new pair of school shoes that don't fall apart after a month of use. Let's get really real here- maybe earning more means you can hire an assistant to help you out, so you can get home from work earlier and actually spend some time with your kids. Let me say this one more time:

PRICING IS NOT JUST ABOUT YOU
IT'S ALSO ABOUT THEM

You need to stop thinking that pricing correctly and charging what you charge is only about you and how you feel about it. It's not. It's about wanting to give your clients more and better things than you already give them - and if it weren't for them, you would have no business in the first place.

The more money you make, the more you can create and
give - and that's why we're doing this in the first place.

Let Me Tell You A Story About Pricing

The products you create tell a story. They tell a story about your client and their tastes and interests, but they also tell a story about you as a creator - are they big and colourful? Quiet and understated? Covered in flowers? Expensive or affordable? Whatever we are creating, be that bakery goods or quilts, artworks or emails, they tell people something about who we are.

Similarly, the way you price your products tells a story. To the customer and their guests, a $15 sheet cake from the supermarket tells a very different story to the $150 custom made cake. Pricing is not an exact science. I've got loads of spreadsheets which give me a whole lot of information about what my cakes cost me to produce, but none of them tell the whole story. They just don't account for the human factor (other than a rate per hour for labour.) You *must* do the maths on these basics, but once that's done there is a very large grey area in which you can shrink or expand the profit you make on a cake.

All good stories should have a "Who, What, Where, When, Why and How" answered in them. Today's post is to answer those six questions as they relate to pricing your creations and the story they tell.

WHO: Who you are as a baker/decorator is a vitally important component to how you can price your cakes. I'm talking about your reputation, your portfolio, your name. At the beginning of your baking adventure, if you have no reputation and no 'street cred', you just can't charge as much as the well-established businesses and people in your area even if your skill level is the same. The very same cake made by someone with an established reputation can be sold for more than one made by someone just starting out. A non-cake example for you: Tiffany and Co. can charge what they charge for things *because* they are Tiffany and Co.! The exact same silver bracelet with a locket sold from someone other than Tiffany's will likely be less expensive.

WHO v.2: Who your clients are will play a big part in your pricing. Look at your target market, look at their spending habits, look at the neighbourhood your business is in. Certain demographics are just plain willing to spend more to get what they want, and quality, perceived value, and 'look at me' all factor into it. To borrow my friends at Tiffany and Co. again - in part they charge what they charge because they *know* their clients are willing to pay those prices because they can *afford* to.

WHAT: This is where your skill, style and the product itself will come into the story, as will your competition and what else is available in your market place. In my case, I much prefer making high-end kids' cakes - and in knowing my target market, I also know about how much my target market of parents is willing to spend and so I price accordingly. I've got to take into account that there are plenty of my competitors who will charge less (or more) - so my pricing is a reflection of the quality and skill of what I make and where my company sits in the marketplace. "WHAT" also refers to the product itself: some products are meant to be sold as lower end, lower price but higher volume - and there is nothing wrong with that. I'm not about to go putting Callebaut chocolate in a $1. 50 cupcake, though.

WHERE: It's an unfortunate fact of life that humans perceive things firstly based on appearances. Whether we like it or not, most consumers will expect to pay less if they are buying a product from a home-based business. I'm not saying this is fair, I'm saying this is how it is. The average consumer who walks into your kitchen to order a cake is NOT thinking they're going to pay premium prices, EVEN if it's a premium product. Sell them the same cake from a fancy looking cake shop (or just premises not located in a home) and they'll automatically be expecting to pay more. Like it or not, working out of home may affect your ability to price beyond a certain level. Plus, you're competing with lots of other home based businesses who aren't charging enough for their products in the first place. This is true in other instances as well - what you can charge for a cupcake sold at a local farmer's market is not the same as what you can charge for a cupcake sold at a local upmarket cafe. Location matters.

To put this on an even bigger scale: you can't charge the same for a cupcake in New York City as you can in Sydney.

WHEN and **WHY**: The event itself (why) - and when the product will be consumed - have a direct correlation to what you can charge. Many cake makers will charge more for a wedding cake than they will for a birthday cake (even if they require the same skill level), simply because it's for a wedding. Wedding clients are likely to have a bigger budget and are therefore usually "willing" to pay more. Plus the importance of the event itself dictates how important the cake is to them - this isn't just a cake meant for the family to have at dinner. So the reason why the client is buying from you may affect what you can (or will) choose to charge them. Similarly, if the client is buying it last minute and you've got to run around like a crazy person to get it done - then "when" they ordered it is going to affect the price. The time of day/week/frequency with which they are buying the product makes a difference as well - if your muffin is something they are buying every day as they grab a morning coffee, they're not expecting to pay very much. If they're driving across town once a week to especially buy your muffins because you make the best muffins in town, they're going to be willing to pay more.

HOW: One of the reasons online shopping has become so big is that it's convenient to purchase and receive the products, and you can look for a good deal faster and easier than walking into ten shops and taking notes. How a customer purchases from you will affect the price. If there is no way to order other than making an appointment, you're telling them the "my product is awesome enough to make you take the time to come in, " story and frankly you're also telling them that time=price. If they can order over the phone, there is probably a limit on what they're going to spend on something without meeting you or seeing the product in person. If they can order online, they're probably not hugely fussy about customised options, but they do want it quick and convenient and probably not too expensive. In my case, the less expensive, less customised products are all available for online purchase but the customised fancy stuff is going to require more effort (and more money) on the part of the consumer. How they get the product from you affects how much they're willing to pay for it.

So there's the basic story on pricing - it's as much about knowing the financial ins and outs of your business as it is about knowing your story - the story you tell with every product you make, and the story your client is telling you with their spending habits.

If you're charging close to nothing, OR you're willing to negotiate the price with everyone who calls you, OR you're charging so much nobody is buying anything ... your pricing is perhaps telling a story you would rather it didn't tell.

What story is your current pricing telling?

The Promise Of Future Work

Recently I've had a lot of people asking about setting up wholesale agreements with other vendors - event planning companies, kids party venues, corporates, other businesses who are in your industry but who need a product you specifically make. My own experience with this has been that almost all these agreements are set up on the promise of future work, which then somehow does not materialise.

Over the years, I've put a whole lot of effort into developing standard product lines for various companies, for example, 3 kinds of 'girl' cakes and 3 kinds of 'boy' cakes that local play centres can offer as a standard item in their party packages. I've created whole pricing structures for companies that have assured me that they are going to buy literally thousands of cupcakes each month for every event they hold. This also happens on a small scale, with the client who tells me I should give her a better price because she has three kids and ALL of her friends (who also have at *least* three kids and they also know people with at least three kids ...) are only going to order from me forever more because I gave Alpha Mum a really good deal. I can't actually think of a single situation in which the work that was promised came through - and as for Alpha Mum, she just told all her friends with hordes of kids that you'll discount for them, too.

Here's my feeling on it. You can't really price products today on *what may or may not happen* in the future. These kinds of deals usually end for a number of reasons, including the vendor finding a different or cheaper product elsewhere, or the corporate company changing staff, or cupcakes falling out of fashion. Whatever the reason, you lack the crystal ball to see why or when this deal might end or even if it will get off the ground as promised in the first place.

Here are a couple of ways to handle setting up these kinds of 'deals':

1. Offer them a value added bonus OTHER THAN a discount. One of the best deals I ever made was with a kids' party venue - I told them if they offered to put us in the #1 spot on their preferred suppliers list, we would deliver for free to the venue. The client still had to call me for pricing, but the venue knew we were reliable, recommended us with a, "Oh, and they'll take care of the delivery for you at no extra charge", and that way I wasn't really out any money. I could also deliver several orders in one shot, which minimised the cost to me. Added bonus, we advertised them on our social media and they advertised us. Client is happy, my company made money, venue looked like rock stars for organising it all. Win, win, win.

2. Sliding scale pricing - this works really well for companies who are just starting out but who are SURE that they'll need hundreds of your products within a few months. Create a pricing list (which starts out at full retail) for them. The price goes down as their order numbers go up. As an example:

1-50 cookies: $5. 00 each

51-100 cookies: $4. 85 each

101-200 cookies: $4. 50 each (and so on and so forth.)

You can count their order numbers in a few ways - either cumulatively (from the very first order ongoing) or each month if you invoice them monthly. Either way, it ensures you are not selling products cheaply, encourages them to not only stay with you, but also place the bigger orders with you, and everyone is happy. Also, don't get it down to ridiculous pricing, there should be a cap on it somewhere, "All orders over 500 = $4. 25".

3. Offer them a trial period - make your products full retail price (because you lack the crystal ball) and offer to re-assess after a fixed amount of time. "I'd love to give you a discount, but without any real idea of what your order numbers might be, it's hard to work out how good a deal I can give you. Let's start off at retail pricing and see how we do, I'll call you in a month and we'll review it. Once I know more about quantities I can work out the best possible price for you." If it's you they want, and the work really will come your way, they'll be willing to wait a bit to get a better deal from you. Don't sell yourself short on the promise of future business. (I so want to put that all in caps. Oh hell: DON'T SELL YOURSELF SHORT ON

THE PROMISE OF FUTURE BUSINESS!)

4. Don't offer the mother who claims her friends are all like the Duggars any discount whatsoever. Smile politely, give her your normal price, and that's it. If you've got a loyalty or referral program (which I recommend you do) then tell her so - "Every time we get a recommendation we send the referrer a little discount card of thanks/a free movie ticket/whatever, so don't forget to tell your friends to mention you by name," and leave it at that.

and lastly:

5. It's the OTHER COMPANY'S job to get orders in, not yours. If they are asking for free samples for their clients, or they want to do giveaways or something like that - they've got to pay for it. They should have a marketing budget which allows for the purchase of these things. If you want to give them a bit of a deal on the price for this sort of thing, go ahead but also negotiate something a little extra in it for you. "Jane's Sweet Tables is thrilled to be celebrating reaching 5000 likes with a prize pack of cookies from Cookies Central!" (and there had best be a link there to your business website ...)

As for the companies that want you to create whole product lines for them ... I would be very selective about the companies I would do it for AND I would keep the parameters of it VERY tight (e.g., they can't have a list of demands as long as your arm). I would also work out the pricing very carefully. Offer to make them sample cakes but again, they've got to pay something for them! They are giving their clients an added value service, so it's in their interest to use your services.

Ultimately at party venues the cake maker probably gets the smallest piece of the client's pie (ha!) so make sure you've developed the product and priced it all correctly so that you do not become resentful of either the product or the relationship. Too often, very well meaning potential customers offer us the moon - and the moon they're offering is endless tsunamis of work coming our way.

Too often, those tsunamis of work are really more like a small puddle hardly worth jumping in. If working with other vendors is a space you'd like to work in, that's great - just remember that they are not working for free or cheap so neither should you. It should be a mutually beneficial relationship. MOST important of all, make sure you've got the same target market as they do. If they are doing things for cheap and ugly and your customers and clients are not like that ... don't align with them. Align with companies and products that share your values share your demographic and share the understanding that this needs to be a win/win relationship, not an opportunity for them to exploit you.

Confused in Cakeland - Pricing for Wholesale

Confused in Cakeland

Hi Michelle,

A local restaurant wants to buy my products, but I'm not sure how to price them since I've never sold anything wholesale before. Plus, I don't want them to sell them for cheaper than I will be. How do I price for wholesale?

Signed,

Confused In Cakeland

Hey there Confused in Cakeland,

I've always used the basic rule of thumb that your wholesale price should be no less than 20% below retail. So if you would sell 1 dozen cupcakes to the general public for $10, the wholesale price should be no more than $8. You may choose to make this percentage higher or lower based on who you are selling to, how much they are going to buy from you, or what your profit margin is. The thing to remember is, wholesale pricing still means you make a profit, it just means you forego a bit of that profit in order to both secure more sales and get a wider distribution than you might otherwise.

I've met a number of people who sell their items AT COST rather than wholesale - and this really isn't the right thing to do for this industry. You need to make a profit, AND the company you are selling to needs to make a profit. In a handmade industry, there is no value in selling something at cost unless there is a very compelling reason to do so (e.g., the exposure would be enormous ... and good luck evaluating that!). Unfortunately, you can't dictate what they will sell your products for but you certainly can give them an RRP - recommended retail price. It's up to them if they use your recommendation, but once you've sold it to them ... you no longer have a say in the pricing of it.

Personally, I've always stayed well away from selling wholesale because I do not operate a volume business - and I've preferred to sell to clients directly rather than have distribution. That being said, finding outlets for your product can be a GREAT way to both sell more and get the word out more, so it's worth determining your wholesale pricing policy from the get-go.

Michelle

Should I Charge A Last Minute Order Fee?

The question of charging an additional fee for last minute orders seemed like a total no-brainer to me. Until I got an email which said this:

> "A few days ago, a lady posted a question on a Cake Decorators FB page, asking for a bit of advice. She received a last minute order for a cake (to be completed within 24 hours) and was not sure whether it is reasonable to charge a late order fee considering her workload she already had. The responses were all for charging the extra fee (a few suggested not to take the order on). The main arguments were:
>
> • The customer needs to learn not to make orders in last minute.
> • She (the cake lady) needs to compensate herself for the stress she will have by taking the order, working under pressure and until late hours.
>
> I was the only one arguing the opposite, answering following: "Charging more just because they approached you with a last minute order does not make sense. It is up to you to decide whether you can physically and emotionally do it and if you agree to take the order on, **you are responsible for the decision you made** (cannot see why they should pay for it). You do not have to say yes."

So I did a bit more reading on the internet - online chats on the same topic - and it seems that it is widely supported by the cake decorators to charge more if they accept last minute order. Well, I still struggle to accept that, thinking ... hold on, **why would you want to educate your customer by**

price "punishment" about making orders well in advance next time. The customer's circumstances could have been such that they too did not know until last minute they will need a cake. Additionally, most cake decorators sound as if they have to take the order on and because it is going to be terribly stressful for them, the customer must pay for it. Again, hold on, nobody is forcing them to do it. In my opinion, there is no such thing as for example paying overtime when a person is self-employed. You either want the business or not. You can either do the cake or not. I am still convinced that charging extra for last minute order (with exception of incurred extra expenses caused by the late order) is unprofessional, but I feel under pressure from so many opposite opinions."

I have to say, it's rare for an email to stop me dead in my tracks like that. I really stopped and pondered on this one for a few days, because it made me think hard about my "of course late orders pay a late fee" idea. She makes some VERY valid points in this email.

First let me say that I agree entirely with the first bit - your business, your rules so if you want to take the business, take it and if not, well, not.

However I still think a last minute fee is a good idea and here's why I think so.

In my mind, the last minute fee isn't really just there "because you can" charge it. It's there to cover the fact that last minute orders will often require more of you - more running around, adjusting your schedule, getting things last minute, working longer hours, getting someone to help, etc. So the extra fee is covering the extra time/work/effort that it may take you to complete the order in a shorter time frame - which is time/work/effort which would NOT BE THERE if they ordered on time. More work = more money. Of course in some instances, because you're not busy there may not be any extra effort involved beyond a normal cake order - but then the issue is one of consistency. You can't really charge someone a late fee because you have not much on that weekend, and then the next time they order you are busier so you would charge them. Also, there is the issue of, "Well if I ordered with 24 hours last time, why can't I order like that this time?", so there is something to be said about the late fee also helping with educating the customer to order with plenty of notice.

Honestly, I don't think a late fee is "punishing" the customer. Ultimately it's their choice if they want to go with the order or not just like it's your choice to give them the option to order in the first place. When we order online, they give us the same option but it's not a "fee" per se. For example, standard shipping is $10 but express shipping is $20. We're not being punished, **we're being given a**

choice about how soon we want to receive something. Same applies here. I find it's quite rare for a person to not know they need a cake within at least a week of their event - and quite honestly there are a LOT of options for those kinds of instances. Supermarkets, local bakeries, etc. you can walk in and buy a cake that day. It's rare for someone to need a highly decorated, custom made cake with less than a few days' notice.

So do I think a late fee is warranted? Yes, I do - but I don't see it as punishment.

With all that said, let me tell you how I did things in **the real world of my business**.

If someone called my business last minute and needed something, and I could easily fit it in with no extra issues, I just did it with no fee, however, I would make a point of saying that we prefer and appreciate one week's notice for orders. If they called last minute and it DID require me to do extra running around etc., then I'd be really upfront about it and say, "Because I'll need to do XYZ especially for this order, there is a late order fee of $25. Would you like to still go ahead with the order?" and at that point, it's up to them. They still have a choice, right? To go with me, or to go to a local supermarket and pick up a ready-made cake. Most of the time, people still ordered with me so it was a win/win situation - and if they didn't, well, I didn't lose much other than the irritation of having to run around.

So should YOU charge a last minute fee?

By now you know what I'll say, right?

YOUR BUSINESS, YOUR RULES

Confused in Cakeland – Show Me The Money

Dear Michelle,

How do you deal with deposits for orders? Do you insist people give you a deposit, and if so - how much? How do you tell people what the policy is without seeming demanding or grabby?

Signed,

Confused in Cakeland

Hey there Confused in Cakeland,

I'm one of those very trusting people who thinks everyone is nice and nobody would ever shaft me. In the beginning I didn't take deposits, I just took people at their word that they would pick up their item and pay for it.

It took exactly one person shafting me for me to realise that while I was being nice, I wasn't being terribly business savvy.

That being said:

1. I always take a deposit. The only exception (which is very rare) is when it's for a very small order from a client who I have a long-term established relationship with.

2. I take a 50% deposit. Even if their order is $20. It's about my sticking to my stated policies more than absolute dollar value. Plus even at $20, there is still some investment I've got to make to get their order completed.

3. At the end of every consultation (in person or via email), I say, "If you'd like to book your order in with us, we appreciate you paying a 50% deposit. We do not consider an order confirmed until the deposit has been received. This can be paid via the following methods: (etc.)" It's rare that someone complains about this, but when they do I just politely explain that the deposit procedure is there to protect both them and me. If they've paid a deposit, nobody else gets their spot (they don't need to know how many or how few spots actually exist.) It's all about THEM, remember?

4. I decided early on what my refund policy would be - e.g. they get a full refund if they cancel before a certain date, or what the reasons I might be willing to refund a deposit would be, etc. If you've taken a deposit, and you limit your orders and they cancel ... that's an order you did NOT take because you committed to them. You shouldn't refund it. If they change their mind entirely about what they want (from cake to macarons or something) then just apply the deposit to the new order. When you're deciding how much deposit to take, also decide what the rules around that deposit are.

5. Publish your deposit policy - in the footer of your emails and on your website. That way most potential customers will not be surprised when you ask for the deposit. You've got to be in it for your customer, but you've also got to protect your investment.

Show me the money,

Michelle

CHAPTER 7

CUSTOMERS

Don't you think that if we had no customers, our businesses would be so much easier to run? No endless emails to answer, no Bridezillas to deal with, no people wanting cake for 100 people on a budget of fifty bucks. While it's a nice fantasy, we all know that no clients = no business. I don't think any of us really anticipated this part of running a business, or understood how much energy and effort it would require. We might have had an inkling about the financial stuff, and the time management stuff, but in no way did we anticipate just how frustrating and rewarding it would be dealing with the human side of our business.

My clients were one of the main reasons I stayed in business as long as I did. I love, love, loved the people aspect of it. I loved hearing their stories and telling them mine, I loved the smiles and the hugs and the appreciation. While I didn't love the occasional complaint or difficult personality, I still appreciated those people for the lessons they taught me and the stories interacting with them created for me. I am no artist – so my business niche was very much about the customer service, or as I like to say, I loved the shit out of my clients.

In my opinion, as an industry we either do not do enough or we do too much about customer service. Because our perspective is that of a maker, our focus often lies in the product rather than the people the product is for. We carry on worrying about the wrinkle in the fondant, or the line which is not perfectly straight – when our focus should be on the customer and what they will notice, appreciate, and be willing to pay for. Sometimes we do the opposite, where we let our customers cross a whole lot of boundaries and we give, give, give to the point of exhaustion, so that by the time the order rolls around, there is not much money left to be made. Customers are what keep us in business – so my general advice on this is, love them as much as you possibly can but maintain boundaries. You are a business owner, not a slave.

Finding The Right Customers

In the great online debates about pricing cakes correctly, someone always says, "If they don't like your prices, they probably aren't the people you want anyway!" There are various versions, like "you don't want people like that as clients", "people who care about price are not your ideal client", "the people who want your products will just come to you" and "your product will naturally attract the right kind of client". Is it just me or can someone please show me the golden unicorn that all these 'right kind of clients' are riding in on?

So ... I'm going to stand in the middle of the street with some seriously sexy and really expensive cakes and the sparkly jewel-encrusted carriages filled with the right kinds of clients whose wallets are bursting with cash are just going to roll on up, kay kay?

No.

Yeah.

It doesn't work that way. Here's the deal. Attracting the magical, mystical 'right kinds of clients' does not happen by accident, nor does it happen by just creating stuff and thinking that they will come. This is no *Field of Dreams* moment.

The way to get the kind of clients you want is a three step process.

Step One: Figure out who the heck these people are. Don't be ridiculous and tell me that they are people who ask no questions, make no demands, hand over a stack of cash and are so happy with what you give them that they go tell people like Oprah to order from you. For real, you need to know in great detail the demographics of your ideal clients. By "ideal clients" I mean the kind of people you want to order from you or come to your store. Are these people women? Are they mothers? Are they local to you? How old are they? What kind of event are they planning? Do they have a lot to spend? Do they care about fancy flavours? Where do they shop? Do they throw parties once a year, or more often? Would they buy their child a cupcake as a snack once a week or more? Are they all about value for money or are they happy to spend more for quality? Write an entire story about what your ideal client might look like. I'm not saying this means people unlike that won't shop with you - of course, they will - but this is about being real about the kinds of people who are likely to purchase from you. You've got to know who it is you're wanting to sell to. This may change a little as your business grows, your skills change and you find your happy place, but overall you've got to have a clear idea of who is going to buy what you want to sell. Here's my hot tip: be realistic. If you hate doing wedding cakes, then your ideal client is not a bride. Similarly, if you're a beginner and you're building your skills up, your ideal client may not be the person who is attracted to you right this minute but that's who you should be working towards attracting.

Step Two: Get in their head and figure out how they might find you. If you or someone you know were behaving like that kind of person, where would they go to find out about you? What might they expect when they got there? What would they be looking for on your website - would it be pricing information, beautiful images, information about allergen friendly cakes? You need to get as much detail about your client's shopping habits as possible. When that ideal client walks in (and they will) ASK them how they found you and keep track of the answers. Do some research on brands that are in a similar bracket to yours (or are in the bracket you are aiming to be in). If the kind of people who buy from Tiffany and Chanel are the clients you want to buy from you, go and look at how Tiffany and Chanel attract clients. Where are they advertising, how are they advertising, what is their client experience like? Go check out the website of the fanciest, most expensive bakery you can think of even if it's not in your city. What's the overall feel of their website? What does their packaging look like? Brands at every level of pricing do things entirely differently - a place like K-Mart advertises entirely differently to Macy's just like a suburban gourmet cupcake store would advertise differently to a chain bakery. All of them manage to be in business so please do not think that your only choice is to be high-end.

*The most expensive dessert does not
come in a plastic box ...*

Step Three: actually BE that kind of business in every possible way. So often I hear people say things like, "Why do people think I make cheap cakes? I am not Wal-Mart!" and then you see that their cakes (while nice looking) are photographed on a messy kitchen bench in a cheap box, their website doesn't exist (other than on Facebook) and they answer client quote requests via text message. I'm pretty sure Chanel does not do ANY of that. Suppose your ideal client is a bride with lots of cash to splash. She's going to be looking at (and judging) your business based on what the website looks like, what the photographs of your cakes look like, what others have said about you, what venues you work with, what magazines you are featured in, and mostly about the process of dealing with you. Did you give her samples wrapped in plastic, or did you serve them to her on a lovely plate with a nice cake fork and pretty napkin? If you gave her a sample box to take home, was it in a cheap looking plastic 'oyster' box, or a glossy white box with a nicely printed flavour guide inside? If you make kids' cakes and your target market is local mothers, did you have a box of books and toys for her kids to play with while you consulted with her? Did you give her the option of a nut-free cake? Did you provide free birthday candles with every cake? Did you offer free delivery to save her the hassle? *You need to actually be the business your ideal client is looking for.*

You've got to <u>work at</u> being the business you want to be,

and <u>actually do things</u> in that manner.

Mystical ideal clients do not just appear at your door - they know to come there because you've told them to, and they stay and chat to you because you give them exactly what they were hoping to find.

This entire blog post really boils down to one question and one answer:

Q: How do you avoid being labelled as the cheap cake lady?

A: Stop acting like the cheap cake lady.

Buy. Repeat. Share.

You want to avoid your customers doing this!

In business, it is both cheaper and easier to keep a customer than it is to *get* a new one. Think about your own buying habits for a minute. We're inclined to stick with what we know, what we can rely on, what is familiar. Usually, the only thing which keeps us from sticking to the same brands and products is when something comes along to shake it up. The price changes significantly, the quality changes, that item is no longer stocked locally, or we are enticed (through various means) to try something different. Brand loyalty is not just something we all really want, it's something we should be actively working on. With so many people getting into the cake business, we can't rely on being the only supplier in town any more. Instead, we've got to cultivate relationships with our clients so that they become loyal to our brand and return to us time and again.

So - how do you build a loyal following of clientele, ensuring repeat business?

You work on developing and maintaining lasting relationships and connections with both your clients and your potential clients. In specific, here's how I did this in my business:

I was consistent. I delivered *what* I said I would, *when* I said I would, *how* I said I would. I gave them expectations and then met them. Every. Single. Time. This sounds SO simple but it's amazing how many companies don't do this. Human beings LOVE the familiar - that's why McDonald's and all other franchises work so well globally. People know exactly what to expect AND they have those expectations met every time they walk into that franchise, no matter where they are in the world. McDonald's fries taste the same everywhere for a very good reason! In my case, the process for ordering, the love and care they got throughout the order, and the attention they got all the way to the end was always the same. They knew what to expect of me, my business, my employees and the products they were getting. If for some reason I couldn't deliver on something I said I would, I called and told them. I also told them how I was going to fix it so that again I set expectations and I met those expectations.

Everything in moderation.

Except Awesome. You can never have too much Awesome.

I almost always went that little bit further for my customers, and people remembered being loved that little bit more. The bit extra was something simple - I'd help them to the car with the cake, offer to refer them to a good photographer, gave them some websites to look for cool cake toppers, gave them some birthday candles, gave them a free gluten free cupcake for that one guest who needed it. Every single cake that went out the door of my shop also had a good quality plastic cake server attached to it which had my company name and phone number printed on it. They cost me something like 11 cents each to have made, but I can't tell you how often people told me they loved their free gift (and some even washed and brought them back to me because they thought they were worth a lot more than they were). I gave my clients a bit of extra love and people *remember being loved*.

I communicated with them. I stayed in contact and not just via social media. I wrote a monthly newsletter and encouraged people to sign up for it. I'd start each newsletter with a "letter" telling them what was happening in the shop and thanking them for their ongoing support and custom, I'd usually have a few pictures of recent cakes I was proud of, plus I listed the upcoming class timetable.

If I had one, I'd include a special deal or an offer, but plenty of newsletters were just newsy and fun. Every month the newsletter got sent, so every month those clients were reminded about my business *directly into their Inbox.* Even if they missed my Facebook post or tweet, it was hard for them to miss the email right in their Inbox. We all know how much the reach of social media is declining, and newsletters give you an immediate invitation to be in front of the very people whose eyes you want to be in front of.

I cultivated the super loyal ones - at the end of the year, I went through my order book and made a list of all those clients who ordered more than once that year. I then emailed them individually, giving them a voucher for 25% off their next order. Why did I give a discount to people who would order from me anyway? Because I truly wanted to *thank them* for CHOOSING ME when they could have chosen any number of people, and it encouraged them to come back again and tell their friends about it. They deserved a reward for loyalty and they got it - which in turn usually made them love me a bit more. Win/Win.

I followed up. I asked EVERY SINGLE PERSON how they heard about my business. If it was a referral, I asked who referred them - I then contacted that person and thanked them personally (usually by phone, sometimes by email) for supporting my business. That's it. A thank you. Why? Because I really was grateful and they deserved that gratitude and love and it also encouraged them to keep on referring me. I ran a small, personal business - so I gave people small acts of personal gratitude. One option might have been for me to give a reward for the referrers but I was indecisive about what to give so that didn't happen (it should have. I let my indecisiveness get in the way.)

I was authentic. I let my own life into my business a tiny bit. No, I don't share a lot of my personal life with my clients - but if they mentioned having twins or triplets, or going through IVF, or having travelled to the US recently, or loving a certain type of food I loved or anything at all I could relate to, I'd tell them a story about my own life. It meant they got to know me, and allowed them to feel they were a part of my (business) family. More often than not they would mention it the next time they saw me. "Hey Michelle, how's your Mum? Is she still in ballroom dancing? Because I just won a silver medal, too!". "Hey, Michelle did you end up doing the Minecraft cake for your son that we talked about? Because my younger son now wants one." They remembered to come back to my business in part because they remembered me and our shared interest.

I asked for feedback and I acted on it. This is so important and yet SO forgotten about. I used an external review website for my business and asked everybody to leave a review for me there. I attached a "please review us, " flyer to every single order, and as a result, I had well over 100 reviews on that website. Those reviews gave the people reading them a sense of ALL of the above - because in those reviews my clients talked about the service, the love, the consistency, the communication. They told potential clients exactly what to expect from me ... but it didn't come FROM me, so it was even more powerful a message. This wasn't me taking the time to toot my own horn, it was other people taking the time to do it. I replied to every single review on that website. Everyone. Why? Because they took the time, so they deserve my thanks in return - and it showed readers that I was engaged with my clients long after the last bite of cake had been eaten. Added bonus of that review site was that I learned a lot about what was working well and what needed improvement in my business ... so again, a win/win situation.

Here's the really important part.

I have a very simple theory about repeat customers, and it goes like this:

> If it looks good, people will buy it **at least once**.
>
> If it tastes good, people will buy it **a second time**.
>
> If it looks good, tastes good and *it makes them feel good*, you've **got a customer for life**.

Make sure you're doing all three of those, and repeat customers will become not only your livelihood ... but also your marketing team. No money in the world can buy loyalty like that.

Promises, Promises

I've gotten several phone calls in the past few weeks from people who tell me that their cake maker backed out on their order. I've heard stories of bakers returning deposits to clients for the following reasons: they just got too busy, the order was too hard for their skill level, their child got sick, they just "couldn't do it anymore", they'd gotten out of the cake business or "something came up". I'm currently hearing variations on this story about once a week (seriously.)

I'm going to step onto my soapbox and say: THAT IS TOTALLY UNACCEPTABLE.

Yes, I advocate having a life as well as a business. Yes, I strongly advocate communicating with your clients when life gets in the way (which it will. Life has a habit of doing that.) However, the frequency of these stories is really making me scratch my head in wonder - and I'm sure some of them have two sides to that story (I am not so silly as to believe every person who tells me this kind of thing). However, I'd like to believe that before returning a deposit to a client, my fellow bakers will do *everything* they can to make the situation workable for the client, INCLUDING paying another cake maker to complete the order for them.

Why do I believe that?

The very moment that you take money for an order, you are effectively signing a contract. You're making a promise to deliver what you said you would, when you said you would. As consumers ourselves we expect that when we hand over our hard-earned money, we're trusting that we are going to *get* something in return. As business owners, we have a legal and moral obligation to actually *give* that something in return.

I think because we are often micro business owners (e.g., the staff consists of "me, myself and I") we have an even bigger obligation to fulfil our promises. They are choosing to support "the little guy" over the bigger companies and their continued loyalty is a major part of our success and so we need to honour that by doing the right thing and getting the order done as promised.

Why do I believe that?

On a personal level, I firmly believe I am in the business of happiness, NOT just the business of cake. Therefore, I consider it a great honour that my clients allow me to be a part of their lives, to bear witness to their milestone events, to become a part of their memories both remembered in their minds and in photos, to play a part in their family stories and often to be welcomed as though I am a member of their family. I have clients for whom I've made their engagement and wedding cakes and I'm now making their children's birthday and baptism cakes. We're talking YEARS of relationship building here, and I think that is a privilege.

I take this privilege very seriously. They TRUST me with all of that. I have an obligation (not only financial) to respect that trust. It's taken me a while to earn that trust, and as you all know, clients who love and trust you will come back to you and support you AND tell all their friends to do the same. I *rely* on these clients for my business's continued growth and success.

This isn't to say that clients don't occasionally piss me off or drive me mad. Of course they do. This IS to say, though, that I believe they pay me for way more than just cake. When I deliver a cake, I'm not just delivering the third course of their meal. I'm delivering happiness, memories, respect, love and a whole lot more besides.

To dishonour that by reneging on deposit for reasons as ridiculous as "I'm just too busy", is frankly appalling.

Yes, life happens - but unless you have a reason of near-catastrophic proportions, there is never a reason to betray your client's trust.

They trust you.
You need to honour that.

It's what they're getting other than a cake which is ultimately is worth a whole lot more than their orders ever will be.

Confused In Cakeland - How To Deliver Cakes Via Plane

Confused in Cakeland

Hi Michelle,

How do you handle a cake order which would require delivery at a distance? Specifically, a cake which would require several hours of transportation, perhaps in the heat, and then set-up at the destination.

I'm asking because I've been approached about the possibility of doing a wedding cake on a Greek island and I work on the mainland. I'm potentially willing, but obviously, the logistics would be challenging, and there would be additional costs, possibly significant.

Should I simply turn it down, or go ahead and quote, adding in my best guesstimate of the extra costs? I wouldn't travel with a big cake already assembled (the wedding is for some number of guests in the high hundreds) but either air or sea travel would necessarily be involved and, at least to some extent, temperature control as well.

Thoughts?

Signed,

Confused in Cakeland

Dear Confused,

I started to get hives about this question when I got to the whole "heat" bit of it, and then I started to itch like mad when I got to the "planes, trains and automobiles" part, too.

I write this reply as someone who hates deliveries. I die a little bit inside every time I've got to take a cake anywhere (even a one-tier) and when I watch those episodes of Cake Boss or Ace of Cakes and see cakes and humans bobbling around in the back of the van, I start to hyperventilate.

In short: there is no amount of money on earth which would convince me to take a cake for several hundred people on a trip for several hours (via air, sea, land or anything else!) Seriously, I'm pretty sure that stress would kill me ... I'm a nervous wreck on deliveries an hour away, let alone several hours!

I would offer to make it if they organise their own transport and accept no liability for once it goes out your door. That being said, if you really want to do this one, and you're strong of heart and mighty of will: send me a postcard proving you're still alive after the stress of it, okay?

Yours in fear,

Michelle

You Need It WHEN?!

One of the more entertaining aspects of my job (and yes, my "day job" is, in fact, running a successful cake business) is the clients who call asking for the impossible, and they want it tomorrow morning. Apparently it's very easy to forget you need a cake for the 200 people you've got coming for a 50th birthday party. DJ? Check! Poster board with embarrassing childhood photos? Check! Platters of pigs in a blanket? Check! Enough alcohol to make your speech bearable for you and your guests? Check! Candles to stick in the ... Oh. Damn.

As a cake maker, a HUGE part of my job is customer service. I spend all day making people happy, even if "making them happy" just means I answer the phone and give them an answer to their question (no, you cannot substitute breadcrumbs for plain flour in a cake ...). Managing customer's expectations is also a big part of what I do, and I make it a point to tell people exactly what's going to happen. First, we'll do the quote. Then, I'll tell you the terms and conditions. Then, you'll hand over your cash so I can afford to eat (and make your cake). And so on ... We're going to talk about managing customer expectations (hint: it's about training them well) a little bit later on, but for now, I just want to manage your expectations by letting you know more about how this blog is going to work.

Here's what you can expect. I'm going to post once a week, on a Tuesday. Why on a Tuesday?

You're cake makers, right?

You're telling me you have the free time to read my wit and brilliance any time between Wednesday and Saturday?

Yeah, right.

95% of our orders are geared towards weekend events. This means that most weeks, from Wednesday to Saturday, you're highly likely to be covered in flour and butter and have a streak of bright pink staining the underside of your arm from the gel colour which leaped off the side of the bottle and onto your skin. You have no time for blog reading (trust me on this one) and hardly enough time to pee (trust me on that one, too).

Suppose you've not yet reached that stage of having cakes to make every weekend - I'm still posting on a Tuesday for you, too. Why? Because Monday is when you catch up on all the stuff you shoulda, woulda, coulda done on the weekend, and by Wednesday you're planning your weekend or you've been sucked into the vortex of this thing we call "having a real life".

My real, live, nitty gritty, let's-talk-cake-business post is going to come right at you - on Tuesday this week (this should come as no surprise). Yes, there are weeks where I'll post more often, but for now, you know that at the very least, we've got a standing date to hang out together every Tuesday. BYO coffee and the cupcake that fell onto the floor (two-second rule!) and I'll see you then.

And just because it seems a little mean to leave you all when it's just starting to warm up in here. . . let me tell you that this Tuesday, I'll be talking about how <u>your friends are NOT your clients</u>, and that your friends have the potential to become your business's number one frenemy[18] (even if they don't mean to.)

---

18   See *Friends with Benefits* in Chapter 3.

I'm Just Not That Creative

I've got a confession to make.

I'm just not that creative. Don't get me wrong, I'm a skilled, talented, capable cake decorator and chef. Other people do describe me as creative, but I know that I am no artist. When a client came to me saying, "I don't care what you do, you're so creative, I trust you! Just make me anything as long as it's pink!" I wanted to run for it. "Free reign" to me was like saying, "Freedom to lose your mind". I was MUCH, MUCH happier with the clients who brought me heaps of pictures of cakes they liked, designed their own, or gave me instructions down the last sprinkle. One of my most hated jobs was coming up with a theme for my front window display, and then having to magic out of thin air 6-8 different designs to go with that theme. At culinary school, I loved cooking but hated plating up. Sounds crazy, right?

Aren't all cake decorators meant to be artists?

Nope.

Many of them are, but just as many of them are not - and I am firmly in the "are not" category. This does not mean I didn't produce beautiful things my clients loved, nor does it mean I lack the "creativity" gene. It just means that while I'm very good at what I do, I'm simply not in the league of the Karen Portales or Zoe Clarks of the world. I got into the cake business because I loved cake - and I still do - but for me, *it was never about the actual cake*. I've written about that a few times now, how I never believed I was in the business of cake, I was in the business of happiness. The part I loved most about my business was **the people**. I loved seeing a kid's face light up, or the beautiful pictures of brides cutting their cake, or even seeing my cakes on the front of a corporate newsletter in a picture about their recent celebration of their company's birthday. I loved teaching and nurturing other cake makers, mentoring other cake business owners, and being a part of people's special moments. Sure, I loved cake too- and I loved that I got to work in a creative field - but for me it was more about the people than it was about the product.

This past week in my Facebook group, someone (http://www.facebook.com/ groups/BakingBusinessConfidence) asked if the rest of us ever get a bit down when we look at Pinterest (http://www.pinterest.com/bizbake) photos and think, "I'll never be that good". I had to smile at that question because I knew from the very beginning that I'd **never** be that good so it never bothered me. I simply do not have the artistic aesthetic of the world's best cake decorators ... but you know what? I didn't really need it. My business was about being my own boss, making a living from it, being available to my kids and creating a name for my products in my home town. I didn't need nor want an international profile, didn't need or want to teach (other than locally to beginners). I just wanted to make people happy, do something I enjoyed and earn a living while doing so. That purpose didn't require me to be the next Van Gogh of the cake world, it really didn't.

What I needed to have was amazing (fast!) technical skills, fantastic customer service, ability to trouble shoot, knowledge about marketing and costing/pricing, some creativity and love for the industry and my clients. I had ALL of that. Would it have been nice to have all those things **plus** that amazing artistic "X Factor" talent the artistic ones have? Sure, but I didn't need it in order to be successful to the degree I wanted for myself. Early on I knew that there were artistic skills I lacked, so where possible I went and did classes about those skills - and learned to adapt those skills to my own strengths and weaknesses. I admire the artistic talent of the world's best, but in my heart of hearts, I know that when it comes down to it, I simply don't have the soul of an artist. I wanted to make people happy, give them what they wanted, and be an entrepreneur - all things I could do even if I'm not the kind of cake maker whose cake sketches look like they should be framed on someone's wall.

So what do you do when you find yourself looking at incredible pictures online and thinking, "I'm never going to be that talented"? The solution here is to figure out what your superpower is in your business and take ENORMOUS pride in that, and use that superpower as a selling point to your clients. We've all got different, special skills to bring to the industry and it's a matter of recognising that those *different skills appeal to different clients*. I built my business on giving clients EXACTLY what they wanted (and yes, I used that as a tag line) - and that's what I delivered to them, every single time. I didn't claim to be original, artistic, "out of the box" or anything like that. I simply claimed to make wonderful things to their exact needs and give it to them with a smile. If it became clear that what they wanted was someone who was going to sketch for hours and talk about the 'creative process', I'd simply refer them onto one of the many talented cake artists in my area who I knew would love being a part of that.

You don't need to be as talented or as creative as others are out there. You simply need to be amazing at YOUR skill or talent, and go about delivering that to your clients with a smile on your face and in your heart. Trust me when I say that not everyone needs to be Picasso - there's a reason why there was only one of him, but the world's galleries still hang with the work of many others.

Ugly Cakes

For those of us who have not yet found our personal style (or in my case, will never find one[19]), or those of us just starting out, most of our orders will be things the client has seen elsewhere, or something they have come up with themselves. This isn't usually a problem until they design something or give us a picture of something which is, well, plain old UGLY. Sometimes we think it's ugly because it's not to our taste, other times it might be something that offends us, and sometimes it's just, well ... gross (I'm looking at you, zombie cakes). So what do you do when a client asks you to do something which isn't your thing? As I see it, you have two choices here:

1. **Take the order**. If the cake design is just not to your taste, but it's not actually offensive to you - you can do the order, but make sure the execution of it is amazing. Sure, purple and green gingham with a crocodile eating Minion might not be your idea of a beautiful cake, but if you do it - ROCK IT. Make sure it looks and tastes as amazing as you can get it. Take pictures so that you have a record of it, but don't share them publicly. When you're starting out, you need to practice your skills and these orders are an opportunity to push yourself out of your comfort zone. If you're worried about your name being on a cake that is ugly - stop worrying about it. Not every cake will be your thing, and it's not like there will be a light up sign with an arrow which says, "JANE MADE THIS UGLY THING". Seriously. It's not a big deal and not worth stressing about.

2. Politely decline the order. If it's something that's offensive to you (for

---

whatever reason), you don't need to justify that. Either tell the white lie that you're all booked out that weekend, or if you'd prefer not to lie - tell the truth. "Thanks for the enquiry, unfortunately, I don't make zombie cakes," and leave it at that. Some people will question you as to why you won't do it. To them, I'd say, "It's just not my thing," or "It's just not my style," or "Zombies freak me out". Just keep it simple, politely say no thank you and you won't offend anyone. Don't start ranting, don't be mean, don't be a jerk. You then should refer them to another cake maker who is happy to do that kind of thing. Also, if you have very specific rules about what you won't do - you can put that on your website on the FAQ page. In my business, I would never make makes that looked like real people or pets. To me, there is never a good reason to eat your best friend's face or Fido's butt. My website said, "While all our cakes are custom made, we do not make cakes that look like real people or beloved pets, so please do not ask us to."

Saying no to a customer - for whatever reason - can make us feel bad. After all, we want to please them - and we want the order. The thing to remember here is, being in business is about solving the customer's problem. In the case of a cake order, the problem is that they want a cake that you can't make. Since you can't solve this problem, help them find someone who can. Don't take it personally, don't spend a bunch of time stressing about this. Either say yes and suck it up, or say no and move on. Most of the time people are okay with it because ultimately they want the problem solved. At the moment, there are a lot of bakeries getting into trouble for refusing to make same-sex marriage wedding cakes. These kinds of situations (where it ends up in the press, and a big legal and financial mess) are the exception rather than the norm. For the purposes of this article, I'm referring more to design than matters of the heart - but in most cases, being kind and polite is usually the best way to solve differences of cake opinion. A simple "no thank you, but here's a solution for you", usually works - and saves you from making that hideous creation.

Confused in Cakeland – Giving Out Samples

Confused in Cakeland

Hi Michelle,

Do you give out samples to your potential customers for free or do you charge them? I'm only a one-woman band so the sampling can get costly. I've seen other business charging for samples, but makes me uncomfortable to do that. The cost of sampling is pretty high for me, though, so I'm torn.

What do you do?

Signed,

Confused in Cakeland

Hi Confused in Cakeland,

It's clichéd to say so, but it's true that you often need to spend money in order to make money. This situation is a perfect example of where that's relevant in a small business in a competitive industry.

I believe that giving your potential customers samples is a marketing exercise and you should think of it that way, and budget for it.

Especially when you are first starting out, you've got to prove your worth to people (and particularly in a crowded market) and one of the easiest ways to do this is by being generous. Pictures won't tell them what a cake tastes like, and consumers these days are getting pickier about the taste of things. I have SO many clients come to me because they went to someone else first, but the other person's cake didn't taste good. I have yet to have a client tell me they abandoned a different cake maker because the cake didn't look good. I think offering samples (for free) is good practice, is a relatively small investment, and helps build your reputation.

However, sampling CAN get a bit pricey when you consider that my company currently offers about 12 flavours of cake and 14 filling options. There is no way I'm going to offer ALL of those as samples, I'd go broke and waste a lot of time preparing all that. So, at the time of making the appointment, I ask them to nominate 2-3 flavours from our offerings that they would like to try, and I provide those (plus usually one flavour that I'm trying to up-sell) at the appointment. If they are not fussy, I'll just make our 2 most popular ones. I do this via cupcakes, not slices of cake. It looks generous when they sit down to a plate of 2-3 cupcakes, it doesn't cost me too much, it's quick to prepare, and it's easy to keep cupcakes on hand or whip some up.

I have met many cake makers (generally high-end wedding cake makers) who sit their clients down to an entire plate of cake pieces matched with an entire array of fillings, and the consult takes an hour or more. I tried that a couple of times and it just didn't work for me - all that choice ended up doing was confusing the hell out of my clients, taking up a LOT of my time, and for the life of me I could not discuss cake flavours for that long without wanting to pull my eyelashes out one by one. I'm there to sell them on the idea that I can create them something which looks and tastes good, NOT get into a discussion over salted caramel made with sea salt versus kosher salt. I have found that you can generally tell very early on in an appointment if the person is going to give you the gig, and I feel no need to drag that on into eternity. I either want to make the sale, or set them free.

Sometimes people will ask to try things they have not asked for - so if I can whip one up (e. g. I have one in the freezer) I'll ask them if they are willing to wait a few minutes while I grab a spare. If they can't, I'll offer them to pop back another day and I'll have one waiting. They almost always order the cake at that point, because I'm being generous and generosity is a GREAT feeling to get from someone who is making you a cake. Cake is often ALL ABOUT THE LOVE, where love = great customer service.

Personally, I think if your cake samples cost you that much that you need to charge for it (and I've seen charges of up to $50) - either your costing is out of whack or you're offering too much time and/or cake. I realise that some cake makers have a fee because they've been stood up by people - but a simple confirmation call the day before is a good idea anyway. I also know some cake makers do it because it weeds out the non-serious buyers, but your website and initial contact with them should do that anyway. Some cake makers do it because they think it makes them more 'exclusive' ... but for me, that's ego talking, not business.

I will say this - over time, you will find that fewer people ask for samples. A VAST majority of the new clients I get now never ask for a sample, although I do provide it at every wedding appointment as a matter of course (but not appointments for anything else unless they ask). A majority of my clients (and please note, I do not specialise in the high-end wedding market) won't taste even a crumb of my cake before cutting into it on the day of their celebration. Why? Because I gave out lots and lots of samples in the early days, have therefore developed a great reputation for delicious cake, and in all my online reviews and testimonials people talk about the look AND the taste of my products. I started - and continue to - run my business in the spirit of generosity and love and that ALWAYS comes back to me in spades.

It's not about the cake. It's about the love. Love your client, give them cake, they'll tell their friends about you. Seems like a pretty good marketing investment to me.

With love from my buttercream encrusted soul,

Michelle

Confused In Cakeland - Sneaky Peeks

Confused in Cakeland

Hi Michelle,

Should I send my client a photo of my cake once it's finished? How do you feel about those "sneaky peek" photos?

Thanks,

Ellie

Hi Ellie,

Well, there are two questions there.

1. *Sending a picture to the client: I wouldn't do it. All it's doing is opening you up to letting them make changes, change their mind, or basically drive you nuts. It's really not worth it. Plus chances are you would be sending them that picture via phone or email outside of your normal work hours - and establishing boundaries with clients is important. If they ask for a photo when you're done (or to watch while you create it - WTH? - I've seen this before, though ...) then just say, "I don't want to ruin the lovely surprise! I love seeing my client's reactions when they see their cake in real life for the first time," and leave it at that.*

2. *Should you post sneaky peek pictures? Honestly, I'm not a fan of it,*

although some people do it to generate a little bit of excitement. I'd prefer to do this for orders which are NOT a specific client's - so a 'sneak peek' of some flavours you might be developing, a dummy cake you're working on, a whole pile of sugar flowers on your bench or a class you're developing are all okay. I really think private client's orders should remain a little, well, private!

In other words. . . don't be so quick to snap a pic!

Michelle

You Couldn't Pay Me Enough

I've been in this business long enough to know from about one minute into a phone call if the person I'm talking to is going to make my life a living hell. I've answered enough emails to know it just from their initial enquiry, and I can almost always tell within a minute or two of meeting them -either they're awesome, or I want to run a mile from them. You learn to develop a sort of sixth sense about your clientele and I can guarantee that the ones you think are going to be painful ARE going to be painful. I can also guarantee that it's the painful ones whose cakes will slide, melt, break or fade, whose deliveries will go astray, whose payments will be incorrectly credited. It's like the Universe knows and just tries to smack you in face with reminders that you never should have agreed to their order in the first place.

Karma. It exists even in cake.

In the early days I used to take on every single order even if I knew the person wasn't going to be worth it. Hell, I needed and wanted the money and the practise and couldn't really (or didn't think I could) afford to be picky. A paying client is a paying client, right? These days I deal with this fairly simply- I charge them an exorbitant Irritation Fee (or what my husband calls, in a very Australian sort of way, "the embuggerance factor"). Basically, I quote them an obscene amount of money - enough which will make dealing with them worth it. 99% of the time they run for it and never come back to me, in which case it's a problem solved. 1% of the time they take me up on it ... and then if their cake survives the Universe kicking it around, they end up loving me and always willing to pay ridiculous amounts for the love. Win, win.

Here are the clients to whom I am likely to charge the Irritation Fee:

- The "Do You Know Who I Am?" client - she promises you that if you give her a good deal on her order, she'll bring you *lots* of business because she has more friends and family than, you know, God. Or Justin Bieber. And because she got a good deal with you, ALL of them are going to come beating down your door demanding cake (never mind they're going to want a good deal, too.)

- The "Too Cool for School" client - she tells you that she normally would make the cake herself, but she's SOOOOO busy/important/talented/ egotistical/genius that she just isn't going to be able to this year, so you - her inferior slave labour - is being granted the honour of doing it.

- The "Something Simple" client - she tells you she wants 'something simple' and then reads you a list of 72 features this cake needs to have, including being able to fix her marriage and teach her kid to read. But it's just something simple, really, so it shouldn't cost too much, right?

- The "I Trust You" client - who tells you that you've got creative free reign to do whatever you like, as long as the cake is pink. And round. And 8". And has an owl on it. A purple owl. With blue wings. And spots. And stripes. And looks *exactly* like the one in the picture she sent you, but feel free to do whatever you like. Really.

- The "I Really Can't Afford It" client - the one having a wedding for 500 people but her cake budget is $200 and she doesn't understand why you're so expensive. It's flour and sugar, right? She can afford 500 guests at $100 a plate, but can't afford to spend more than 50c a serving on the cake.

- The "Prest-o Change-o Rearrange-o" client - the one who agrees with a design and price, pays the deposit and then continually (but slowly, so apparently you won't notice) changes or adds in more and more elements to her cake and is surprised when you gently tell her that three more tiers might cost a wee bit more than you originally quoted.

- The "Never Going to Learn" client - no matter how often you tell her you need 48 hours notice, she always calls the night before the party. Because apparently it's easy to forget you have 100 people coming round tomorrow, all of whom are expecting cake to be there.

- The "Hold My Hand" client - the one who brings her mother with her to the design appointment and asks her mother for an opinion on every single element, then goes with what her mother said even if she disagrees with it. Hard to tell which is your client here, really (but it's going to be the mother who complains later. Guaranteed.)

- The "Is She Serious Right Now?" client - the one who asks for something completely impossible and is miffed when you politely explain that you cannot bend time, defy gravity, time travel or make cakes bake faster. (I had one of these recently. A client called and gave me less than 18 hours to produce a scale model of the Sydney Opera House, on a budget of $200. I might have done it had she added an extra zero to the end of that budget.)

- The "Do You Know Who I Am?" Client, Version Two: the name dropper. I'm so sorry, but being Ashton Kutcher's 1st-grade teacher does not entitle you to a discount.

This entire post does of course come with the disclaimer that I've got loads of lovely clients, and I treat everyone with respect ... but it's amazing (and amusing) to me how many times examples of the above come up.

You Couldn't Pay Me Enough - Part 2

Previously, I wrote a tongue-in-cheek list of the types of clients who get charged my Irritation Fee - and I called it "You Couldn't Pay Me Enough." It's currently the most-read post on this entire blog, mostly because we can all relate to it. We've all had that kind of clients, haven't we? The ones who make you never want to bake another cake or macaron, the ones who make you doubt yourself, the ones who irritate you and get under your skin and frankly, just piss you right off.

Some of you left me some hilarious comments - naming a few types of clients I'd missed. Of course since writing that post a few more have come to mind so I thought I'd share some new little gems with you. Plus, like it says above, it's not always rainbow sprinkles in here and it's about time we took a moment to have a laugh (or ten.)

Clients I want to THROW rainbow sprinkles at:

- The 'Desperate Till Dollars' client: The one who calls you in a total panic because she either forgot she had a party for 100 people happening tomorrow, got let down by another cake maker (or claims she did), or frankly just plan forgot to order her cake. She's totally desperate, needs it exactly one minute from now, and the order has a details list as long as your arm. She'll beg, plead, demand, whine, ask and wheedle until you agree to make it on short notice. As soon as you tell her the price, she suddenly finds she "needs to speak to her husband about it" and will never call you back. Your phone grows cobwebs while waiting for her call.

- The 'Unique and Different' client: She will make you crazy from a design point of view and a flavour point of view, because she needs to impress ALL her friends by being different and original and special. You'll pull out ALL your baking superpowers to please her and give her something different, and you'll agree to try things you've never tried before in her quest to be the best Real Housewife she can be ... and then she'll order a round, chocolate cake which looks exactly like the ones her friend ordered last week because 'everybody likes chocolate, right?"

- The 'You Decide' client: She hands you two designs and can't pick between the two, so, in the end, says, "I can't decide. They're just both so amazing. YOU decide." Against your better judgement, you decide on one. She doesn't like your decision ... but nor does she like her own decision, either. Best to give-up here, she'll never win (nor will you).

- The "Is it moist?" client: She asks you what your best selling flavour is, ask you what flavour is your favourite, and then insults you totally by saying, "But is it moist? All cakes are dry, aren't they? I don't want a dry cake." Or my personal favourite, "Is your cake nice to eat?" Umm ... no, lady, I sell crappy dry cake AND I tell my clients that it's crappy and dry. WTH?

- The "Complainer" client: She comes to you with endless complaints about other companies who did her wrong, whose cake sucked, whose service was bad, who charged her too much, blah blah blah and she is hoping that YOU are the one who will represent the entire industry and turn all her other experiences around. Rest assured you can create her the world's most amazing cake and give her the most amazing service, but next year she'll be complaining about you to someone else.

- The "Progress Report" client: She calls you. A LOT. To check how you're doing, how the product is progressing, to make sure you've got the details right, to see if you're done yet, to see if you've started yet, to see if you remembered the shade of blue, just to "check in. " You want to say to her, "Seriously lady - it's a dozen cupcakes. GET A GRIP. "

- The "She Who Must Be Obeyed" client: She won't take no for an answer. It doesn't matter what you tell her (you're booked out that week, you do not make orange cakes, you do not make penis cakes) - she's convinced that for HER, you'll do anything. Including making her a cake the same week you are on vacation, in a flavour you don't offer, in a shape you don't make. Because, you know, it's her cake.

- The "I Know What I'm Talking About" client: She went to another company and got a quote on a cake, and she's now shopping around this idea to everyone else. So she emails or calls asking for things with very specific industry specific information she clearly does not understand - "How much does a 12" cake cost?" "Well, depends a bit on design. Tell me, how many people do you need to feed?" "Ummmm ... I've got 10 guests. I think 12" will be enough, right?" I'm not sure where these kinds of people get their information, but it's always wildly out of proportion to what they need. The opposite is also true - "I just need something small, like 7" or so? It's for 280 people." "I need faux tiers." Really? Why? "Because this design requires them."

- The "Nobody Eats Cake" client: I get this one daily! People who call and ask for quotes, hear the price, then assures me that NOBODY ever eats the cake, so they surely can get away with less cake? Yup, because at a wedding with 300 people it looks really fabulous if the cake is smaller than a lunch box. Nobody eats it anyway, right? (Apparently this must be because all cake is dry, right?)

- The "Refund Me" client: Either her husband saw the bill, or her sister insulted her choice of cake, or she needs a couple hundred bucks to pay for a new handbag. Either way, it only occurs to her to call and ask for a refund *weeks* after the cake has been delivered and eaten. Because, you know, it wasn't cooked, or was crooked, or ... whatever. She just wants (needs?) her money back.

What crazy clients have YOU had lately?

Close The Deal And Make The Sale

On Facebook, I recently shared a story of a woman who called me for a quote on a cake. She did not understand that a "decorated" cake meant that it has things done to it - she asked for details like borders and a message but then kept saying "I want a simple, undecorated cake."

Funnily enough, all the comments (and thanks for commenting) had nothing to do with the actual reason for my post. I was posting to make the point that sometimes, the hardest part of my job isn't making a cake - it's *communicating with people* about cake. Nearly everyone who replied commented that it's the word "simple" which makes them the craziest when it comes to client interaction. "I just want something simple," seems to be client code for, "I want it cheap and I also want it amazing, and did I mention I want it cheap?"

The average person has no real idea of what kind of effort goes into making a cake, and they don't realise that the simpler something is, the harder it is to make! (You just can't hide mistakes behind flowers or stripes ...) They see decorated cakes in Costco, Wal-Mart or Safeway, which sell for twenty bucks and think that you should be able to do the same, but better or cheaper. Some people have a really weird reaction to this, too - they get annoyed or pissed off when you say you can't meet their budget (a budget which is frankly unrealistic in the first place.)

Many of the people commenting on that post said that they tell those "I want it simple (and cheap)" clients to go to a supermarket. Me? I think this can be dealt with in a different way entirely.

Basically - I would ALWAYS rather tell a client what I CAN do versus what I CAN'T do. Why? Because I'm a saleswoman and *I want to close the deal*. Guess what? ___You're a salesperson too___.

Here's how I do it:

1. Educate them and use that as a way to show you're better, not that the other companies are worse. They have no idea what goes into cake which is hand made as opposed to one made by the thousands at WalMart. Don't justify your prices, educate about your prices. "My prices reflect the personalised service and handmade nature of my product. It's quite different to what you can get at the supermarket, so it's priced differently to the supermarket. It's kinda like buying a Ferrari versus a Ford. My cakes are Ferraris." Notice there's not a huge amount of detail in that sentence, but it talks in language most people will understand. We're trying to educate, not belittle.

2. Concede defeat but still be helpful and leave the door open. There are ways to nicely tell someone they can't afford you or they are being unrealistic without YOU getting all defensive and pissed off about it. "If you're needing something simple and quick for a small dinner party, I'd suggest you go to XYZ bakery. They make really lovely things and you can just buy them on the spot. Next time you need something fabulous and something with more wow-factor, give us a call and we'll be happy to help." I've even said to a client, "I'm a Mum too so I understand that not every party needs the super-fancy cake, they're kids, right? Try XYZ bakery this time, and come back to me next time you need something a little fancier." This is a great way to show them that you're a decent person, and you're trying to help even if it's not you who can help this time. They will remember that next time - that you gave them great service, NOT that you couldn't help with their cake.

3. Offer a range of cakes which are at a lower price point - which might not be at their budget still, but might be closer to it and they might be able to stretch that little bit. Basically, it's a good idea to have something to bridge the gap between you and WalMart until such time as enough people have been educated.

4. DO YOUR COSTING so that you know what your minimum cake charge is. Be clear about the kinds of cakes which will fit into that entry price point - *and the benefits to ordering them*. "Our minimum cake charge is $50, but for that you will get 20 servings, you get to pick from 10 flavours and fillings, and we give you birthday candles for free." If you get them in at the ground level NOW, they'll love you enough to keep coming back and by then they'll understand and value your reasons for your prices. Even if they come back and only ever order the minimum, that's still a client you have versus a client you lost, and if you're cost is right, you're still making money.

5. Ask for a budget then tell them what you CAN do for that budget, don't laugh or say "You're dreaming babe!" If their budget is ridiculously low, either offer them another product, "I can't make a fondant covered cake within that, but how about a buttercream cake?" OR concede defeat (see #2.)

Your aim here is to KEEP the client, not LOSE the client - but your aim is also to MAKE money not LOSE it. A big part of your job is convincing people why they should go with your company - not justifying, *__educating__*. Make no mistake - you are a SALESPERSON. If all you ever wanted was to be in your kitchen quietly making itty-bitty flowers and never having to talk to other humans ... do yourself a favour and just keep this as a hobby.

Of course, there is always a percentage of people who frankly just want it fast and cheap and who will only ever pay for fast and cheap and you've got no hope of educating them. Overtime you'll be able to spot these guys from a mile away, but you should still at least have one good try at educating them - you're helping yourself, you're helping the industry as a whole, and it's just good business practice.

There will always be a time, place and customer for whom the WalMart cake is perfectly fine - hell, I have bought plenty of supermarket cakes in my life. I also know there is a time, place and customer for whom AWESOME cake will be needed. My job is help people *understand* the difference and come to me when it's time for the awesome cake - which they'll do <u>because I educated them to do it</u>.

Haters Gonna Hate, Cakers Gonna Eat (Oreos)

Today I want to talk to you about a skill we all need: dealing with negative customer feedback. It's probably one of the hardest things to deal with in a cake business, especially when that feedback comes long after we can do anything to fix it. We work in a creative industry which has a very high personal and literal "touch" factor. We've spoken to our clients from their initial enquiry all the way to the delivery of their cake. We've spent hours in the process, from the creative design drawn on paper all the way to the carving and covering of the final product and then delivering it without a heart attack. We get intimately involved in the big moments of our customer's lives - our work is in their wedding photos, we get to meet their friends, parents, children. That's a lot of honour and a whole lot of responsibility, and I defy any cake maker to not take the work they create personally. You know, I'd say even those of you reading this who make smaller items of a less custom nature take it personally - it's just the beauty (and the pain) of being in a small business.

By the way: if something goes wrong and it's your fault and you can fix it in time for the event, FIX IT. This post is about the times when the problem or feedback occurs after the fact.

Here's what I want to tell you, but can't: You need to focus on the many, many positive reviews and client thank you notes rather than the one negative call you got. You need to let it just roll off your back. You need to realise that some people just love to complain. You need to remember that it's inevitable that within a large number of orders, there is bound to be a complaint or two - cakes are not always rainbows and unicorns. You need to remember that even Ron Ben Israel has had a client complain - probably more than once.

I can't tell you that stuff because this blog is about honesty, and while all those are true, they teach you nothing about how to deal with negative feedback in any real way. Other blogs will tell you all of that and they are certainly right, but they aren't REAL.

In the current age of Facebook, Twitter, Yelp, Urban Spoon and so on - feedback is immediate, has a very wide spread, and is almost impossible to delete entirely. The cyber footprint, both good and bad, is very, very big. That's great if ALL your feedback is awesome, and it sucks when some feedback is less than awesome. Regardless of how the feedback comes - over the phone, via email, in a public forum where others can see it - you MUST deal with it.

Here's how I do it (and over the phone, you've got to be able to think on your feet):FIRST:

- Thank them for their feedback, and be sincere about it.
- Acknowledge their feelings, and be sincere about it.
- If it's over the phone, do not interrupt them. Let them get out their entire thought before you reply, and use that time to gather your wits. If it's online, resist the urge to shoot off a reply immediately. You need to reply in a timely manner, but not in the same minute they've sent their missive.

Then BEFORE you get all upset and start freaking out, think hard about their complaint. Does it have ANY basis at all? Could you have done better? Did you really forget to write the message on it? Did you get the flavour or colour wrong? Did you know at the time you weren't doing the best job you might have? Does this client's complaint have ANY basis in fact, or are they just blowing off steam and you are their nearest target?

You need to figure that out before you can proceed. Be brutally honest with yourself.

If their complaint has any basis in fact <u>and you are at fault</u>:

- Decide how you're going to make this situation better for the both of you, and that's NOT always via a refund. If you are at fault, you still want to make them come back to you AND tell their friends about the amazing service they got but nor do you necessarily need to lose money.

- The resolution needs to be equal or only slightly bigger than the problem. You got the flavour wrong but they still got a great cake? Offer them a discount on their next order. You forgot to write Happy Birthday on it? Apologise politely but don't offer any recompense. You got the colour wrong and the whole party had a colour theme so it did not match at all? Offer a partial refund. The entire cake collapsed in a heap because you failed to give it internal structure and so they had no cake at their wedding? Refund the entire amount, send some cupcakes AND offer a discount on a future order. You've got to make them happy, but not have the 'reward' exceed the offence too much because that's both an admission of guilt and sets up the future interactions. Frankly, not writing Happy Birthday on what is clearly a birthday cake had no real impact on their event, but they deserve a sincere apology at the least because you didn't meet their expectations.

If their complaint has NO basis in fact and there is <u>NO way you are at fault</u>:

- Say as little as possible. The less you apologise, defend yourself, express your embarrassment, tell them you feel awful ... the less you are feeding the fuel of their emotions. You want to avoid having this become bigger than it needs to be.

- DO NOT offer recompense of any kind. If you are not at fault, there is no reason for them to get compensated ... and you don't want them as a client if they are the type of person who complains about things you have no control over.

- Tell them what (if anything) you are going to do about this situation should it ever arise again, and tell them you're grateful that they are helping you improve your business practices (if you're a business owner worth your salt, that bit is actually true.)

In either case, don't let the conversation drag on. <u>Come to a resolution as quickly as possible</u> and then act on it if you said you would. Keep it short and keep it about business - no matter how many tears you might have shed over it (and if you're like me, you have definitely shed some.) Be sincere, be authentic ... but above all be professional about it. This is true in EVERY forum you get feedback in. Negative feedback online is horrible because so many people can see it - but it says a lot about you and your business if people reading that feedback can also read your reply to it, and if that reply is done in a polite, respectful, businesslike manner.

Above all - you MUST:

- Thank them for their feedback, and be sincere about it. ALL feedback is useful feedback.

- Acknowledge their feelings, and be sincere about it. They want to feel loved. Even when they are pissed off.

I'm repeating those two because they are vitally important. They are complaining because -above all else- they want to be heard, and FEEL like they got heard.

That being said - no customer has the right to abuse you, which is why I say keep it short, keep it straight forward, and keep emotion (yours!) out of it as much as possible. There are some people who seem to revel in beating a dead horse. If you notice that happening, make the choice to exit the conversation. If you have already resolved it - there is no need to keep on talking about it.

Here's how I deal with it emotionally:

- I get upset. I let myself feel annoyed, angry, hurt, or (insert emotion here) about it for a little while. I take it personally even though I know I shouldn't - because I'm human, and I work in a high-touch industry. I actually do try to remember all the great feedback I get, but sometimes it's just easier to wallow for a bit. It's totally okay to feel like crap for a little while. Remember, being in business is not always fun.

- I call someone I love and trust who is NOT involved in my business and I vent about it. Letting it out feels really, really good. I probably then emotionally eat (remember I said this blog is honest? I'm an emotional eater. So a complaint from a customer, justified or not = too many Oreos.)

- I deal with the problem in a timely fashion by replying to the client (as above) or just taking care of it (actioning the refund). The faster I end the conversation and action the resolution, the quicker it's over and I can get back to clients I love and cakes that need me.

- I set a timeline for how long I will allow myself to be emotional about it - and you'd be amazed how well this one works. "I'll be grumpy today, but by tomorrow, I'll need to be done with it." Giving yourself a timeline for irritation is a pretty neat trick AND it totally works because by the next day, I've got other things to worry about and I've given myself permission to be irritated in the first place. I find trying to convince myself to "get over it" does not work as well as just being grumpy for a defined period of time.

Most of all:

- I wait a little while (long enough for the initial emotion to pass) and I think about what I've truly learned from this, and then I take action so that it doesn't happen again. All feedback teaches me something, even if the lesson is about getting practice in dealing with unreasonable people, or improving my contract or disclaimers. It may not feel like it, but every bit of feedback is doing you a favour.

Let's face it, negative feedback is no fun at all, but it's inevitable. *Knowing how to deal with it makes it a lot less painful and makes you a much more effective business owner.*

Since I never let you all leave here without at least one real life example - about two years ago, I made a stunning wedding cake for a demanding client. THREE MONTHS LATER I got an email from her about the cake. This email went on for pages and pages about how it was a total show-piece, how her guests went back for fourth and fifth serves, about how she got compliments on it all night. This email was really pages and pages of good feedback. The final page, however, was a complaint that the ribbon used on the cake was "too peachy, not pinky enough, " and, therefore, it did not match the rest of the decor of the event. The shade of ribbon was not pink enough ... and apparently I RUINED HER ENTIRE WEDDING as a result. She will never be able to look at those pictures again, I should have called her about this "major design change, " and apparently her disappointment is not going to go away. All because the shade of light pink ribbon we used was "not pinky enough. "

I wish I was making this up. I'm not.

She got a polite, short businesslike email back which thanked her for taking the time to send me the feedback, expressed pleasure that her guests enjoyed the cake so much, and acknowledged her disappointment about the ribbon. I then told her that it's taught me to always ask for a colour reference for ribbons in all future cakes, and thanked her (again) for helping me to improve my business. I then wished her and her new husband all the happiness in the world.

I then went and called my husband, had a good whine to him about it, and then ate a few Oreos (but not too many. Anyone who thinks the colour of board ribbon on their cake ruins their entire wedding day is not worth the calories.) That story has now become one of my favourite to tell - because it makes you want to laugh and cry at the same time.

Haters are gonna hate. Let them. Just learn how to deal with them and it won't bother you quite as much, I promise - either that or stock up on Oreos.

CHAPTER 8
MARKETING

Nothing scares a cake maker more than if I ask them what kind of marketing they are doing to grow their business (unless of course I ask them how they work out their prices). Most will sheepishly look at me and say, "Ummm, well I KNOW I should be doing more marketing. But I HATE talking about myself." Again, because we work in such a high touch, personal industry that we take everything personally. We forget that marketing is often focussed on our business as a whole or our products, not just ourselves. We think marketing means we have to drone on and on about who we are and how special we are, when really the products should be in the spotlight more than our personality should be. In a small business, who you are is important as it forms the basis for how you do things, but it certainly isn't the thing you use exclusively as your point of difference. There's an important difference there. I can't imagine saying to someone, "Buy my cake because I am really awesome!" I'd much rather say, "Let's talk about how your event will be even more awesome because of the cake." In that second sentence, it's about the client's happiness and how the product meets their needs. It's still very much a reflection of my personality (using the word awesome in every sentence I possibly can) but the focus has shifted to them and their needs rather than me and my ego or lack of self esteem.

Without doubt I find that our biggest barrier to marketing isn't the "how" or the "when" or even the "why", our biggest barrier to marketing is fear. Many of us also have a fear of failing around marketing, we're worried either about getting it wrong or about it not working. "What if I spent a whole lot of money on this advertisement, and no orders come from it?" Some of us fear succeeding because of what might result – what if I do a bunch of marketing, and then I get so many orders I can't handle it? I'll have still failed, because I won't be able to meet the demand. Some of us fear being seen, because as long as you are hiding behind the cake and not marketing, you feel safe. We all know that to keep our businesses going and growing, we've got to be out there telling potential customers that we exist. That's not a new concept and anyone reading this knows it. This chapter has a whole lot of practical know-how and advice which will teach you marketing, but what it can't teach you is how to get out of your own way. We are the biggest barriers to our success because we are so stuck in the crystal ball thinking of "what if?" that we simply avoid taking action. If you get only one thing out of this chapter, let it be this: if you're wanting to build your business, marketing isn't an optional activity. Get out of your own way and get going.

Marketing For Bakers

I started my business because I was good at making cakes, not because I was good at business, and over the years, I've made it a priority to learn about *business* more than I've made it a priority to learn about cake. One area I needed a real education in was marketing - or what I would have probably called 'advertising. ' It's something people ask me about all the time, "Where should I advertise?", "How much money should I spend on ads?", "Are Facebook ads worth it?", "Do Google AdWords work?", "Are print ads worth it anymore?", and so on. All these questions made me realise that most owners of baking businesses have no real idea what marketing actually is - because nobody ever taught them, and because the common wisdom is that marketing and advertising are the same thing.

They're not.

I recently heard this quote which I think explains it beautifully: "If the circus comes to town and you design a sign saying, 'Circus Coming to Town Saturday' that's **advertising**. If you put the sign on the back of an elephant and walk into town, that's **promotion**. If the elephant walks through the Mayor's flower bed, that's **publicity**. And if you get the Mayor to laugh about it, that's **public relations**. If the town's people go to the circus and you show them the many entertaining booths, explain how much fun they'll have spending money at the booths, answer their questions and ultimately, they spend a lot at the circus, that's **sales**. And if you planned the whole thing, THAT'S **MARKETING**. "[20]

In short, marketing is about the big picture.

Successful marketing is about _planning_ the how, when and why of getting your business's personality to shine through all the other personalities vying for attention at the big baking party. It needs a defined plan, it needs a defined goal, it needs to be the driver BEHIND the ads, the promos, the press releases, the sales.

Now that you know what marketing actually is - start thinking about the ways you currently market your business. What methods do you use to get your message out to your clients or potential clients? Have you got some activities planned for the future? For those of you not at that stage, what activities would you like to be doing? For marketing to work, it can't be a case of you suddenly deciding you might try to promote a post on Facebook (although promoted posts might be a part of the overall plan).

---

20   Attributed to Lee Solters.

Next week I'm going to talk about how to go about creating a marketing plan[21] - so this week, take stock of what you're doing (planned or not) and also think about the story it's telling your potential clients. Is it telling them the most amazing circus is coming to town and they should save their pennies especially to spend money at the big top? Or is it telling them that the two-bit flea circus with the half-dead horses and no-longer-performing seals are limping their way into town?

---

21   See *Five Steps To Writing A Marketing Plan* in Chapter 8.

Confused In Cakeland - Best Marketing Idea Ever

Confused in Cakeland

Hi Michelle,

I know I need to do some marketing, but I'm really overwhelmed by it. I don't know where to begin. Some people say I should pay to advertise on Facebook, then other people say that's a waste of money. I've heard you say that things like letter drops and local newsletters can work, but I'm not really convinced by that. I want to get my pictures into a wedding magazine, but those ads seemed very expensive and I don't have a lot to spend. What do you suggest? What's the best kind of marketing to go for first? I don't want to spend a lot of money on something if I'm not sure it's going to work. What are the best marketing ideas you've got?

Signed,

Mixed Up Marketer

Hey there M-U-M,

You're not going to want to hear this, but I really can't just give you a "do this, this will totally work" guide to marketing (I wish I could, I'd make a fortune.) The truth of it is that there is no one size fits all solution, because good marketing depends on two very simple principles:

1. *Knowing who you are selling to, and*

2. *Going to where those people are.*

What do I mean by this?

If you are not clear about the type of company you own and products you make - are you budget? mid-range? premium? - and the type of people likely to want or need those products - soccer mums? big budget brides? corporates? - then frankly, ALL marketing you are doing is going to be hit or miss.

Nobody likes to hear me say this but it's true - your marketing choices must come first from those two pieces of information and knowing those is <u>where the confidence will come from</u>. In the Facebook example, sure, you can just hit that "boost post" button and then watch as the random hairy men from the Virgin Islands like your page, and then get peeved that you wasted money on people who are nowhere near your business. OR you can use the Ads manager to target those same Facebook dollars to females within 5 miles of your store, who are between the ages of 25-45 and who are recently engaged and who are probably looking to purchase cake or cookies for their event.

A little bit of effort into research at the beginning of your marketing makes the rest of your decision-making a LOT easier. While I can't guarantee it will absolutely, definitely, 100% work - I can guarantee it's going to be <u>a lot better</u> than if you decide to do things randomly because "everyone eats cake". Everyone does not eat cake (especially not all those ridiculous "I quit sugar" people ... but let's not go there). You're going to be a heck of a lot more confident about your marketing if you know your money will be spent on getting your amazing creations in front of the eyeballs of the people you want it to be in front of.

By the way, I was an epic fail at this in the beginning of my business. The very first place I ever paid to put an ad was in the Yellow Pages. I'm serious. I PAID BIG MONEY (well, for me it was big money) to place a fancy ad in the YELLOW PAGES. Like that big ass book that lands on your doorstep once a year and is equal to like five trees. Seriously, what is this, 1957? In my head it made perfect sense. Everyone needs cake, not everyone uses the Internet (really Michelle?! Umm ... Google was around even back then) and I thought that if I wanted to find a local cake store, I'd probably use the Yellow Pages.

Yes, because apparently *I* am actually from 1957 as well, and all my customers are too. I wasted a bunch of money and two years of marketing time on the Yellow Pages. Embarrassing but true.

The very best marketing in the world is: planned, targeted, trackable, and most of all, actually doable by you. Don't get totally overwhelmed with HOW you're going to do it yet. First, decide who your product is for. Second, figure out how that group of people finds things to buy and where they hang out to do so (live or digital). Third, go there and hang out too! And fourth, don't advertise in the Yellow Pages.

Love,

Michelle

Five Steps To Writing A Marketing Plan

This week I'm going to give you 5 simple steps to writing a marketing plan. There is a WHOLE LOT, which goes into marketing, so this might be a little far along the path for some of you. I'll re-visit the marketing topic probably quite a few more times, so if this is over your head - just bookmark it for a later date.

Full disclosure: I had no idea what a marketing plan was or that I needed one until I hired a clever business coach a few years ago. Once he pointed it out to me, the light bulb went off and I realised that I HAD, in fact, being doing this, just not in an organised fashion. **The key to great, effective marketing is, in fact, planning and organisation**.

Here are the five steps to becoming better organised when it comes to your marketing (I did this activity via some very simply created tables in Word):

1. **ASSESS:** Work out what activities you are already doing and how often you're doing them.

   - Make a list of all your marketing activities. These can include but are not limited to: paid ads on social media, paid ads in print media, events (such as wedding expos or market nights), charitable contributions, customer loyalty programs, Tweeting, blogging, pop-up shops, joint ventures with other businesses, daily deal websites, online competitions, voucher books like the Entertainment Book, handing out flyers, writing a monthly newsletter. ANY activity you are currently undertaking which gets your business' personality out there in the world.

   - Note down how often you're doing them - are they once a week blog posts, are you Facebooking daily, do you advertise once a year, how many expos do you exhibit at and so on. Just work out WHAT you do and HOW OFTEN you do them.

2. **ANALYSE:** the current activities for the following things: cost, purpose, effectiveness, effort.

   - Cost: What does it cost you, if anything, to do these activities? This might be money or product.

   - Purpose: What is the point of doing it? Is it to raise your profile, bring in some cash, influence potential clients, drive people to your website, improve your Google ranking?

- Effectiveness: Go back and check if the things you've been doing have been meeting their purpose. ALL your marketing activities must be somehow trackable - if you can't track if they are working or not, you're wasting a lot of time and money. Did your clients mention seeing your ads in Bride magazine? How many orders did you take on the day of the expo? How many clients did your sponsored Facebook ad get you? How many readers did your blog get after your last post? Did anyone mention they saw you at the Kids Market? How much money did you earn at the Bake Sale? Did anyone take up the offer in your newsletter? (... and so on).

- Effort: Compared to the effectiveness of it, how much effort was involved? So if it took you 3 months to prepare for the wedding expo, it cost you $1000 to run and you only got one order out of it, this is important stuff to know! However if the activity takes only 5 minutes each day but gets you a new order each week ... you need to know that too. Figure out how much effort is involved in these activities.

3. **DECIDE:** Based on the information you found in step #2, work out which of your current activities you want to keep, and which ones you want to ditch.

   This is also a good time to do some research into activities you have not currently tried but would like to try. Call and get some quotes on having fliers printed, find out what ads cost, contact some local suppliers about setting up joint ventures. Do your research and then decide what new things (if any) you would like to try out this year (hint: if you've decided you're going to do them, ALSO work out how you're going to track their effectiveness).

4. **CREATE:** Create a 12-month long marketing calendar.

   This is basically a chart which along the X axis (horizontal) you list all the months of the year, and along the Y (vertical) axis the activities you've decided to do. So as an example, suppose you want to run a sponsored Facebook ad for products you'll sell which are attached to the major holidays of the year. Along the Y axis you'll have "sponsored Facebook post" and along the X axis, you'll have an X under February (Valentine's Day), April (Easter), May (Mother's Day), December (Xmas). For year-long activities such as ads in print media, you'll have an X under every month of the year.

This also will give you an idea of which months are stacked full with activities and which months seem to have not much happening. It gives you the chance to perhaps come up with ways to 'boost' your marketing activity during currently quiet months, or spread out activities so you're not doing too much in certain months. For example, if you look under April, run your finger down the line and there's only one X, that's a quiet month. If you did it for December and every single row has an X, that's a busy month. You might want to add in a few marketing activities for months which are traditionally quiet for your business (e.g., run a winter special) or spread out some activities.

5. **MAKE IT HAPPEN:**

- Go to your normal planner (diary, electronic or otherwise) and about 2 weeks before the next month starts (e.g., in the middle of April for May), block out some time in which you will check on the current month's activity (is it working well, not working well) AND either set in motion or plan the next month's activity. This might only take you a half hour, but actually put it in the diary or it won't happen.

- Some of these activities might be year-round (e.g., an online listing you pay a yearly fee for) and should be 'checked in' with maybe only once every quarter (not monthly) - for example, if you pay yearly for an online listing, make sure you're checking the stats for that listing. Tweak that ad once in a while - change the wording, add an offer, swap out the pretty pictures.

- Some activities need to be planned more than 2 weeks in advance and need more than one call to action - for example, you want to work out your Xmas product line probably sometime in September but don't need to promote it just yet. So this activity will appear earlier in your diary and should appear more than once - in September you might have "develop Xmas products" but through November, you'll have "insert Xmas products add into local paper" or "run Facebook promo on Xmas products."

- Actually, PUT IN some time in your calendar for ALL OF YOUR marketing activities. I write a monthly newsletter - so on or near the 21st of each month, my diary says, "Write newsletter" in it. If I didn't write it down like that (and yes I do this a year in advance), it would likely get lost in the shuffle.

Any big task like marketing can very easily get overwhelming and, therefore, shoved into the "when I get around to it" category. If you take the time to do this activity of creating a marketing plan just ONCE a year, this seemingly big task leads to a whole bunch of smaller, more manageable things which you can do over the course of time. Some marketing advice says to "do a little bit each day" but I've never been very good at that. By creating a year-long marketing plan, I'm at the very least making sure the bigger, longer term, more important activities are *definitely* happening, which frees up my time for making some smaller activities happen as an added bonus.

In future posts I'm going to go back to some marketing basics -working out your target market and so on - but in the meantime all of you should be able to create some version of a marketing plan to work with (it's not the size that matters, it's the discipline of doing it in the first place!).

As the old saying goes, it's better to plan to succeed, than fail to plan.

The Table

The baking industry as a whole (and custom cake/cupcakes in specific) is experiencing massive growth at the moment. Thanks to the magic of television, it's the scrap booking of the current era - everywhere you look cake has become sexy and it seems like everyone is doing it. Now more than ever before, actually getting into the baking industry is also very easy. The products are way more accessible than ever before - where craft stores used to have two shelves of cake tools, they now have two whole aisles. Skills are more accessible too - if you can't afford a "live" course, you can buy one online for $24. 99 or watch YouTube tutorials for free. People who otherwise can't or won't afford a real website use Facebook as their primary business page and it doesn't cost them anything.

In my opinion, the baking industry is at an absolute saturation point. Let me be frank here - for someone like me who has been in the business for many years, this situation sucks. There are people who are more talented than I am doing cakes for half the amount of money I can. There are many, many more people doing things themselves that a year or two ago they would not have even attempted to do themselves. In short, this is a very crowded marketplace to be at the moment.

I'm not willing to just give up, so what the hell am I going to do about it?

I'm going to bring something new and different to the table and I can do that based on my existing reputation and client base.

But ... what do YOU (who is probably not in this biz as long as others have been) bring to the table? How do you stand out when you are in crowd? And not just any crowd, but a crowd where people may be cheaper and way more awesome than you are ... and a crowd where nobody knows your name?

Simple: work out what is special about you and sell the hell out of it. (In business this is commonly referred to as working out your USP - your "Unique Selling Point".)

What makes your cakes better than the next guy? What makes your business as a whole stand out from the crowd? With the amount of accessibility in the industry, just being good at making cake isn't a compelling enough reason any more. Used to be there were some good cake makers, and a small handful of GREAT cake makers - and now there are plenty of good ones AND plenty of great ones.

In order to make it in this saturated industry in the long term, there must be *something* about you or your business which stands out, something which you can shout about from the rooftops. If you can truly stand out on skill or technique innovation - do so - but be mindful that in this environment, skills are easily learned (and thus easily copied and therefore no longer unique). So innovate if you can, but realise that your cake super power might have a shelf life to it. I can think of a few cake makers who stand out because of their unique skills - Dawn Butler from Dinkydoodle for her airbrushing, the stunning 100% buttercream work of the girls at Queen of Hearts Couture Cakes, the construction and 3D skills of Mike from Mike's Amazing Cakes ... you get the idea. Talk to any of those people (all of whom are teaching internationally) and I'm guessing any one of them will tell you that teaching their unique skills is a double-edged sword. It's a great way to make money, see the world, share the joy of cake making, and increase your profile - but you're also educating the people who will become your competition.

Without truly unique skills, what have you got?

Maybe you're the first person in your area to offer custom cakes covered with fondant (which is a real possibility - as pointed out to me by the readers of this blog from small Caribbean countries). Maybe you deliver further than anyone else does. Maybe you have a flavour which is unique, you offer a service not currently offered by others, your customer service goes above and beyond, you only use organic ingredients, you offer cupcakes suitable for people with allergies, you work with other vendors to create amazing events, your retail shop is open late nights ... maybe you are the only cake maker in your city who specialises in cakes for kids. Whatever your USP, you need to find a way to make it obvious to the consumer - use that Unique Selling Point to bring people to **your** door and not to anyone else's. Let me put this in really simple terms - it's the squeaky wheel which gets the grease, and so once you work out your USP, you should:

SQUEAK AS LOUD AS YOU POSSIBLY CAN.

There has got to be *something* about you which stands out - something which you then need to make your potential customers want.

I can't tell you exactly what that is, only because we haven't met so I don't know your story (but don't worry, that's going to change soon). You've got to work this out for yourself - and you've got, to be honest about it. Suppose you are sitting there thinking that there really isn't anything better or different about you - that secretly you think other cake makers are better than you, cheaper than you, and you're wondering what the heck you are doing in business in the first place.

First, that's bullshit. By reading this blog, you're proving that you're better because you aren't just relying on your cake skills to get you through. You're taking the time to learn, to grow, to seek help.

Second, realise that at some point there HAS TO be something different about you, otherwise you probably wouldn't have gotten this far in the first place. It's just that uncovering what that is might take a little time to work out.

If you honestly think you can just do exactly what everyone else is and somehow still make it in the long run (and this business IS a long term goal, is it not?) then you are kidding yourself. Let me tell you a story. Actually, let me tell you TWO stories. Several years ago now I did a class with a big cake company. One of the skills the class involved was how to coat a cake using ganache. I asked the instructor if you can do the same technique with buttercream and she said an unequivocal NO. I then asked, "Well, what do you do if a client does not like chocolate?" and her reply was, "I tell them to go away! I don't want them as clients if they can't understand that the only way to get things looking perfect like this is with ganache!"

I was gobsmacked. One way and only one way only to cover a cake? REALLY? (I also couldn't imagine speaking to a client like that, but that's another story.) It occurred to me that this company had a USP (sharp edged ganache covered cakes) and was busily teaching an entire generation to make cake in their style and *only* their style - thus diluting their USP *spectacularly*.

Even back then I knew it was useful to learn this skill, but that there was no way it could be my only skill (besides, I love butter cream and would not give it up that easily!)

My second story takes place four years later. One of my best friends lives in the same city as that big cake company. I decided I wanted to get him a cake for his birthday and have it delivered, so I started to look online at cake companies based in that city. I looked at no less than TWO DOZEN cake companies online. All of whom I knew immediately had to have been owned by people trained by this big cake company. Why? Visually, all these cakes looked pretty much the same - it was almost as though they had all rolled off the mass production factory floor. Make no mistake, these cakes were gorgeous - really great work - but not one offered an option other than ganache covering. I clicked and clicked and clicked and eventually I just gave up because I couldn't find one which said "BUY ME!" above the others. There was just <u>no real compelling reason</u> to go with any one of those companies. They all made beautiful cake, they all delivered ... so how on earth do I choose one to give my business to? (I didn't. He missed out.)

The point of these stories is to demonstrate to you that in order to make it in a crowded marketplace, you've got to: 1) work out what is unique about your business AND 2) communicate that to your potential customers. (A secondary lesson: think hard about teaching your special skill if you've got one. We'll talk more about that later.) Even if you are similar in skill style to the others - what are YOU going to bring to the table which the others aren't?

The weight of the razor-edged ganache covered cakes on top of the table will collapse it soon.

If I were you, I'd make sure that in the aftermath, your cake is the one sitting on its own table, under the spotlight, yelling "BUY ME.

Not The Bad Cake Lady

Last week I asked my Facebook community to post a picture of their first ever cakes. I was honestly expecting to see an entire catalogue of cakes that were made from Women's Weekly cookbooks or displayed on foil-covered trays and covered with candies and plastic toys. You know, the kinds of things our Mums made for us back in the day.

Holy mazoly was I wrong about that!

Every single one of them was made with love - but a whole LOT of them had plenty of skill, too! Some people even posted "then and now" pictures with their first cake and their more recent ones ... and my jaw just about hit the floor with those. First, I want to acknowledge that you are one heck of a talented bunch of people and you should all be SO proud of what you have achieved, even with that very first cake.

Second - I was reminded in seeing those pictures that this industry has changed A LOT in recent time. With the rise and rise of online schools like Craftsy (http://www.craftsy.com), and with a whole lot more amazing cake books out there than there used to be, people are getting ever more skilled and ever more talented. The end result is that consumers are getting a WHOLE LOT MORE but paying a WHOLE LOT LESS. We all like to think that the cheap cake lady is making cake wrecks. She's isn't.

I don't think there is anyone to blame for this, not really. Those who charge less than they should do so for a whole lot of reasons - maybe they don't know how to cost things, maybe they don't consider it a business, maybe they are truly in it for the love and are thrilled to get a bit of cash in hand, maybe they simply don't know what they are worth, or maybe they think people won't pay "proper" prices because they are home based. The truth of it is, we don't know (and will never know) why people charge so little for things. I'm working on changing that - but it's going to take a while, and as each day goes past I've got a whole bunch of new people to teach. :)

An early (and terrible) cake wreck of my own. :)

You know the cheap cake, lady? She's not necessarily the BAD cake lady. Actually, she probably doesn't even know she's cheap - or if she does, she thinks it's because she's not good enough, professional enough, or legitimate enough to charge more. As for her cakes? Yes, sure there are some cheap cake ladies who also produce crappy quality work ... but there are plenty of them producing stuff which easily out-skills many of us.

Today I want to give you a bit of homework.

One, I want you to decide to stop hating on the cheap cake lady - because you know, that was all of us at some point! Teach her. Send her to this blog, or politely offer to explain pricing, or nicely answer her "what should I charge for this?" questions on social media. If YOU are the cheap cake lady (and you know it, you really do) then you can consider coming to my business class.

Second, I want you to reconsider your own business. If you cannot compete on price, and you can no longer compete on skill ... what are you going to compete on?

It's the "X Factor" that ONLY YOU bring to the market which is going to keep you in business.

Being the best or being the cheapest just isn't going to cut it anymore.

I Spy With My Little Eye

Recently one of you asked me if it was ever okay to pretend to be a potential customer in order to find out what your competition is charging for their products. She called doing this "cake espionage" which is an expression I immediately loved. In my mind I'm imagining people wearing all black, picking locks with metal ball fondant tools and meeting people in dark alleyways to trade recipes. All joking aside, it's a valid question - is it morally okay to pretend to be a customer and ask for a quote, knowing full well you will never order from them, and knowing that the information you get will probably help your business out?

In a word: yes.

In a few more words: you probably do this already. Every time you 'like' a company similar to yours on Facebook, visit their website, read their blog, follow them on twitter, look at their images on Pinterest, sign up for their email newsletter, or take time to interact with them at all, you're engaging in research (cake espionage!) which will benefit your business. Most of the time you don't need to pretend to be a customer to find out pricing information because plenty of their customers will talk about it online, and plenty of businesses will happily publish their pricing (mine included). You can tell me all you like that you're "building friendships", "getting inspired", "helping each other out", by doing these things - but really, you're gathering useful information and LOTS of it.

I'm even going to go so far to say that if you're NOT checking out your competition AND not using that information, you're making a big business mistake. Yes, no question, you need to do proper costings in order to work out what you should be charging. But without knowing what sorts of prices the marketplace will tolerate, you have no idea if you have any business being IN the marketplace to begin with. It's no different to selling a house and looking at what comparable houses in your area recently sold for. You've simply got to have a feel for where your product fits among your competition. If, for example, you decide your product costs $5 per piece - and your nearest competitor is selling (and successfully selling) them at $7 ... either you've got your costing wrong, or they are making some real profit (or both). If, however, yours can't be sold for less than $5 to cover your expenses and your nearest competitor is selling it for $2 ... your costs aren't right, or they're going to go out of business soon. It's imperative you know both what the market will tolerate AND what is out there in competition to you.

I imagine some of you are thinking, "But two weeks ago, you told me[22] I had to

---

22   See *The Table* in Chapter 8.

stand out! Can't I stand out on price?" Honestly? NO, unless this is your *defined* marketing plan. If you're setting out to be 'discount' 'affordable' 'wholesale' etc. as a business model - that's totally okay, and your prices should reflect that. Nobody uses "being more expensive than everyone else" as a marketing plan unless their product justifies the price - so in that end of the market, price can't really be your unique selling point. I also said in that post that this is a flooded marketplace, and standing out on price alone isn't really going to cut it anyway.

Let's step away from pricing for a second, and look at the other information you can get simply by keeping your eyes and ears open. You can see what's trending (frills? ombre? rustic? vintage?), you can see what products are getting well received (cupcakes? macarons? cake pops? push pops?), you can see what skills they've got which you don't (3D building? realism? armature?) and you can see what marketing schemes they're using to get ahead (give aways? picture competitions? tagging days? charity drives?). Of course you might see any of these things and say, "no, that's not for me," or "that didn't seem to work so well," and decide not to try any of these things. That's fine. I'm NOT telling you to copy everything you see (please don't!). I'm telling you to be aware of your competitors and what they're doing, and use that information to drive you to be better. TRUE competition does that - it moves us forward. It should inspire us -not to copy - but to think of concepts which are different, better, newer, more interesting. I told you how important it is to stand out, but you can only do that if you already know what's out there.

I don't see ANY of this as cake espionage. I see it as being a clever businessperson. If you're going to bury your head in the sand about what is going on in your industry and with your competitors (and your ego tells you that you're good enough to justify that), you're doing your business no favours at all. I don't think this is ANY different to a consumer comparing the price online with the price in store, or looking at several different websites to find the best deal, or Googling for pictures of football cakes to see what is out there of interest to them. If the CONSUMER is aware of what's out there, YOU need to be aware - simple as that.

Does it irritate me that a large portion of my Facebook followers are my competition? Not at all - because I *expected* that to be the case. Does it irritate me that some of my phone or email enquiries are probably from my competition, fishing for information? Not at all - because I treat everyone calling or emailing the same way, so it makes no difference to me. Frankly, plenty of legitimate calls and emails I get will not result in a sale, so a few more makes no difference - because legitimate customers fish for information, too! That there is competition wanting to know what my company is up to is actually flattering. If I was really terrible at it, or not successful, would they even want to know in the first place?

To demonstrate my point - good delivery service is a major issue in my city. It's expensive, hard to find reliably, and basically, most companies end up doing it themselves out of sheer frustration. Some years ago an industry contact complained bitterly to me that a rival company ordered cupcakes from her just so that when the delivery guy showed up, the rival could get the details of the delivery company and use that same company. My first thought (after, "Damn, why didn't I think of that?") was, "So?" I don't see the problem here. It's a third party delivery company anyway, there is no risk to her current set up with them (they might even be grateful that she managed to get them another gig), it's effectively telling her that she's onto a good thing anyway, and nobody loses out in this. Is it annoying? Oh heck yeah, it's annoying -but ultimately it has ZERO impact on her business.

So - pull on your black chef coat, file down your ball tool - and get out there.

You need to know what's out there in order to be better than what's out there.

How Do I Find More Clients?

Today I'm answering the question that most people ask, which is, "How do I get more business?" It's the one thing we all want to do: grow our businesses and get more orders.

I'm going to ask you ONE question: What are you doing to get more business? The reason I ask is because it's the first thing you should be working out. Not, "Why am I not getting more orders?" but *"**What am I actually doing** to get orders and grow my business?"* I ask this question of everyone who tells me they want to grow their business, and most of the time they look at me and say, "Well, so far word of mouth or Facebook has brought me most of my business," and that's about it.

That's just not a good enough answer any more. It might have been good enough for a while, but as I've been saying for months now, the industry is far too crowded and you simply cannot rely on what USED to work for you. Facebook's news feed is so crowded now, and organic reach has all but disappeared. You can still use Facebook as a marketing tool, but it certainly can't be the only tool you're using. Word of mouth is brilliant, but word of mouth also relies on people remembering to actually talk about you. Word of mouth needs to be cultivated just like any other form of marketing.

Both of those strategies are great but if what you want is to grow your business, you need to grow and change your marketing strategies as well.

Also - that neighbourhood lady, the one who undercuts you all the time? She's not going to go away anytime soon AND her skills are getting better by the day. When I opened my business ten years ago I was able to build my business on my reputation and skill - pricing didn't even come into it. I was the only one around who could do what I did. The neighbourhood lady was cheap but she also wasn't terribly good. These days, reputation counts for much less, I'm not the only person with the skill anymore, and pricing is more important than it ever was. Let's be honest, the neighbourhood lady is now real, serious competition and *she's only getting better*.

If I could shout this at you in real life I totally would: you MUST market your business if you are going to succeed. In fact, it has to be the BIGGEST thing you do other than creating your product. You have simply got to suck it up and market the hell out of yourself, your business, your products. You don't want to hear that but it's true - you want more orders and you want to grow your business - so you've got to work on marketing your business.

You will not survive in this industry if what you want to do is sit in the corner using your wafer paper scraps as tissue to dry your tears.

I want you to do a little exercise for me. Sit down with a piece of paper and a pen (yes, I'm old school) and write down ALL the ways in which you get your orders. How do you currently get people to your door? How do people know your business exists? What action, right now, are you taking to actually bring those orders in or make people aware of your brand? In short, what real, tangible, actual work do you do to grow your business?

Be honest with yourself. I think you might find that you probably haven't been working hard enough on marketing. You might have come to rely on things which aren't working as well as they used to, or you might just be doing the same things your competitors are doing. It's totally normal to do that, but I'm here to push you forward into success, not let you rest on your laurels.

Once you've written those down, then come up with at least 3 more options you can try. PUSH yourself on this one. Think a little harder about how to get in front of your ideal clients.

Here's the bit I want you to remember: The single best way to get more orders and grow your business is to work on selling your stuff as hard (if not harder) than making your products.

SELL IT, BABY.

Who Is My Ideal Client?

Many of you have heard me (and most marketing people) talk about how important it is to find your ideal client. What exactly IS an ideal client? In fancy terms: your "ideal client" is the specific segment of the market you're selling to. In plain English: It's the *type of customer* you are going to sell your stuff to. Why is this important? It's important because it helps you make decisions about a lot of things, like how and where to advertise, what your company logo and colours are and so on. Knowing your target market sets the tone for your business overall.

Briefly, let me say that sometimes this is called "niche" - but I tend to use that word to apply to **the kind of work** you do - the style, the feel, the types of events. For the purposes of this article, I'm going to talk about niche from a customer point of view.

When we first get into business, we think our ideal customer is, well, everyone. After all, doesn't everyone like cake and cookies? **Doesn't everyone have a birthday at least once a year?** When we work in custom products, we can sometimes feel like we don't have a single ideal type of client because every order is so different. Sometimes we don't want to define our ideal client because we think that it will limit the number of enquiries or orders we get. We all start out wanting to be all things to all people, but that needs to get more defined as we go on so that we can start to create the business we want. I recommend starting out simple with this and then getting more detailed - because as your style evolves, so too does the picture of your ideal client.

You're going to have an ideal customer even if you're starting out because, at least on a basic level, it sets the direction you're going in. You want to **create that picture so that when it comes to making decisions** about marketing, you can ask yourself - would this appeal to my ideal client? Would they read the magazine I'm going to put this ad into? Would the colours of my logo appeal to them? How should I target my social media ads? You're aiming to build what in fancy terms is an ICA - Ideal Client Avatar. In plain English: A picture in your head of what your customer might be like.

One of the best ways to define your target is to **look and listen to your existing client base**. While the orders might differ, the people themselves will have commonalities. The easiest way I found to define your target market is old school - sit down with a piece of paper and a pen and ask yourself a bunch of questions about this person. Start off nice and basic:

- Are they male or female?

- How old are they? (For this one, think about who makes the buying decisions. So while your cakes might be for kids, your client is actually the Mom, not the kid - because the Mom is who you will deal with.)

- Where do they live? Are they within 50 miles of you (that's how far you can deliver) or within your country (for example, that might be for cookie makers who can mail their products)

- Are they likely to be very price conscious? (Not everyone is!)

- How far in advance are they planning to purchase? Are they likely to be planners, or are they "pop by on my way home" type of people?

- Do they have kids?

- What's more important to them - the way it looks or the way it tastes? So are they foodies for whom you might need to have a ton of crazy flavours, or are they people who are more concerned with appearance and are really happy with 4-5 basic flavours?

- Do they have a lot of disposable income? (are they wealthy overall? Or people who will splurge on a special event but otherwise not really.) Similarly, will they be paying for this themselves, or is it an event (like a wedding) where someone else holds the purse strings?

At this point you can start to get more detailed:

- Do they work, and if so, is it full time or part time? What kind of job?

- What kind of stores might they shop at? (Anthropologie or WalMart? Target or Bloomingdale's?)

- What do they do in their spare time?

- Where and how do they socialise?

- What is their personal style? Is it classic and elegant? Quirky and fun? Bohemian?

- You can consider race/religion, but this will really depend on where you are located geographically and if you offer special items - for example if you sell only Kosher or Halal products, or if you specialise in Greek sweets.

- Where do they go to shop for things like the kind you are selling? Do they shop online? Search via Google? Or do they prefer real life stores?

- What do they read? Blogs? Which ones? Magazines? Which ones?

- Are they the kind of person who would attend a bridal fair, and if so - a high-end one, or a more local one?

You get the idea - we want to get to know them as best we can so that we can then SERVE THEM as best we can.

HERE'S AN IMPORTANT THING to be aware of - even if you define your target client down to the teeny tiny details, there will ALWAYS be outliers. Always. The outliers are people who just don't fit your mould for some reason, and that's totally fine - hey, an order is an order, right? So use your target market to define your website style, where you advertise, etc. but don't obsess over it if "everyone" does not fit into that exact description. So in my own case, I hated wedding cakes - still happy to do them but they were not my target market in the least. So I never pushed them at all - but I left it as a category on my website (which was all bright, happy colours, kids cakes and words like "rock star" and "awesome") and if I got an order or enquiry for a wedding cake, I just did it (provided I had the skills and time). I neither worried nor cared that this person wasn't at all what I pictured my clients to be like.

Here's the point: Your target market is who you AIM for but not always who you get.

And lastly - the way your cakes and website or Facebook page look will attract that target market as defined above, which is why I say that while you are happy to take whatever order comes your way, only display or make a big deal of the kinds of orders you want to be doing. If you've got a website full of superhero cakes, then a super high end, couture, very traditional bride would look at your things and think, "Ehh, not really the style I'm after" and would move on - she's unlikely to even send through a quote request. Figuring out your ideal client in part also helps you to begin to define your style.

Where Are My Customers Hiding?

A comment I've heard a few of you make recently is, "I'm waiting on my first customer," or "I'm nervous about my first consultation," or "I'm all ready to go but I haven't got any orders. " When you are working from home, just starting out, it can be very frustrating to have hung out your shingle and then watch as the tumble weeds float past your open door. You're excited, you're nervous, you've got a box of 500 business cards at the ready and yet nobody is coming to order from you.

Worse than this is when you've been in business a while, your shingle has some dust on it, you've used half the box of business cards ... and yet it still feels like a struggle to get people ordering from you.

Where are all these customers hiding out, exactly?

Here are 3 steps to finding your first - or getting more - customers (also known as, "A crash course in Marketing").

STEP ONE: Figure out who your ideal client is.

Before we can work out WHERE these customers are, we need to work out WHO they are. Your 'target market' are the people who are most likely to be your customers, based on what you are offering. Figuring out who your target market is is a vital step in working out how to find them - and while it's by no means a new idea in business, it IS something which can be a challenge for cake makers to do. Theoretically, every single person you meet could be in your target market - who doesn't like cake, everyone celebrates birthdays, etc. In reality, sure, everyone likes cake and everyone has birthdays but not everyone is willing to or can afford to buy a custom cake. Some people who love cake and have birthdays might live rurally and so can't access cake companies. Some think a cheap supermarket cake is just fine. Some will be able to afford it but prefer to do it themselves ... you get the idea.

The key to working out who your customers are lies in working out not only what you sell, but what the limitations of those sales are. So, for example - if you sell very expensive cake but you have no means to deliver it - your target market will be all the people with a high disposable income who either local to your area or are willing to travel for it. Or, if you sell make-your-own cake kits which you can ship all over the country - your target market is going to be time-poor parents who can't (or won't) get a custom cake but who are happy to pay more than just a box mix will cost them. They probably also shop online.

This is where your homework comes in - sit down and outline exactly what your product is. Then work out who is most likely to buy it. How old are they? Are they male? Female? Stay at home parents or working parents? Are they cake makers? (That's entirely possible - especially if you teach cake decorating or sell figurines.) Where do they live? Do they have children?

It's entirely possible that your target market fits into more than one category - you might be targeting brides (who don't have children) but also mothers (who do) - but the important thing is to start to build a picture or two of who will buy what you are selling. Get as detailed as you possibly can about what these people are like. A good way to get the ball rolling on this is to look at your existing client base and see if you can pick out common traits they have. If you don't have any clients, think about the kind of person you think is most likely to buy your product. Get very real about this. I can't stress enough how knowing every detail about your target clients will shape a whole lot of business decisions.

STEP TWO: Figure out where these people are hanging out.

So now you know the kind of person your business needs to have walking in the door. Now you need to work out how they spend their money, where they spend it, and mostly importantly WHERE THEY GO to decide how to spend it.

Hint: They are not all on Facebook.

Let me tell you about my own business and how I learned the "they are not all on Facebook" lesson. It's my policy that every single person who comes through my business gets asked, "How did you hear about us?" I ask *everyone*, even if they are buying something worth five bucks. Why? Two reasons: because I want to get more detail about how my customers spend their "spending" time, and it's also a great way of knowing if the advertising I pay for is working for me. I also write down their answers so I can get some cold, hard statistics to look at. In preparation for this post, I went and looked at how many answered the, "How did you hear about us?" question with "Facebook, " and the answer was: 3. THREE. (Out of several hundred.) Many of our customers are currently our fans on Facebook but generally only because **they found us somewhere else first**. So for me, the stats are clear that while Facebook is a great way to stay connected with our clients, it's not a great place to generate actual sales for me.

Now - Facebook might work really well for you if you are, for example, a cake decorating supply shop who relies on cake makers. For me as a custom cake business, it doesn't get me much in the way of sales. I worked out who my target market was and then I worked out where they hang out and guess what? Most of them are too busy for social media. A lot of my target market is people with kids and so this directly affects where they hang out. Local schools, local sporting clubs, local dance classes, online parenting forums, online directories for kids' events, local radio shows, they hang out in cafes and they read parenting magazines - my target market hangs out in and does purchasing research in a whole bunch of places which are not always the obvious ones.

If *you* or your friends fall into your own target market (and you might), where do you go when you want to purchase something? The local mall? Do you research it online first? If so, where? Do you ask your friends for referrals, and if you do, where do they get their info from? Ask your customers! Ask ANYONE who falls into this category.

Find out where your ideal clients are - and be prepared to be surprised at what you hear.

STEP THREE: Go to where they hang out, spend some time there, and don't leave too soon.

Once you've worked out what your product is and you work out where your ideal customers spend their time - GO THERE. By whatever means are appropriate for that place. Go there, spend more than five minutes there, and for heaven's sake don't leave too soon.

Let me explain. Suppose you work out that your target market is local parents with school-aged kids. You decide to take out an ad in the local school newsletter. You do it for a month and only get two enquiries. You're disappointed so you decide never to run that ad again, it didn't work, right? WRONG. These are busy parents - they probably don't read every single newsletter which comes out. Good marketing and advertising need these things: consistency, clarity, and certainty. You've got to be running that ad, with a clear message or offer in it, for longer than just one edition - and then you've got to deliver on whatever it is you said you would. I'd probably recommend (depending on how often the newsletter comes out), giving it a good run of time before deciding it is or is not working for you - say 3 months for a monthly publication, 6-8 weeks for a weekly one. Then, when people walk in the door - deliver on what your ad said it would deliver and make a point of acknowledging that you are happy to support the local school.

Guess what happens then? Those parents have a great experience with you, and tell other parents about it, and then it snowballs because your advertising starts to generate word of mouth AMONG YOUR IDEAL CLIENTS (and it's backed up by the newsletter ad appearing again next week!). Word of mouth is the best sort of advertising because it's entirely free, but it definitely costs you something if the word is getting around to the wrong people.

Suppose your ideal clients hang out online somewhere - bridal websites, for example. Advertise there and follow the same basic rules of being consistent, clear, and certain. Maybe your clients hang out at bridal fairs. Maybe they are on Facebook. It doesn't matter - what matters is that as long as your marketing and advertising is going to exactly the RIGHT people in the RIGHT place, over a reasonable period of time - it's not a waste of time or money, it's an investment in a longer-term plan.

This post is not about if you should pay for advertising or not or how long you should do it for, it's not about magazines versus online, it's not even about if you should bother to advertise at all. It's basically about working out how to shape your business and find some customers to build that business. It's entirely possible that you can find customers and not need to spend a cent on advertising - but if you don't know WHO they are and WHERE they are, you'll find yourself staring at an empty doorway regardless.

If you forget everything about this post, I want you to just remember this:

There are 3 steps to finding customers.

1. Figure out who they are.
2. Find them.
3. Hang out there.

How To Sell Without Feeling "Yucky" About It

I recently posted this meme on our Facebook page and I was surprised by the response - it seems like a lot of us have a hard time telling people about what we do and what we make.

So here's the thing. If you make (or are starting to make) some amazing stuff, and you don't go out there and tell people about it ... well, you're not going to be able to afford to make amazing stuff for very long. If people do not know it's available to them, how to they go about buying it? Being a successful baking business owner is AS MUCH about sales as it is about anything else.

I think the feeling that we don't like or know how to get ourselves and our business "out there" is due to two things.

The first is we think we need heaps of confidence - we think that the ability to sell means you are somehow brimming with heaps of extroverted confidence. Let me let you all in on a secret. If you've ever watched a webinar of mine, met me in real life, or come along to one of my classes, you would think I'm extroverted, very confident, and great at talking to people. That's only partially true. I am in fact sometimes quite introverted, I'm confident only some of the time, and I'm great at talking to people only because I've had to train myself to be. Kinda hard to believe, but I promise you it's totally true! It's really just that I realised early on in my career that orders were not just going to come flying in the door just because I was good at making cake. I had to get it out there somehow, even if what I really wanted to do was hide under a rock and wait for someone to find me under there!

The second issue around this seems to be the 'yuck' factor. For some reason we perceive sales and salespeople as being a bit 'yuck' and none of us want to be seen that way. We get sold to ALL day and ALL the time - in ways that are overt (TV ads) and ways that are not (competitions on social media.) There are plenty of ways to sell in ways that are not yuck! Somehow when thinking about sales, a whole lot of other negative words or phrases come up - pushy, demanding, 'too sales-y', greasy, untrustworthy, 'only in it for the money' etc. Nobody likes the feeling of being 'sold to' all the time. We want to be loved, appreciated and have people be attentive to us just because of who we are, not because we might buy something from them. We really, really don't like this idea of having to sell to people, mostly because we have all encountered that salesperson who just rubbed us up the wrong way.

Since I can't give you a confidence boost (although I like to think reading this blog DOES help that a bit) and I can't make the idea of sales less yuck, here are a few tips and tricks to help you get yourself and your business out there:

1. If you don't want to sell it, do you really HAVE to? I wrote about staying a hobbyist a few weeks ago[23]. If the idea of selling really fills you with dread, sit and have a think about whether or not you really want to be selling your products in the first place. Are you in business *just because* your friends or family convinced you that you can make money off your creations?

2. Stop thinking of it in terms of sales. Just think about it in terms of making connections, having conversations, getting to know people. Word of mouth is WONDERFUL but it needs to start somewhere, and that's usually with you. Next time you meet someone new, ask them what they do … and when they ask in return, answer with, "I make custom cakes." We're very fortunate in that most people know what cake is, they've probably seen a cake or cooking show on TV, or at the very least the idea of cake making for a living is a romantic one- so more often than not they will then ask you more questions. Or, next time you make a cake and also attend the party, chat about your creation to anyone who is curious (and they will be). "It was really fun making that figurine", "This is a new flavour I tried out", and so on. You're not selling to them, you're chatting to them. It's THOSE types of connections which "get you out there" and conversation by conversation, the ball rolls onwards!

3. Get other people to do it for you. Every time you complete an order (even

---

23   See *Don't Run A Baking Business If You Don't Want To* in Chapter 1.

if it's for a friend or family member), ask for written feedback. Either collect those on an external site (Womo, Yelp, etc.) or via email. Post a picture of the cake and the words from the email to your Facebook page, to your business blog, on the website of your business on a "testimonials" page - or really wherever you can put it that other potential customers

4. will see it. That way it's not YOU who is saying you're awesome, it's other people - and in the current marketplace, we rely very heavily on reviews when making purchasing decisions.

5. Make sales to your existing customers - it's a lot easier to retain an existing customer than it is to capture a new one. Build on that loyalty - offer a 'frequent buyer' card, have a 'members only' special, offer a holiday-themed range of products, etc. Once you've captured them as customers, work on *keeping* them as customers! The more they use your services, the more they'll become loyal - and the more that loyalty will encourage them to share their experience with others, which again means it's not YOU having to spruik directly.

6. Find opportunities to sell and market that you're comfortable with. If (like me) the idea of going to a networking event fills you with dread - find other ways to network! Comment on blogs, put an ad in the local paper, make some baked goods for a charity event, help your local Scout troop earn their cooking badge by teaching them to make cupcakes, volunteer to make a cake for Teacher Appreciation Day, etc. Remember that with marketing, everything you do is getting it out there! Find some creative ways to get yourself and your business known and make sure that you are a) comfortable with those ways and b) that it directly leads to your target market! In the example of the Scout troop - those kids are going to go home to their parents, thrilled with their creations. Give each kid a flier about your cakes for kids range, put your sticker on the box they take home, offer a "Scout discount" on any order they place ... and so on. You're not directly selling, but it's an activity that can lead to sales and gets your business some exposure to the local community.

7. Not everything needs to be sold - sometimes 'selling' is about giving things away for free. If you look at any of your 'big name' companies out there, you'll find that a lot of them do things for free alongside selling. For example, they might sell tutorials but also have free tutorials on YouTube, or offer free samples at a wedding expo. Or they might give a free box of birthday candles with every order, or offer free shipping on orders over a certain dollar amount, or they give people a voucher for $10 off to give

to a friend. Sometimes the way to sell more is actually to give stuff away. Of course I wouldn't do this so much that you go broke, but sometimes offering a free "taster" in your business is a great way to then drive sales to your business as well. If they love the free tutorial, they might buy one next time.

8. Put on your big girl pants and accept that selling is just part of the job of a business owner. We all have to do it. Some are better at it than others, but many like me had to TEACH themselves to get better at it! I'm still a bit of an introvert, and I still have days when it seems like my confidence has just flown out the window entirely - but on those days, I remember WHY I'm in business in the first place. Remembering why I'm doing this makes it a lot easier for me to be confident enough to get the word out there. There is a picture of my kids on my desk - and every time I feel like it's all a bit too much, I look at that picture and I remember that this business isn't just about me. It's about providing for my family, inspiring other people, and a whole lot more - and suddenly the need to 'get it out there' isn't nearly as scary as it otherwise might be.

When you're doing this on your own, getting the word "out there" is one of the more daunting things we've got to do - because, at the heart of it, most of us started in this business because we were good at creating things, not good at selling things. That being said, there are a number of business skills we've got to learn in order to make a sustainable profit from our passion - and learning to sell is one of them. The key is just to forget about being a salesperson so much and instead think about being someone who shares their passion with others (a baker/decorator), but also does so with the bigger picture in mind (a business owner).

MMM Business

Photo credit: lifelounge.com.au

A good friend and colleague of mine (**cough* Sharon *cough**) is a MEGA FAN of the boy band Hanson (http://www.hanson.net). Seriously. Hanson, as in the long-haired brothers who sing the 90's song that never dies, *MMMBop*. She's such a fan that she's going to concerts in more than one Australian city, and she's trying everything possible to get a photo with the boys (including offering free cake, so you know the obsession is real, right?) She was telling me about how they own their own record label, they've sold over 16 million albums and how they've grown up into one heck of a business and a band. Because I was intrigued, I started to do some research, and discovered that she was right about all of that ... and that they even have a connection with our industry - they were **judges on Cupcake War**s! (This automatically makes them even cooler to me than they were when I was a teenager ... and they were pretty cool then.)

I started thinking about the music business, and Hanson in particular, and then of course I can't get **that song** (https://www.youtube.com/watch?v=NHozn0YXAeE) out of my head. We can learn a lot from the music business (and the Hanson boys in particular.) As in our industry, the music business is crowded with lots of extremely talented people, all trying to make a living doing what they love. Music is also a creative business, so they too have the issue of trying to put a dollar value on a talent and skill. The music and cake industries are very similar, except perhaps that the musicians who make it big are making a heck of a lot more money than the cake people who make it big.

So, with more respect for Hanson than I've ever had, here are 3 business lessons I think we can all learn from the boys:

1. It's really about being a resilient Entrepreneur: Since 2003, after a split from their major record label, Hanson have been a fully independent band. Rather than look around for another label to take them on, they formed their own company and have paved their own path ever since. Sure, they took on additional risk, but this also opened them up to additional reward. The thing about true Entrepreneurs is that they don't give up - because it's actually about the creating, not about the details of failing and succeeding. Hanson decided to move on and do things their way, they didn't just decide to give up music altogether simply because they were dealt one seriously difficult blow.

At the moment we are in a crazy time in the industry and it seems like every day I see posts on social media saying things like, "I'm beginning to wonder if it's worth doing this anymore", and "I'm just going to give up, there's no way I can compete against the others who are undercutting me." I've said for a long time now that staying in business is a lot harder than getting into business - something I'm pretty sure Hanson would agree with.

When I read those posts, I think to myself, there's someone who has not worked out *why they are in business in the first place*. Is owning a business what you really wanted, or is it a case of having given in to the pressure of "You should SOOOO sell those!"? Hanson had a massive setback in their career, but because for them *it was about being able to make a living making music*, they just set about doing it in a different way. They got knocked down. They stood up again. Why? Because they wanted to earn a living doing what they loved. They were in it for the long haul, determined to succeed even if it meant taking big risks and suffering potentially big failures.

Longevity in this industry - in any industry - has less to do with the product and more to do with your willingness to take the knocks and keep coming back for more. It's about being an <u>entrepreneur</u> more than you are a cake maker or cookie baker. Hanson, and every one of us reading this, is trying to carve out their corner in a crowded market. Where we have unregistered home bakers or newbie cake makers to contend with, their equivalent is shows like The Voice and X Factor. Getting into cake and getting into music are now easier than ever, but it's the ones who KEEP GETTING UP after being knocked down who will succeed in the long term.

2. It's not just about the product, it's about the people. Hanson are BRILLIANT at looking after their fans and cultivating a whole group of people who love and support them. They've got an active fan club, they have several 'members only' events and activities, and in all their interviews they talk about how grateful they are for their fans. They also involve their fans in the creative process - allowing fans to vote on their set list and be a part of what they create. Isaac Hanson recently summed this up beautifully, saying, "As long as fans understand that the goal is to have your favourite band be successful and for you to be as involved and engaged in that process – because the fans need to appreciate the bands and the bands need to appreciate the fans – as long as you can create a well connected relationship, everybody's going to win."

They have worked really hard at building a fan base from the very beginning of their career. In the early days, they sent CDs to fan club members, created a members-only magazine - and in 2000 when their record label pulled their funding to tour, rather than disappoint people they self-funded their touring.

Photo from esquire.com

How does all that translate to the cake industry? Two words for you: customer service. I don't think cake companies focus on customer service and building tribes enough. We spend more time sharing cakes with each other rather than building relationships with our fans. I fully believe in creating a community, but that community must include the people who are going to buy from you and shout about you from the rooftops to others. We all talk about how word of mouth is such a powerful marketing tool, but word of mouth needs to be cultivated. It doesn't just happen like magic, it happens because you invested in giving your customers a great experience. Hanson adore their fans, understand that without fans there are no record sales, and they invest heavily in their fan base. Us cake makers should be doing exactly the same thing.

Hanson produced a documentary - *Strong Enough to Break* (https://www. youtube.com/watch?v=arfx4i-050I) - which chronicled their leaving the record label and getting their album released as independents. In their words, they "wanted to show people what's involved, show them what it takes to get an album released." This reminds me a bit about those of you who struggle with the constant explanation of pricing and what work goes into making one of your creations. Just like music fans have no real idea about the process of releasing an album, your customers probably have no real idea what the process for building a 3D cake is. It's your job as an artist to help them understand that process so that they understand it's worth it. Isaac's take on this is, "People *don't value what they don't purchase* so you need to encourage people to see the products that you are making as valuable," - which is a pretty basic premise in selling anything at all. If people don't see the value in it, they aren't going to buy it! Is it annoying to keep explaining? Sure it is - but we've got to do it not only because it helps people value us but because it also helps us to build our tribe of fans.

Photo from: http://www.theaureview.com

3. It's About The Long Term Plan. It was 18 years ago that Hanson came out with *MMMBop* (I KNOW! 18 years! Makes me feel old ...), and since then they've recorded 6 studio albums, have several Grammy nominations and continue to tour globally (among other things.) They still consistently sell out concerts all over the world ... and yet it's fair to say that Hanson is not a band you hear on the radio all that often these days. Until it was mentioned to me I had no idea they had as much of a back catalogue as they did, nor did I even know they regularly tour. I truly had no idea how big they actually are and continue to be.

This is a brilliant lesson in the importance of having a bigger picture in mind and remembering that you're in it for the long term. I'm sure the boys would love to have #1 hits on the radio all the time, but they've managed to build a career doing what they love and between them they have 11 children. Have they reached the dizzying heights of the 90's *MMMBop* fame again? No. Does it matter? No.

Sometimes in our quest for fame (and fortune) we feel the need to just create, innovate, create, innovate endlessly, never truly being satisfied with what we've got and keeping up with the Joneses. We flutter from order to order, we get overly excited about reaching social media milestones and we endlessly chase the "oooh ... shiney!" factor. If what you're aiming for is to have a *long-term, sustainable, successful* (to you) business, then <u>that's what you've got to build</u>. Stop looking at how others are becoming superstars and think about what is important for YOU. How do YOU define success? In Hanson terms, would you rather be the one hit wonder or accepting the Lifetime Achievement Award?

When I started my business, I wanted a career doing what I love, which also was flexible enough for me to raise my kids and which would pay me a decent salary. I also wanted to be able to bring happiness to people's lives, influence the next generation of cake makers and feed my creative soul. I then actually succeeded in doing all of that because, for me, that's what success was about. Rather than be a one hit wonder, I wanted to stay in this industry, consistently earning a living over a long period of time. Hanson's goals are much the same, in so far as it has always been about doing what they love (music), earning a living (touring), having a life (becoming parents and starting families) and making a connection (fans). You've got to have the long term plan in order to actually take the steps to getting there.

Photo from: vulturemagazine.com.au

In the last week or so, I've learned more about Hanson than any one person should actually know ... like that they had a cameo appearance in Katy Perry's music video for Last Friday Night. In all the things I've learned, the biggest lesson of all came to me when I kept finding similarities between their business values and mine. Ask anybody working in a creative industry - from big (Hollywood and movies) to small (Etsy and crafters) and the challenges are much the same although the scale is different. Think back over your favourite artists, in any number of creative industries, and you'll find that their long-term survival has come down to the same three things: resilience, building a fan base, and committing themselves to the long term.

While Hanson might not be your thing (although hello, how completely gorgeous are those men!?) - look around at other musicians, actors, artists and I think you'll see their challenges are much the same as ours are. The 'cake world' can be such a bubble sometimes that we fail to see that it's not just us that deal with customers who don't see or value, tons of competition (some great, some terrible) and plenty of set backs.

Yes, I believe we're all in this together ... only now I know that the "we" goes beyond bakers and decorators.

First, Best, Only

Photo credit: www.campaignasia.co

Get your thinking caps on, today we're talking about *innovation*.

I recently attended a two-day course where the parting words of wisdom were this:

To succeed in this business, you must either be the FIRST, the BEST, or the ONLY.

(It's best if you can be all three of those.)

So how do you do that in this industry, an industry which seems overrun with people who can do what you do, for cheaper than you do it?

BE THE FIRST:

I think it's fair to say that in the baking industry at the moment, it's pretty hard to be the FIRST at the more tangible things. There are definitely people who innovate with product (Bakerella (http://www.bakerella.com/) and her cake pops, the dude who created cronuts), or technique (Valeri and Christina and their buttercream skills (http://www.queenofheartscouturecakes.com/)), but unless you're crazy clever (or lucky), innovating an actual product or technique can be difficult. Not only because it's got to be a wicked amazing innovation to get any traction, but because you then need to sell the heck out of it and hope like hell you can do that before someone else beats you to it. I'm pretty sure there is no way Bakerella could have predicted how many people OTHER than her would be producing books on the topic of cake pops.

So if you can't be the first on product or technique, you <u>can</u> be the first with location. You can be the first in the area to offer a certain type of product or service, or you're the first one who offers a choice of flavours. Look around you and see what the others are not yet doing - and do it. One of the best ways (I've found) to do this is take inspiration from other countries and other industries. Read food blogs and design blogs and see what's trending - then be the first to bring those trends to your area. For example - Pantone recently announced the colour of the year. Be the first in your area to design an entire dessert line around that colour scheme. Being the first doesn't necessarily mean being the inventor, sometimes it can mean being the first to DO something in your area which already exists out there - be the one who brings the trend to the locals.

BE THE BEST:

This one is easier to do, but harder to market. You can by far be the best at a certain style, skill, flavour or specific product, but you've got to cultivate that reputation and it may take quite a while for it to reach "the best" status. After all, the competitors around you are also going to be claiming that theirs is the best, too. This one is really less about product and more about marketing because you've really got to work hard to earn that "best" badge AND let people know about it. "Jenny's cakes are the BEST in town!" is exactly what you're wanting people to say about you, but you need to earn that reputation and that takes a while.

So if it's going to take a while to become the best, in the meantime figure out what you are best at and make a plan for how you're going to earn and celebrate that badge. Maybe you'll be the best at customer service (this is, in my opinion, a huge, underutilised and high potential for impact area within the baking industry) or maybe you really do make the best macarons this side of the Rio Grande. Whatever it is, if you're aiming to be the best, I want you to make damn sure your product or service not only IS the best available, but that you are prepared to market that fact till the cows come home (and even then.) This might mean doing stuff like entering competitions (awards are a great way to prove 'best') or sponsoring taste tests, or giving out lots of samples, etc. Stuff which right now won't earn you money but is worth it if you're going to build your brand on the idea of 'best'.

BE THE ONLY:

Being the "only" anything can often just mean a little tiny tweak of what you're currently doing. Suppose there are 10 cupcake companies in your city. One of them was the first to open and has been around a long time, the other has a reputation for making the best red velvet cupcakes ... but you, you're the ONLY one who offers gluten free cupcakes. Sometimes being the only company who does something can be easy - but bear in mind it means it can also be easier to copy as well. If you're the only one doing something, the others will jump on board pretty quickly if they see you are getting any success at it. This is where I think that if you're going to be only at something, you'd bed either be prepared to keep coming up with "only" items, OR pair that with being the best at it. That being said, this industry is one in which it's virtually impossible to be the 'only' for very long - and that means you might not have had enough time to establish yourself as the best and not been there long enough to be considered the first.

A lot of the international teachers at the moment are very fortunate to be ALL of these - they developed a technique or style (the first), then got better and better at it (the best) and now are the only ones teaching it all over the world (the only). The problem with this is (and as any of them will tell you), it's a double-edged sword, because the more they teach, the less they become the only, the less they become the best (their world is full of untapped talent) and while it's still great to be the first at something, things like price will start to come into play. There are consumers who want the product for a price more than they care about the pedigree - all of us have experienced this when someone tells us they can get the same thing for cheaper somewhere else.

So - for this week - start to think about innovation and how you can bring innovation into your business - OR - if you're *already* the best, first, or only - start to think about how you're going to get the word out there about it. If nobody knows you're those things, then you're missing out on a vital piece of the marketing puzzle. You might be using that best, first, only ... but if you're not shouting it from the rooftops, I can guarantee you someone else will be.

Confused In Cakeland – Using Pictures From the Internet

Hi Michelle,

I'd like to offer some Christmas products to my customers. I've never done these before, and I don't have enough money to make real or dummy ones to take a picture of. If I use pictures from the Internet of cakes that I am sure I can make, but I make it clear that I haven't done them yet (I can for sure make them though), would it be okay?

So far I've only posted pictures of cakes that I made. I'm just starting out and I've got so much to learn! Is it okay to do this?

Thanks, Noel

Hi there Noel,

No, I would not use photos of other cakes from the internet - when people see a picture they expect to get exactly that. Plus frankly, it will just look bad if you say, "This is a picture of a cake not made by me, but I am sure I can do it." Your clients want to be able to trust that you can deliver what you said you will (by proving it with a photo of something you actually made yourself).

You can offer things without a picture of a cake, though - like a cute picture of Santa or some elves (just to get their attention – please credit those photos if they are not your own) and say "I'm now offering Christmas products" and give them the information about the price and how to order. Some people will happily order without a picture of it because they know and trust you. Once you do get an order - do a great job of it and take a picture! That way next time you already have a picture of your Christmas stuff ready to go.

It's <u>never</u> okay to "borrow" cake pictures and claim they are your own work.

Happy Holidays!

Michelle

Eventful

I recently received an email from someone asking me for help with a big event she's been asked to do. The event expects 3000 attendees, and she wanted to know how much product she should make. It's a great question and one which lends itself to a blog post, since we've probably all be asked at some point to participate in this kind of thing.

Let me preface this by saying that I am a little bit anti-events. By "events" I'm not referring to things like wedding expos where it's a clear opportunity to personally meet your direct target market and get exposure to those ideal clients. I'm talking more about events like "Girls Day Out" afternoons, carnivals at schools, charity events, etc. Basically, anywhere where you have been invited to come along and sell stuff. I'm a little anti-event because I've found (after doing dozens of them) that they often don't pay off as much as you might like them to.

That being said, I think every offer you get to participate in something beyond the four walls of your business is generally worth considering, but don't jump into them just because you are flattered to be asked. I still consider every offer even if I don't take up many of them.

Here's some tips on how to decide if you should even attend in the first place:

- Before you do anything else: decide WHY you would attend. It's either a) because it will raise your profile among your target market, b) help you raise some much-needed cash, or c) both. Deciding why you would bother to go in the first place will then affect how much you'll be willing invest in the event.

- Who is attending the event? Are they in your target market?

- Has the event been run before? What was it like? Did they get the attendance numbers they thought they would, or can you see growth in numbers if it's been run for a while?

- If a company selling a product similar to yours participated the year before but isn't doing so this year - call them and be honest. Why aren't they doing it again? (Making this very phone call saved me a heck of a lot of money.) Of course, maybe they didn't do well because their product was crappy, but if their reason for not returning was "not enough people attended to make it worth it" or "the organisers did not advertise it, the event was a hot mess" you've got to take that into consideration. Inside knowledge is priceless and don't get that info from the company running the event, they just want you to sign up for a stall.

- Think about what the fall out might be if (for example the weather sucks) and you don't sell anything. How much will this affect you, financially or otherwise? Can you afford for it to fail?

- If you've done this event before and it didn't meet your goal of profit or profile, ask yourself was it the *event* or was it your *product* which was the problem. Be honest! If you went again but changed things at your end, might there be a different outcome?

- When is the event? Is it at a time of year when you have more time to devote to it, or is it at a time of year when you already will be working 100 hours a week? If it's at a busy time but you think it might be lucrative, can you sacrifice staff or hire more staff to do the event?

- Write out a budget of what it will cost you to attend and be brutally honest and detailed about it if you can. Labour, product costs, gas to get there, stall holder fees, insurance fees (often you need different insurance for public events), hiring of trestle tables, etc. If the number at the bottom of the budget makes you suck in your breath - I personally wouldn't do it.

Here's some tips on how to work out the 'nitty gritty' of products to take and things to think about once you have committed to being involved:

- Has any other food company sold stuff at the event? If so, it's worth giving them a call to ask what their experiences were with sales. If you are honest, e.g., "I'm thinking about holding a stall at this event," most people are very willing to help, as long as your product is not in direct competition with theirs. This once worked very well for me, as I called a coffee company for inside info and ended up 'partnered' with them to have stalls next to each other. Coffee and cake are easily co-sold. Win-win!

- If you decide to go ahead even though a similar product company pulled out, ask how many they sold and reduce it a bit. Cupcakes are cupcakes. If they sold 500, don't bring 1000 because you think yours are better than theirs. Bring 500 or less and then sell out. It's always better to sell out and create perceived scarcity in the market. If you go a second time, people who come a second time will know to buy your stuff early or risk missing out.

- If in the above points you said you're going to the event for "b": to raise some cash - then work out the minimum number of products you will need to sell in order to actually MAKE some cash. Costs you $3000 to attend, your cupcakes cost $5 each - you've got to sell 600 of them just to break even. Is that even realistically achievable?

- If in the above points you said you're going to the event for "a" - to raise your profile or "c" - profile and profit - then work out the minimum you need to sell to break even, and brainstorm ways to keep your profile top of mind for the people who attend. Gather business cards for a prize draw, ask people to sign up for your newsletter, donate something to the auction, give away free fridge magnets, etc.

- Experience has shown that about 1 out of 3 people will buy non-essential things at events- of course, some will buy none and some will buy 3 or more products, but the 1/3 is a good rule of thumb. Generally speaking, I would not make more than 1 per 3 - so if 3000 are expected, 1000 items is probably more than enough. For me, I tend to do 1/3 then reduce that by an additional 20% because I prefer to sell out and minimise wastage. That being said, if the event has never been run before, take the organisers "estimated attendees" number with a massive grain of salt.

- Come up with a plan for what you're going to do with leftover stock. Donate it? Sell it? Trash it? Things which have a long shelf life and are wrapped (granola bars, cookies, etc.) can be on-sold later but freshly baked cupcakes cannot.

- Find a way to track the ongoing effectiveness of the event. You should be asking every single client how they heard about you anyway, so keep track of how many say they heard or saw you at the specific event in the months afterwards. Events can be just about cash flow, sure - but you should be seeing if they actually raised your profile as well.

- Is it worth selling something you are capable of, but don't normally produce? Events can be a good way to get an immediate reaction to a new flavour or new product line.

Events can be a great way to get your product in front of lots of people who may not have encountered it before, but they're often a big investment of time and money so it's worth thinking about carefully before committing. Events can also be a part of your bigger marketing strategy - perhaps you do events only in the winter, when it's quieter and cash flow is needed and you're trying to 'recruit' summertime clients. Just don't immediately jump at the opportunity without first doing some legwork about it.

A tip of the day for you - most bigger events will sell stalls off at a fraction of the price the closer to the event that it gets because they need to sell as much space as possible. If you have an event you'd like to be a part of, but can't afford the fees ... about 7-10 days before the event, call the sales office and see what they've got and don't be afraid to bargain them a bit. Might not be your ideal location or ideal stall size, but it might also be a great way to get your foot in the door at a much cheaper price.

Selling At Markets Successfully

One of the best ways to start generating word of mouth about your business, get immediate feedback about your products and start to make connections with local potential customers is to have a stall at a market. By "market" I mean a monthly farmer's market, a local school carnival, family fun day or other public event where you are invited to have a stall and sell your wares. You may choose to start out this way and as private orders grow, scale back the markets - or it may form part of your long-term selling and marketing plan. Either way, **I am a huge fan of starting out this way** if you can. If however you're not going about this in planned, smart way it can be an easy way to lose a heck of a lot of money and time. Events like these have some drawbacks, especially if the weather where you live is variable or the amount of people they are expecting don't turn up.

Here are my **top ten tips for successful selling at local markets** and events - and at the bottom, I've included a free resource for you to use next time you're planning your event.

1. **Check what the rules are** around selling publicly - I know more than one person who set up, only to be shut down moments later because they did not have the correct permits to be selling to the general public. Also, check the food laws where you live. Do things need to be labelled and if so, what information needs to be on those labels? Do you need to be insured? This is the kind of stuff you can't afford to screw up.

2. **Attend the event yourself first** and OPEN your eyes! Go on a recon mission and take notes (no I'm not kidding, write it down or you'll forget stuff.) Are there others selling similar things to what you want to sell? What kinds of people are coming? Are they the kinds of customers you

want to attract? Do they appear to be spending money, and if so, what are they buying? Which stalls seem to have a buzz around them, and WHY? Is the event of the calibre you thought it would be? How many people are there? What are the best positions for stalls?

3. **Be very clear about your cost-benefit analysis** - what is it going to cost you to do this event? Is there a fee for a permit, a fee for the event, will you need to buy extra packaging? Figure out the costs to attend before you say yes to it, then work out how many pieces you'll need to sell to break even. As a very simplified example, if it's going to cost you $1000, but your items sell at $2, you'll need to sell 500 to break even. Is that even realistic, given the numbers of people who come in the door? These events can and should be used for marketing and profile raising, but you've got to at the very least be aware of what it's costing you to do the event so you can decide if it's worth it.

4. **Not everyone will buy what you're selling**. I've heard people use stats like "only 10% of people will buy" but I've found that to be quite variable depending on the event and the product. For example, if it's a hot day and you sell popsicles at a family friendly event ... you'll do better than the 10%. Still, find out the numbers of people they expect, and make no more than enough for about 20% of those people. Example - they expect 1000 attendees, I would not make more than 200 cupcakes at maximum. You don't want your stall to look empty but far better to sell out than to have to re-pack the car with hundreds of cookies or cupcakes you have to throw out later.

5. **Don't only have one product available** - where possible, have a mix of products with a mix of uses. As an example, you might have: cupcakes which have a short shelf life and need to be eaten within a day, chocolate

covered strawberries which people will eat at the event, and boxes of cookies that people can take home later.

6. **Branding and marketing** - your stall is an extension of your brand and it should look like it! No dirty tablecloths, no grubby signage, no standing there picking your nose and looking bored. That's not the impression you want to give people.

7. **Use it as an educational tool** - have a few dummy cakes on display with a sign, "Did you know we also make custom birthday cakes?" and engage people in conversation about it! Or a sign, "All of our cakes are baked from scratch, no artificial ingredients and tons of love," and so on. This is a GREAT TIME to educate people. Use this as an opportunity to practice your marketing and talking to people, or bring someone along who is good at that and learn from them.

8. **Make it EASY for them to find you later** - give out business cards or some sort of freebie with your info on it, remind them that you're always here once a month, get them to visit your Facebook page and like it, etc. Make it so that people can EASILY FIND YOU when they want to outside of market days.

9. **Make it interactive:** 1) Take your online media offline: Encourage people to "check in", take a selfie with your product, create an event-specific hashtag they can use and so on. They need a way to remember you and getting them to DO something right then helps with that. OR, 2) Get them to enter a contest to win a kids' cake or some other product. You want them to get involved with you and your product. Make sure ALL of these people are signing up for your customer database. Easiest way to do that

is to give them an incentive - enter a draw, take a picture, etc.

10. **Listen, listen, listen to what is happening and watch, watch, watch what people do when you're there**. Be very mindful of what people say about the product, the price, what they want and so on. Markets are golden opportunities to find out more about your target market and what interests them. Encourage them to try new flavours by giving away free samples of 'trial' flavours and ASKING what they think about it. Did people need napkins, and you didn't have them? Was your stall getting ignored a lot? What kinds of things did people comment on about your stall? At the end of the event, keep track of how many you sold of each flavour and at the next event, make more of those and ditch the one or two which did not sell as well. Keep track of how many you sold this month at this event so that if you decide to do it monthly, you'll have a better idea of how many to make next time. Ask the organiser for info at the end - did they get as many people as they thought? Then USE all that research you gathered (write it down!!) to make your next market more successful.

I think markets are a wonderful way to get your business out there - and it can be a nice injection of cash flow as well. There are a few pitfalls to avoid but on the whole, they are wonderful and many food businesses started life out at local farmer's markets and events.

To help make the process of getting ready for selling at markets a little easier, I've created an event checklist which you will find on the website of this book (www. thebizofbaking.com/BestofBoB). This is a checklist of all the stuff you may need to take with you as you pack up to go to your event. It's also great to use as a guide to gather together all the bits and pieces you'll need to make selling at markets a success. Enjoy!

Wedding Fair Vendors: How To Become An Awesome Vendor

Tis the season ... for wedding fairs! If you are a cake maker who makes cakes for brides, chances are you've either been invited to or you want to go to a bridal fair to showcase your wares. The fairs can often be rather pricey to be involved with, so in this week's article, I'm sharing my top tips for getting maximum value out of attending wedding fairs.

Tip #1: Attend the fair yourself before signing up to be a vendor and go on a recon mission. See if your product will fit in there - are the other vendors of the same calibre as you are? What kinds of people are attending? What's happening at other stalls? Is it crowded? Empty? What was the marketing of the event like in the lead-up? Basically don't consider showing up to this event until you've thoroughly checked it out.

Tip #2: Grab a couple of business cards at the event of vendors you think are of the same style and calibre as you are. Call those vendors a little while after, explain that you really admired their booth and you're thinking of going and you wanted to know their thoughts on it. Find out if they got any business from it, if they think they would do it again, and any advice they might have for you.

Tip#3: Don't just put out a platter of samples and hide behind the table. Be picky about who you give samples to, and try to have a conversation with them before you give them one.

Tip #4: Make it very easy for them to book an appointment with you right there and then (offer it to them!) or if you've very brave and it's reasonable to do so, take a deposit right then and there. You can offer an incentive for this - anyone who books in for a consultation today gets free delivery (etc.)

Tip #5: Gather email addresses - do this by either asking, or offering a prize for which they need to register to win. Then after the fair, FOLLOW UP with these people via email. Within a week of the event, I'd be sending an email to them, and then once again 6 weeks or so later -you can again offer a special incentive if you like. Then add them to your normal mailing list so they are getting regular communication from you. Often the people at wedding fairs have a VERY long lead time on their event, and you can't expect them to remember you 18 months later. Since you should be tracking ALL your clients anyway by asking, "How did you hear about us?" - track this event too. If within 6-9 months not a single person books from you that was at that event, I'd consider not attending again.

Tip #6: If you give something away, try to make it more memorable than just a business card. A magnet, a company, branded bag of candies, a cake server, key chain, pen ... whatever you can afford which is more "keepable" than just a business card. Something they will hang onto rather than something they will recycle.

Tip #7: Involve social media to make your booth interactive. There are going to be lots of people doing a "enter to win" type of raffle - but how boring is that? Create a simple photo booth or have a funny cake and encourage them to take a selfie and upload it to social media with *#yourbusinessname* in order to win.

Tip #8: Do something which makes you stand out from the others and which makes an impression to OTHERS at the event. For example, if people can sample directly from the booth, give it to them in brightly coloured cups or bright coloured forks so people walking around will see it and want to know where the heck all the red forks are coming from. Tie a balloon to the fork - whatever it takes really, to create some buzz around your booth.

Tip #9: Make sure everything about your business actually talks the talk and walks the walk. If you're high-end, your booth needs to look it AND SO DO your website and social media account so that when they check you out later, it's consistent. Also, YOU need to look good and exemplify all your company is about. Don't show up in jeans and a t-shirt and think you're making a good impression. Branding, branding, branding - on everything! Make your booth visually appealing AND useful for the client - perhaps a photo album with more designs, a beautifully printed menu of flavours you offer, maybe price the dummy cakes so people can get an idea of how much they would spend with you and how many those examples would feed.

Tip #10: If you suck at talking to people, take along a friend or family member that is chatty and get them to break the ice, then hand the couple over to you for more detailed talk about appointments and cake. You do not want to go to the event and either hide behind a tall cake or just stand there with a tray of samples looking awkward. You need to do your best to have conversations with people because they'll remember the chat they had with you.

Wedding fairs often cost a lot to do, so if you're watching your marketing budget be selective about the ones you attend. Don't feel like you have to go to ALL of them in your area. For everyone I meet that says the wedding fair they went to was great and they booked a ton of work, I meet someone else who says it was a complete waste of time and money and they would never do it again. Don't stress if it wasn't a success for you the first time around - different events have a different vibe so it's worth trying out a few before deciding which to keep going to and which to ditch. Lastly, wedding fairs are a GREAT place to network, get marketing ideas, and check out your competition and what they've got on offer.

Networking for Cakers

We've all heard the expression, "it's not what you know, it's who you know," and that statistic about something like 80% of job ads never being advertised publicly. So we all know that networking is a part of business these days (and always has been, long before the concept of formal "networking" became a thing). When I think of "networking" I immediately think of a bunch of people in a room, standing around awkwardly holding onto their drinks and business cards[24] for dear life. Maybe it's just me, but I'd rather airbrush my eyeballs with disco dust than network in that way. The last time I went to one of those networking events, I was standing around SO awkwardly that one of the other participants asked me to go get her a drink ... because she thought I was one of the wait staff. (True story - I actually did go and get her the drink, mostly because I was mortified. The look on her face when I then sat down at her table was priceless. Then she was the mortified one. I laughed it off with her, though. I mean, it's not her fault I'm awkward and look like a waitress.)

If the idea of networking fills you with dread, please know that there are ways to network with people which do not involve awkward drink holding. Most of you are probably doing it already to some degree. Networking is really just a fancy word for getting to know people - it's just the 'word of mouth' of the industry. Any time you're posting in a Facebook group for your local area, that's networking. If you go to an event like a decorating class, Cake Camp or a local small business course and meet people there, that's networking. If you sent an email to someone whose work you admire, that's also networking. If you establish a good working relationship with your suppliers, you're also networking with them. If you re-

---

24   See *You Make Awesome Cake. And. Now. What?* in Chapter 1.

tweeted, re-posted, or shared someone's work, that's also networking (but you've got to tag them in it so they know you've made the connection). Networking is

just all the different ways you widen your circle of acquaintances and get to know more people in and around your business. The key here is to actively network by actively reaching out to people.

If you're trying to network with a specific type of person, there are a few ways to do this - either attend an event specific to that kind of person (like an industry networking night) or just approach that kind of person directly. As an example, if you're looking to network with and establish relationships with wedding venues, you might consider attending a local wedding fair. Whether you attend as a consumer or as an exhibitor, you can network! Make it part of your plan for that event to introduce yourself to the vendors that are there. Say hello, introduce yourself, give them a business card when and if it's appropriate. Don't forget to follow up with them after the fact, because yours is not the only card they got that day. Another option for that same group of wedding venues would be to make a list of venues you want to work with and call them. Introduce yourself over the phone and make an appointment to bring them some samples and brochures. That's networking, too -but it's 1:1 networking rather than event networking.

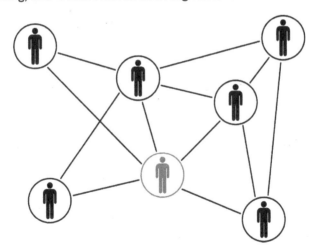

Networking does require a bit of bravery - you will need to reach out to the people you are interested in. They key is to network in a way which works for you. Me, I'd rather network on a smaller scale, either one on one or with group of very specific people (I can't deal with the awkward drinks thing). The other thing about networking is that you've got to be willing to connect the dots. So the people in my network know that I might call and ask, "Hi Jane, do you know any good logo designers?" but they also know that they can call and ask me for referrals, too. I'll call that logo designer and say, "Hi Sarah. Jane sent me, she highly recommends you," and that immediately establishes a little bit of rapport for us because we have Jane in common. I also will occasionally recommend something out of the blue to people in my network. "Hi Jane, I just used this amazing florist and I know you're always looking for good floral suppliers, you should check this company out." In other words, you've got to connect the dots, because one connection leads to another, which leads to another which leads to another. All or none of those connections might be useful to you, but you've got to <u>make them in the first place</u>.

Networking for cake makers is the same at networking in other industries, it's really about making genuine connections with people, but then maintaining that connection into the future. We all lead busy lives (actually I think we all suffer from Busy Disease!) and so the onus is on you to make the connection and keep the connection going. Putting in a bit of effort with human interactions almost always pays off in a big way. It's important to also remember that networking is not just with cake makers - it's connecting with business people in other industries. Through networking, I've made some fantastic connections with people who have nothing to do with cake but who had IT skills, legal skills, admin skills and so on.

Big Obvious Thing: Good networking is just like good marketing, only it's business to business as opposed to business to customer. You've got to follow up, do it genuinely, and make it a part of your business skill set.

CHAPTER 9

SOCIAL MEDIA

Social media is one of the most exciting and fun tools we as small business owners have available to us. It's interactive, it's immediate, it's fun to do. The downside of social media is that it's interactive (so we get trolls and people saying stupid stuff which upsets us), it's immediate (so we are constantly distracted by it) and it's fun to do (so we avoid other jobs because we're sucked into the social media vortex).

I am an enormous fan of social media and in part it's what has grown our industry as rapidly as it's grown. We can now share our creations across the globe with the click of a button, we can collaborate with friends we may never meet in person and we can share our skills with people who might not have access to us otherwise. The biggest mistake I think cake companies make with social media is relying on it too heavily, often at the expense of local marketing. Your marketing should incorporate social media not be entirely driven by it. It's part of the bigger picture, not the only picture. While it's nice validation to see those numbers go up, ultimately it's of no use to us if we cannot sell products to those numbers. There are ways to maximise the use of social media for small business and I cover that in this chapter.

Social Media 101 For Bakers And Decorators

Social media is one of those things us bakers and decorators love to do, because it's fun, you get immediate feedback, and you can pretend to yourself that what you're doing on there is real work. While it is definitely fun, most of us don't fully appreciate how powerful of a tool social media is and how to best use it for maximum marketing effect. In a nutshell, here's what's boring but important to know about it: posting on social media should be part of your overall marketing plan - meaning it needs to have a defined purpose, follow a plan (at least a little bit!), be consistently done and it has to be measurable. Wow, way to take the fun out of it, right?! I promise you that social media can be both fun AND effective - and I'll post more about this in future. For today I'm going to cover the 5 most frequently asked questions, I get about social media.

"Social media" just means posting on Facebook, right?

Nope. "Social media" as a whole really refers to all of those online platforms where people are creating and sharing content - in other words, think of it like the different digital places you might hang out with your friends. There are lots of social media platforms but they include places like Facebook, Google+, twitter, Instagram, Pinterest, Reddit, YouTube, Ello, Cakes Decor . . . and so on (there are WAY more (https://en.wikipedia.org/wiki/List_of_social_networking_websites), but you get the idea ... did you know there is one called *Cucumbertown*?!)

Do I need to have my business on all of those platforms? That seems like a lot of work!

No, you don't. You really should only be on those platforms that a) your clients are likely to use and b) you enjoy using. It IS a lot of work being across all of those places so here's my advice on how to control it all:

1. Reserve your company name/place on every social media site you can even if you don't intend to use that platform (to protect you from others getting it).

2. Pick 2-3 platforms that you know your clients are likely to use. This is based on who they are - for example, you hardly find teenagers under 18 on Facebook these days but you DO find mothers of small children. Also, make sure those platforms are ones you enjoy posting to or are good at using (for example, I suck at twitter and my customers aren't there, so that's not one I'd pick right now).

3. Set up a plan to consistently create and share high-quality content on those platforms. Seriously. KILL IT on there for a set period of time, I usually recommend 1-3 months for real results and that's ongoing, good quality content (more on that coming soon).

4. Once you're up and running on those platforms - and they are consistently doing well for you (the numbers are going up, potential clients talk about your pages and so on) then think about adding in another platform.

Should I pay for ads? Why should I have to? Facebook is KILLING small business with this whole "pay to be seen" stuff. It's not fair!

First, stop whining. Facebook is a business. Businesses are there to make money. Mark Zuckerberg and his college buddies have absolutely ZERO interest in spending millions on running a business just so you can have a free and easy way to talk to your clients. Like ALL forms of advertising and media, if you want to be seen - you'll need to pay a bit extra for that service. Want a bigger ad in the local paper, a colourful and glossy business card, a TV ad on prime time? You're going to pay more for it. EXACTLY like we expect clients to pay a bit more in order to get a bit more quality, social media platforms are no different. If you want it for free or cheap, you're going to get what they offer at the free or cheap end and often what you get isn't all that fabulous. (Do I need to say it? Good cake isn't cheap ...)

Do I think you HAVE to pay for ads on social media? No. I think if you've got a budget for advertising, then YES some of it should probably be spent there - but you're not going to want to just boost some random post and hope for the best. You're going to need to get a bit of education about how those ads work so that you're investing your money wisely. Do I think you need a budget for marketing and advertising in the first place? Of course I do - but you knew that.

Should I allow customers to communicate with me through Facebook messages or Instagram messages? What about things like WhatsApp or BBM?

Personally, I don't think you should allow this - but I do know that in some Asian countries, it's very normal to conduct business via WhatsApp and BBM. I'm still not a huge fan of it, because there is nothing about Facebook Messenger, which says, "good customer service, " to me. I can't imagine a high-end car company or luxury handbag company conducting transactions through Facebook. Also, I've noticed that people tend to forget about those messages really quickly and easily. They miss the notification that you replied or it goes into their "others" folder and so on ... and the conversation just sorta dies. I recommend turning that function off entirely and making sure that it's VERY obvious on your page how people can find you. Your profile on ALL platforms should have a web address and a phone number, plus email if it fits.

Why do I need a website? I get all my orders from Facebook anyway, isn't that good enough? Web pages seem like an unnecessary expense and also, I'm not that great at technology so honestly, it just seems really daunting to do it.

I can't stress this one enough: YOU NEED A WEBSITE because YOU DO NOT OWN FACEBOOK. Someone else owns it, someone else controls it, someone else makes the rules, someone else can TURN IT OFF and delete everything you've got on there right this very second if they feel like it. Do you really want to have your entire business platform in the hands of someone else? All that work and effort ... and you have no say in what happens to it (ask any of the people whose pages recently got deleted what this feels like). Me, I want control over my own business online and while I love and adore social media, there's no way I'd put all my eggs in that one basket. As for websites being expensive and hard to do (etc., etc.) - you can either do it yourself with very user-friendly platforms like Wix (www.wix.com

), or you can be a grown up and outsource this to someone else. A website is a legitimate business expense and should be included as part of your start-up costs. You can get a pretty decent website these days for under $1000. The key is to GET ONE started and not worry too much about it being sparkly and perfect. Lastly, the last time you went and shopped for something, I'm guessing you started your search at Google - not at Facebook. So unless someone remembers you and types in your exact business name, they aren't going to find you easily. If however they go to Google and put in "wedding cakes Pittsburgh" - you'll come up because you've got a website all about the amazing wedding cakes you're making in Pittsburgh. If that in itself isn't a good enough reason to have a website of some kind, I don't know what is.

Confused in Cakeland – Is a Website Necessary?

Confused in Cakeland

Dear Michelle,

Do I really need a website? Isn't a Facebook page enough? Most of my business comes from Facebook and I'm running this business on a shoestring as it is.

Signed,

Confused in Cakeland

Dear Confused in Cakeland,

No, a Facebook page is not enough for you to run a real business from. There are two reasons for this:

1. *Not all of your clients and potential clients are on Facebook and as it's grown in size, it's getting harder and harder to be found on there organically.*

2. *If Facebook crashes tomorrow, so does your way of communicating with your clients. Can you afford to have you one method of communication be so vulnerable?*

So - get yourself a website. They are cheap, quick, and when you have more time and money to invest in them you can make them better - but for now, at bare minimum it needs to have your business name and logo as well as your name, contact details, and some details about your products and how to buy them.

Yours in Cyberworld,

Michelle

Website Essentials

If you're going to be even vaguely legitimate, it's not negotiable.

There are tons of free/cheap platforms you can do it on – Weebly, Wix, Squarespace, WordPress. You don't need to spend a fortune on it, however there are some things I think are absolutely essential to website content. You will expand on these over time and add more as needed – in the meantime here's a guide to website content.

Your first website will likely only be a single, static page:

- A page which clearly states: what it is your business offers, where your business is located, if you have opening hours and what they are and *how to get in touch with you (email, phone number).*

- A few (1-4) pictures which show your current work in their best light.

- Links to any social media accounts you may have.

- Link to sign up to your newsletter[25] (even if you don't have one yet. Start collecting email addresses from the very first minute your website is online.).

Your next website improvement will have all of the above plus:

- An "about me" page – several studies have shown this is the second most read page on a small business website. This is where you can make an emotional connection with the customer. I got a LOT of orders

---

25   See *Do I Need A Business Newsletter* in Chapter 9.

because people liked knowing that by buying from me, they were helping out "the triplet Mom."

- A "contact me" page that has a way for them to submit a form online and also asks them to tell you how/where they heard about you.

- Allergen info and disclaimers – this is especially important if you offer gluten free, dairy free (etc.).

- More photos – but please, don't just throw every photo you have on there. They must be current and they must be good quality. No pictures of cakes in boxes! It's far better to have a few beautiful photos then a ton of crappy ones. Also, your cake skills will improve with time,so update those photos to reflect your current skill and style. Here's some great classes about taking photos:

  - Food Photography Basics - http://www.craftsy.com/ext/ MichelleGreen_4726_CP;

  - Product Photography at Home - http://www.craftsy.com/ext/ MichelleGreen_5069_CP; and

  - Photos with Your Smartphone - http://www.craftsy.com/ext/ MichelleGreen_5322_CP.

Now we've got a solid website, let's start adding in some good stuff to improve the customer experience:

- Your terms and conditions IN FULL. This is so you can give people a reference to go read rather than hand them a ten page document when they give you a deposit.

- Important info about your product – your flavour range, your price range, how to store the product, where it's available (if you have outlets).

- Important info about working with you – how far in advance do they need to order? Do they need to pay a deposit? Some of this might repeat from your terms and conditions, but it's the stuff about how they order from you so that's important to repeat.

- Testimonials or Press mentions – if people think you're great, tell everyone about it!

- More photos, now categorised in albums – wedding, cookies, birthday and so on.

Once you've got all that in place, you can start adding in things like this (if they are relevant):

- A blog.[26]

- Online ordering of products.

- A pop up window inviting them to join your newsletter list with a freebie as an incentive (hint: make it a useful freebie not just something random).

- FAQ – this is a nicer version of important info on how to work with you. It's like a Top Ten of the questions people as you the most often and the things they'll look for first.

- Class info if you teach (and a way for them to sign up!)

In this busy digital social media world, we can be deceived into thinking we don't need a website. Many people started and grew their businesses on Facebook – but in my opinion, that's not a long term strategy for business success. When you don't have a storefront, your website IS your storefront, so keep it clean, tidy, and

---

26   See *Does My Cake Business Need A Blog* in Chapter 9.

a clear representation of your business. Exactly like a store, make sure you go in and dust things and refresh the look once in a while too! (Get rid of those photos from when your piping was terrible!)

You don't need to have all the fancy photos which fade in and out, or the music that starts playing when people visit (god no, PLEASE don't do that!). **You need a solid, informative, <u>mobile friendly</u> website that shows the customer what they want and instils in them a feeling of trust that you'll be able to give them exactly that.**

Breaking Up Is Hard To Do

Henry Ford said, *"It has been my observation that most people get ahead during the time that others waste ..."* - and that quote really embodies the point of today's post. Today's post is intended to get you thinking about where your time as a business owner is best spent, and share with you the hard lesson I learned about this.

Being connected to other bakers and other cake makers online is a wonderful, wonderful thing ... until it turns evil and/or begins to suck up your time in an unhealthy way.

Which it sometimes does, unfortunately.

I adore that I've made some fabulous baking and cake friends through social media and online avenues. I've learned from them, taught some of them in return, and shared inspiration with them. The online cake community can be pretty awesome.

But ... (and you knew that was coming, didn't you?)

Not so long ago, I was a member of a few online cake groups, because like all of you I considered it a fantastic resource and support system, and because owning a small business can be a lonely place. One group mushroomed into two, which mushroomed into three. Then I realised that I was always telling my friends and family about what was happening on the forums ("Can you believe that she said ... and then these other people said ... and then ..."). I realised that I was getting hurt by what people had said, even if it wasn't said directly to me and even if I didn't know these people in real life. I realised I was spending two or more an hours day on cake forums - even more if I had free time in the evening or weekends. I spent time 'liking' other cake businesses, getting involved with "tagging Tuesdays" and sitting by watching as forum threads got longer and longer and sometimes meaner and meaner. I found myself really caring what other cake makers thought about my work. I'd post a picture with some ridiculous self-deprecating comment like, "This is my first time making a 3D car cake, be nice!" or "Of course I look at it and only see the flaws!" and then checking back endlessly to see what "people" had said.

Still, those forums were kinda fun, you know? And then ...

I went to a modelling chocolate class where one of the women confided in me that she was actually afraid to show up at all, because one of the other students had threatened (in a forum) to beat her up had they ever met in real life. I read one of my "friends" in forums calling me a "selfish, unreasonable bitch" because an expensive class my company was hosting had a no refunds policy. I answered someone's question about fondant by recommending my favourite brand and then a cake maker felt she needed to let me (and everyone else) know that she, "would not piss on a cake made with XYZ brand". All this - and more - happens in forums which claim to be supportive. Sad, isn't it? Somehow, being one of the popular crowd didn't seem quite so fun any more - I didn't want to be a part of a community where people are actually afraid to go to a class and some people are nothing more than thinly-fondant-covered school yard bullies.

Yes, absolutely, the online cake community can be great. It can educate you, empower you, support you, and be a valuable source of information - but here's what I began to ask myself after those experiences:

- If I wasn't spending time in these forums, what would I be doing to make my business better? Truly, as a business owner, could my time be better spent?

- Does it matter what other cake makers think of me or my work? Aren't I in business for my clients, not for my colleagues?

- Is it worth the emotional energy it's taking up? Why am I always talking about online people to real life people?

- My business Facebook page is meant to be an avenue through which I move my business forward ... so why am I using it to make "friends"? Shouldn't my personal page be for that purpose?

- Are there ways I can further my cake education without having to get involved in online drama?

I found myself pondering these questions often enough that I eventually decided to entirely cut off my forum-based involvement in the cake world. The time I spent there was doing <u>nothing</u> to advance the bigger picture of my business, was causing drama and heartache I had no time for, and frankly, my time was much better spent elsewhere. I literally left every single group or forum I was in, "unfriended" cake people who were not my actual friends, and now my business page only "likes" suppliers or businesses it directly works with.

Personally, I still look at and admire my competition (of course) but I don't comment there unless it's to say "great work!" when I admire something. Now when I have a cake question? I either Google it to find an online tutorial or email/call a cake friend - you know, the ones who are actual, real people - not bullies hiding behind keyboards.

I am IN BUSINESS. Moving that business forward is the one thing I need to spend my time on. Watching people tear other people's work to shreds just isn't helping my business (no matter how much we all love to see a train wreck of a cake).

Did I miss being a part of the groups? Sure. For about five minutes. Honestly, it was more painful hitting the "leave group" button than it was to actually not be there. For those five minutes, I missed the gossip, feeling like I was a part of the "in" crowd, and hearing about what was going on out there in the wider cake world. Are there times I wish I was still a part of those groups? Rarely. You make a choice to either be involved or not be involved and I choose to use my time better elsewhere. From a social media point of view, I made the same decision - this is MY business, these are MY rules, I'm here to serve MY CLIENTS (not other bakers) - and so I made the choice to turn off the group interaction.

You know, it's an incredibly liberating thing to step away from the time and energy sucking "community" and instead concentrate on your actual business. It's also wonderful to realise that you can learn, grow and be supported and NOT NEED to be in a single Facebook group or other online chat room.

Sounds scary, right? If you need some reassurance that your success or ability has nothing to do with your involvement in online cake communities? Name the top ten well-known decorators you admire and tell me if ANY of them are hanging out in chat rooms. Why are they absent? Because they are running a business and probably aren't interested in or have time for hanging out around the proverbial water cooler.

Like I said, I still read articles, look at cake pictures, watch tutorials and so on - I just no longer immerse myself in the group bit of it because it's just not helping my business. I'm not sure this is the right thing for **you** to do. Honestly, it might be helping you a whole lot. I'm not one to say what works for you. I'm simply pointing out that cake groups are great until. . . they aren't so great. Or until you outgrow them, or they take over your thoughts a bit too often, or they become the place you go to for reassurance. What I'm really asking you to do is look at how you spend your time and ask yourself: what am I getting out of it, and is what I'm getting really worth it?

For me the answer was simple, I had to let go of the outside "community" of cake people and build the inside community of my own business. Was it scary to let go of that community? Yeah. A little. Was it worth it? Oh, **hell yeah!**

Believe me when I say that I am WAY more productive now than I ever was when I was a member of all those cake forums.

Need proof of that? <u>You're reading it</u>. I'm choosing to spend my time writing this blog and helping my business and my community instead of getting involved in petty arguments over which fondant brand is best.

I don't need to even question if it's a better use of my time.

Social Media Overwhelm – My Social Media Experiment

I sometimes get social media fatigue even though I love being online.

Some days I'm just tired of all the endless status updates, content creation and needing to be "ON" every single day of the week. This happens a lot with social media, either because we have FOMO (fear of missing out) or because we think we "have to" be doing a million things on our social media accounts in order for them to be effective. Be on this! Be on that! Update! Update! Update!

When I teach people about social media, the first thing I make a point of saying is that **we live in an incredibly noisy digital space**. Sadly, this means you not only need to talk louder but also **WAY more often** in order to be heard above the cacophony of tweets, likes, shares and follows. It's simply not enough to be loud. You've now got to talk more often than the others do, too.

I decided to test out that theory using my preferred platform - Facebook - as well as 4 other platforms (Google+, Pinterest, twitter, Instagram). Normally I would post 7 days a week, twice a day - 14 a week. I noticed that a page I admire was posting no less than EIGHT times a day (that's 56 posts a week, or a new post every 3 HOURS!) so I decided to see if it was worth making that kind of effort. I couldn't manage that kind of output so instead I decided to double mine, to 4 post a day across those 4 platforms plus as much as I could manage on Instagram (so minimum of 28 per platform). I also decided to give this experiment 3 months and see what would happen in that time.

Result: My following across ALL platforms increased significantly as did my reach, shares, newsletter sign ups and so on. It did not happen overnight, but it definitely happened (I know, I watched the numbers go up). In that time, I also did a lot of work on increasing my online visibility via guest blogging, interviews and other profile-raising activities. I have to say that while I'm happy with the result because my theory proved correct, it also saddened me about how sheer volume alone (let alone good quality volume, because I don't like to just put crap out there!) is <u>required</u> to get any traction. It was also interesting to see that in order of effectiveness, out of the 5 platforms, Facebook was best for me while Google+ was the least effective.

What does this mean for you? It means that if you want to be using social media as an effective marketing tool, you can't just throw up a post every once in a while and hope for the best. No, I don't think you need to do it as much as I did, but I think small business really needs at least a post a day and that post needs to be a good quality one (more on that in a future blog post).

The second thing I tell people about social media is - you don't need to be on EVERY platform that pops up. You need to pick your platforms (the ones your potential clients hang out on) and ROCK those platforms rather than be a little bit on everyone. So for me, based on that experiment - I'd ditch Google+ and see about doing better on the platforms that performed best (for me that was Facebook and Pinterest).

What happens when a new platform comes along? A few months ago I started to use Periscope - not going to lie, I started using it because a whole lot of business mentors I follow use it, and it started to get a whole lot of attention from people I admire. Periscope (for those new to it) is an app that allows you to live stream from your phone - it's just live video that people can interact with by typing into their phone. Broadcasts (or 'scopes') remain live on the app for 24 hours and after that are gone. As the creator of a video, you can choose to keep it and then upload it to YouTube, use it on your website and so on. So for a few weeks there I LOVED Periscope ... and then I very quickly realised that it's a MAJOR time suck. It became totally overwhelming to need to broadcast daily, come up with a topic, make sure I looked halfway normal, watch other people's scopes and so on. I also started to get really overwhelmed with all the scopes I wanted to watch, because several times a day my phone would ping to let me know someone I followed was live broadcasting. I ended up spending WAY too much time watching scopes about everything from how to make more money online to how to make guacamole. (Not kidding, and I already know how to make "guac".)

In short, **I got Periscope fatigue really quickly** and so I've hesitated to jump back on it again. I do think there are plenty of my potential customers on there so I'm going to get back to it - but not until I've worked out some sort of plan for how often I'd like to broadcast so that it does not get out of hand again. For right now, I don't see a massive amount of marketing value in Periscope for those of you making cakes for your local area ... but it's a new platform and I suspect this will evolve as time goes on. It also requires a very high degree of visibility; you can't hide when it's just your face on a video screen talking to people. The visibility factor alone will stress many of you out (if you prefer to hide behind the cake, Periscope is your kryptonite).

What does this mean for you? It can be tempting to jump on board every single platform that comes out (and lord there are a lot of them!) My advice remains the same - see what platforms are out there, poke around a bit with them, but if they either don't suit your style or your clients don't hang out there - don't do them. You will not miss out on anything - because one of the beauties of social media is that most people are across more than one platform, so if they can't find you on one they'll find you on another.

So many platforms, so little time ... choose yours wisely because time is something we all need more of but can't get (unlike social media platforms, which we do not need more of but we can get more).

Marketing Your Business On Social Media

Last week I spoke to you about feeling overwhelmed by social media[27] and many of you asked, "But how do I know what to post? I know I need to market my business on social media, but what do I talk about?" Coming up with content for social media or a small business blog can be daunting when you don't have many orders (so no pictures of cakes to post) or you're just starting out. Trying to think of stuff to say can be as time-consuming as the time it takes to post.

I'm going to give you a few ideas for what to post to market your business on social media, but before I do let me remind you that **your business social media pages are designed to serve your customer or potential customers**. So before posting anything at all, you've got to be quite clear on who that is and with each post ask yourself, "Is this of any use or interest to my customers?" As an example, suppose you make wedding cakes for the local area. If you're posting videos of YouTube cake tutorials on your business page, how is that helping your customers or potential customers? Since they are not cake decorators, they are unlikely to be interested in or see value in cake technique tutorials. Similarly, if you're a local cake business, don't post funny memes about dealing with difficult clients - not only is that of no interest to them but you don't really want to "complain" about clients ... to clients!

REMEMBER THIS: Everything you post on social media has got to be with your brand and your customer in mind.

---

27   See *Social Media Overwhelm – My Social Media Experiment* in Chapter 9

So keeping those people in mind, here are some suggestions of what to post on social media:

- Pictures of cakes you've made with the testimonial from the client

- Close ups on details you are proud of (and that will be interesting to clients -not 20 photos of a single petal.)

- "Behind the scenes" pictures your workspace (note: PLEASE take these pictures carefully. No cats, no kids, no disgusting bench tops!)

- Shout outs to other local businesses you work with (venues, florists, kid's play centres)

- Links to relevant articles that you have written or others have - and by relevant I don't mean "hottest celebrity couples 2014" I mean articles about party planning, wedding cake trends, and local suppliers.)

- Links to your other social media accounts - "Have you seen us on Instagram?"

- Links to products you sell online (if you sell tutorials, etc.)

- Info about your business they may not know, "Did you know we also rent out cake stands?" and include a picture of those other products/services

- Info about your product they may not know, "Did you hear there is an egg shortage in the US? At (business name) we only use free range eggs in our cakes and we get them from the local farm. "

- Links back to your website - "Have you seen the updated wedding cake photo gallery on the website?"

- Ask them to sign up to your newsletter with a link to do so

- Pictures of you at events - "Here we are all set up at the Amazing Wedding Fair!"

- Pictures of you in action, for example, putting a flower on a cake at a venue, rolling out some fondant, etc.

- Updates on your calendar and availability - ""We currently have dates available in November, so please get in touch by calling us on (phone number) to secure your tasting."

- General info that new people will not have seen - "Welcome to the (company name) Facebook page! We are an (insert what you do) company located in (place you do it.) We (insert reason why you're awesome) and we look forward to creating something special for your next event! We can be reached by (contact info)."

- Ask a question - "My favourite flavour is cookies and cream. What do you like?", "I recently made this cake in navy and gold and blue is my favourite colour. What's your favourite colour for cakes?"

Pro Tip: Start to build up a library of images you can use for those days when you really can't think of much to say. When you're taking pictures, resist the urge to post every single one up at the same time and instead start to build up that library. Take lots of pictures when you have no immediate need for them, solely for the purpose of library building.

In the above list, there are 14 items - which means you can do one of those a day for 2 weeks and never need to stop and think about the kind of content you're going to put on each day. That being said not everyone sees every single thing you post (on ANY platform, crazy algorithms or not) so don't be afraid to repeat the same type of posts more than once in a week. For example, in a given week you might have 3-4 cake pictures, not just the one.

Sitting and wondering, "I know I have to market my business on social media but I have no idea what to talk about," isn't doing you or your business much good. Print this list out (or bookmark it for later) so that when you're stuck for an idea you can come back and use one of these. I also encourage you to come up with some of your own!

Confused In Cakeland - How Do I Deal With Trolls On My Facebook Page?

Hi Michelle,

I have a question for you. I have had a negative comment on my page about one of my cakes and upon investigation, I worked out it was a local cake decorator and a couple of other competitors who liked it. How would you handle this? Thanks.

Signed,

Confused in Cakeland

Hey there Confused,

Facebook has a "delete comment and ban user" button for a reason. Use it. It's your page, so it's your rules.

How I handle it emotionally? I generally gnash my teeth a bit, tell a few friends about those losers, then remember that I'm in business for myself, my family, and my customers. I'm here to serve those people, not serve trolls. I'm better off spending my time hitting delete and moving on than I am dwelling on it. I've got WAY more important people who need me.

((Hugs)) because it sucks that these type of people are out there with nothing

better to do.

Michelle

Social Media Etiquette

The Business of Baking Facebook page (http://www.facebook.com/bizbake)
is an interesting one, because it's newsfeed is not cluttered with all my friends
and personal likes (seriously, how many times a day does the Nutella company
post? Good thing I love Nutella.) Therefore, the newsfeed is only filled with
baking companies of every shape and size, and in recent weeks I've seen so many
wonderful and not-so-wonderful posts from those companies (stop cringing, I'm
not going to name and shame.) I also recently asked you all if you thought having
a rant was ever acceptable on a business page - and an overwhelming majority
of the responders said NO, it's not acceptable. But, geez, there are a LOT of rants
happening out there!

Here are my thoughts on social media etiquette for business (any business, not
just baking businesses) and some top tips for how to get it to work better for you.

DON'T:

- Overshare. Be real, be authentic, be you - just don't let it all hang out. An
  occasional post about your cute cat or a picture of you and your kids is
  great and gives your page a personal touch, but we really don't want to
  know that you're having a pap smear or your ex-husband is a loser. Oh,
  and we also don't know and don't care if your business is making you
  tired, stressed or broke. It's *always* rainbow sprinkles in there, right? (Or
  at least, you want your customers to think so.)

- Don't rant. Ever. Turn whatever that situation was around, make it into a
  (reasonable) company policy then nicely, kindly inform people of the new
  policy without saying stuff like, "Because there are people who ruin it for
  everyone, I am now ... " or "Unfortunately there are jerks which make this
  necessary, so ... "

- Don't post pictures of cakes before they have been delivered or picked
  up. I really don't like the whole 'sneak peek' thing for a paying customer's
  order, it serves no legitimate purpose. I don't see a problem with sneak
  peeks it if it's cakes for charity or collaborations. I just don't think you
  should do it for paid orders. Frankly, the time you're spending posting
  sneak peeks can be spent making that cake even more awesome, and
  what we do is MAGIC to our customers, so stop showing people what is
  behind the smoke and mirrors. A magician never reveals her methods.

- Nobody likes to feel like they are being sold to, so if you are constantly
  overtly selling stuff, it tends to turn people off your page very quickly.

Sure, offer stuff for sale - just not on every single post and for heaven's sake do NOT beg.

- Don't name and shame. Deal with the unpleasant stuff on your own, on the quiet, in a professional manner. Naming and shaming gives the bad guys more attention and just associates you with them even more.

- Don't open your page to other people to share their products on your page unless it is a sharing or community page. The ONLY exception is if you sell tutorials to other decorators, then you might want to allow shares of people showing off the cakes they made using those tutorials but otherwise your page pretty much needs to be about you and your product ONLY (plus a bit of fluff.) Don't allow your competitors any space on your page. That's prime real estate in front of your clients, and you're giving it to the other guy?!

DO:

- Remember what the purpose of your Facebook page is and who it's target market is, then act accordingly. As an example, if you sell macaroons to private clients - post about your new flavours, tell them where they can buy your stuff, run a 'name our macaroon' competition, etc.

- If your page's purpose is to influence existing clients to purchase again, showcase your wares to potential clients, or basically be another way to stay in touch with clients - make it about what you can do for them and build a relationship with them. It's a place to show what you and your company stand for and are all about. Your page and it's pictures and posts should be a direct reflection of the values you hold and your company stand for.

- If it's community or sharing page or that's a big part of what your page is for - have some guidelines which you publish and which you actually enforce so it does not become some sort of horrible cesspool of bitchy keyboard warriors. Your page, your rules. Always. There is a "ban user" button for a reason.

- Check out the Facebook 'Insights' page and work out when your followers are reading your stuff. Post at those times (Facebook even lets you time/date your posts into the future). You'll get more traction that way. No point posting at 3 am if nobody is awake to see it. I read somewhere that the average Facebook post has a "life span" of 6 hours. Posting at 3 am means it's dead by 9 am and there are not nearly enough people up in those hours who care what you're posting about even if you worked on that cake for a week straight.

- Don't just post stuff willy-nilly, or post a bunch of stuff sometimes and nothing else other days. Consistency - as with ALL MARKETING - is key to getting people to become part of your tribe.

- Ask people to do stuff - so use the instructions "like this" or "share this" or whatever you want them to do, as more interaction will get you more reach. Humans like to be told what to do. Don't be all demanding about it, though. Recently my business page had a status update which said, "If you love us and what we do, please like this post, share a photo of ours, or tell your friends about us. I really appreciate the support!" It was seen by over 50% of our likers and got a jillion likes ... which is WAY more than usual. Notice I did not demand. I asked in a nice, sincere way.

- Stop whining about Facebook making you pay for posts. It's not free anymore. Get over it. Add paid Facebook ads to your marketing plan and budget and get smart about the best ways to do it. Facebook IS A BUSINESS that wants to make money, and so do you. Stop complaining about it. They have a right to run their business as a money making venture and you, my friend, are their customer who needs them more than they need you. It's not great (because we all remember when it was free) but it's the way forward. Either jump on board or get off the train.

- Post GOOD content which varies, not a ton of content which is all the same (or crappy). A mixture of things - perhaps some talking about new products, maybe a funny (but relevant and not offensive) meme, start a fun competition, ask people for opinions, tell them about a new product you're trialling, whatever. You've got to capture their attention in their news feed and this is getting harder and harder to do, so get better at it!

If you remember nothing else, please remember this: Your Facebook page - which for many of you is your only business website - **is exactly like having a shopfront**. If you would not say those words to a client standing in front of you, OR you would not yell those things into a megaphone while standing at the front door of your shop, DON'T post it as a status update.

We forget that while social media might be quick and (mostly) free, it's not private. Your customers and potential customers *are watching*. Make sure you look in the mirror and pull your undies out of the back of your dress *before* leaving the house ... and always check yourself before hitting the post button.

What NOT To Share On Social Media

Last week I talked to you about the kinds of things you can talk about on social media[28] - and today, I'd like to talk to you about the kinds of things you SHOULDN'T talk about on social media.

"Authenticity" is a term that gets used a lot in the online world, we talk about how we all need to be honest, put it all out there, be ourselves and share our stories with the world. Mostly, I agree with this and I especially think it's important for small business. Our customers LOVE to hear the story behind the business. Did you know that the "About" page is the second most read page on any website (after the home page)? When we own a small business, we can't help but let our personality come through in our emails, our social media updates and to some degree our product. I'm fairly sure nobody would say that my style in real life or in cake is girly and delicate! That being said, no, **I don't think we should let it all just hang out** there for the world to see.

So how do you balance "being yourself" with being professional?

Whenever I'm not sure if I should share something - which is often as I am notorious for having a big mouth - I ask myself one simple question:

If this person were to walk into my store, would I say this out loud to them?

That's it. Is what you're about to say online something you would say to a real human standing right in front of you? If the answer is "no" then there's your answer - don't post it. If your answer is "yes" then go ahead. If your answer is, "I might, but I'm worried they will be offended. I'm really not sure," then my advice is to keep that one to yourself and find something else to talk about OR find another way to word it so it's not offensive. Sure, some people get offended at very small things and you can't please them all ... but we all know to avoid the bigger topics of sex, drugs, and politics when it comes to our small business pages.

I really think that question should apply to **everything you do online**, be that posting on your business page, commenting on a forum, posting a picture and so on. Yes, we all love to have a rant and a snark and a whine, and there are places where that's totally reasonable and appropriate. I'm not the Fun Police. I just think it's high time we started seeing one another as people not just faceless people behind keyboard. So when it comes to your social media (especially for your business) I just want you to remember this:

IF YOU WOULDN'T SAY IT OUT LOUD, DON'T SAY IT ONLINE.

Do I Need A Business Newsletter?

With all the emails we get from various companies, you might be wondering if your business also needs a newsletter. Alternatively, you might already know you need and want one, but you've too overwhelmed by the tech side of it (exactly how does one send 134 emails at once?) or the writing side of it ("I have nothing interesting to say!"). In today's post I'm going to explain why you need an email database (and business newsletter), and next week I'll be writing about the tech side of it, including some sample formats you can use if you struggle with the content of your newsletter.

As small business owners in the era of social media, it would be easy to think that social media is the single best marketing tool you can use for your business. We get told all the time that if we're not constantly active on Facebook, Pinterest and Instagram (and Google+, and ello, and Twitter, and ...) that we are missing out on prime opportunities to market. There are a couple of problems with this thinking. Firstly, we forget that millions of other businesses (from micro to massive) are told the same thing, so they too are across all those media or trying to be. As a result, the online world is becoming an unbelievably noisy place. Secondly, we forget that not all of our target market spends time on one or any of those platforms. It might be hard to believe but, yes, there are potential customers of yours who do not have a Facebook account or use it to make purchasing decisions. Third, we forget that when we signed up to those platforms, we agreed to those platform's terms and conditions, the most important one of which is that ***they hold all the control***. They can turn their platform off, ask you to pay to be involved, delete your posts or pictures, suspend your account, stop showing your posts and pretty much do whatever they like and you have NO say in it. Let me give you the big scary obvious point here: If the only way you currently market your business is via social media, and someone decides to turn that platform off tomorrow. . . well, yeah, good luck keeping your business going. I'm not saying it's likely to happen. I'm saying I don't want to be the guy who is left up a creek with no paddles if it does. Me, I like a good insurance policy!

ALL of those reasons are reasons why you must - today, right now - start building a client database (email list.) An email list belongs to you and only you. You are in total control with that information. Nobody else decides what to do with it and so it becomes an asset of your business. This is vitally important because it means that it's a method of communicating to your clients which will never close down, suspend you, or lock you out because you posted a picture someone thought was inappropriate (but please don't do that). With social media, we've all become very good at endlessly scrolling, scrolling, double tap, like, pin, scroll, scroll, double tap, scroll. We have less than a second to get someone's attention.

So if you've got a client database, should you be sending an email too, if we already get too many emails?

Yes. Yes, you should, and here's why:

With email, you get their attention for way longer than any other digital medium. Firstly, they're spending more than a half a second to see what you've got to say and secondly, many people KEEP newsletters to refer back to later. Yes, the content of your newsletter is vital to ensure that people do in fact open it rather than delete it (we'll talk about that next week). The important thing is that you're getting time in front of their face for a lot longer than your social media post will. You've getting a position of prime real estate in their inbox and the value of that cannot be underestimated.

With social media posts, sometimes it can feel like a very lonely place. We say and share amazing things on our pages, only to be told that 32 (out of 5000) saw that post, or we have no idea how many people saw that tweet. With a business newsletter, we might only be sending it to 120 people, but we know those 120 people KNOW us, LOVE us, and CHOSE to hear from us because they signed up. They're already loving you! You don't need to work quite so hard to convince them of your awesomeness because *they already know it and signed up to hear about it*. It's common business wisdom that it's easier to keep a client than find a new one and nowhere is this more obvious than in a business newsletter or email list. Speaking from my own experience of this, I LOVE that many of my classes are purchased by names I recognised because they are on my list. It means that I'm building a committed tribe of people who like what I have to say, are interested in being a part of my community, and they'll give me useful, honest feedback about programs I launch. I can also more effectively reward them - I can telling them something important, share news or free tutorials and release products directly to my inner circle rather than whoever is wandering around my social media accounts. I know they're more likely to take action and I know they'll appreciate it.

You cannot underestimate the importance of building a list and then communicating with the people on it.

By now you're nodding your head and thinking, "Oh yeah, I should totally be creating this list, but how the heck do I create one?" and the good news is, many of you are sitting on a goldmine of a list already. You've probably got TONS of emails from past clients, people who contacted you to enquire about an order, and so on. Those are the people you start with (plus your Mom and all your friends). This week, your homework is to start thinking about and gathering that list up in one place (Excel is a good place to start.)

Starting Your Business Newsletter

Last week I wrote about why you've got to build an email list of your clients and potential clients[29]. This week, I'm going to give you some 'how to' info on how to get started with doing it. The most common way to communicate with your list is simply via a company newsletter that you send out regularly.

SETTING IT UP:

I recommend using MailChimp (http://www.mailchimp.com), as it's free (for your first 2000 subscribers), very easy to use, and you can easily integrate it with your website. There are plenty of other sites you can use - AWeber, Constant Contact, etc, etc. (there are so many it's crazy) - but I really love MailChimp and no, they don't pay me to say that. The reporting is great, you can easily see who signs up and who unsubscribes, you can link it to your social media and the help centre is one of the most comprehensive I've ever seen or used.

FREQUENCY:

No less than monthly. In my business I send a newsletter monthly but would send out extra ones for special events like Mother's Day cupcakes or Christmas products. Like all marketing activities, newsletters work best when you can schedule them to happen regularly, so in your diary or planner, put "Send company newsletter" on the 5th (or 15th or whatever) day of each month so the reminder comes up for you.

WHO SHOULD GET YOUR NEWSLETTER:

Current and past clients, friends. You also want potential clients to sign up, so you

---

29   See *Do I Need A Business Newsletter?* in Chapter 9.

need to make it really easy for people to opt in. One thing I suggest is that on your "contact us" page, you have a sign-up spot for your newsletter so people can sign up from there. I also strongly suggest having away to sign up on every page of your website so that it's really, really easy for them to sign up and they are encouraged to do so. You don't have to do this as a pop-up unless you want to (some people find them annoying) but I can say that a pop-up will increase your list a lot faster than a static sign up box will.

WHAT TO WRITE ABOUT:

One of the biggest struggles people have is knowing what to write, especially if writing does not come naturally to you. My suggestion here is to develop a really simple formula for your newsletter. A short greeting, something new about your products, something about existing products, and something which will improve the lives of your readers. Let me break that down for you:

- Greeting: A short personal style note saying hello. A way to get your personality across, mention a product or event you're excited about, or share a bit of behind the scenes type stuff.

- Something new about your products or business: your class schedule, upcoming specials for holidays or events, a new flavour you're trying, your new operating hours. Something 'new' which is happening in the world of your bakery. If you participated in a charity event, were recently on TV, etc. This is just something exciting and interesting.

- Something about existing products: A 'cake of the month' feature with a testimonial from a client and a picture of them cutting the cake, a "did you know?" feature where you outline one of the services you offer, a list of your most popular flavours, a photo collage of kids' cakes all around a certain theme.

- Something to improve your readers' lives: This is often the reason why people will keep a subscription or open your newsletter, because something in it compels them to keep opening it. So maybe a funny meme, a simple 'home made' recipe you want to share, an inspirational saying (make it relevant please), an article about wedding cake design trends, etc. Basically, this is the last bit, so you want them to end on a happy note and find a reason to save rather than delete that newsletter. Plus if you're good at it, it makes them want to open the next one that they get sent.

WHAT IF PEOPLE UNSUBSCRIBE?:

Let them. You've got people who love you and want to see what you have to say. Don't worry about anyone else.

WHAT IF SOMEONE TELLS ME I'M BEING "SALESY" OR "PUSHY" WITH MY EMAILS?:

Ask one or two other trusted, long-term customers how they feel about your newsletter content. If they seem to like it, just don't worry about that one comment. If they say it seems a bit pushy, maybe re-think the way you are presenting the bits in it about your products. I think ALL feedback should be "checked" to ensure how true it is but if it's really only one person who is bothered, just unsubscribe them. You're in BUSINESS and you have every right to both market your wares and ask for money for those wares. They are entitled to their opinion of course, but you are also entitled to make a living in whatever way you see fit.

IT'S TAKING UP A LOT OF TIME:

In most email software you can set up a template. It's a bit of work to begin with but once you've done it, you've done it! Then if you follow a bit of a formula to fill it up (as I mention above), it's a lot easier to do. Also, as you get things through the month (like testimonials and photos from clients), file them into a "newsletter" folder in your email so you've got some stuff to choose from when that time of month rolls around again.

CAN I SEND MORE THAN ONE A MONTH?:

Yes, and I full expect you to if something big is coming up. Towards the end of the year, you'll be sending a December newsletter but also at least 2 reminders about Christmas products, since the holiday is close to the end of the year and people do tend to forget.

There is a lot more to the art of writing newsletters and keeping in touch with your email list, but the pointers above are a great way to get started. No, you don't have to have one, but it's a fairly inexpensive and very effective marketing tool and well worth investing a half hour each month in doing. The key is to set it up so that it's almost automatic for you to do it and it does not become a major burden or irritation in your life.

Does My Cake Business Need A Blog?

Blogging seems to be the thing all the cool kids are doing, so you might be wondering if your cake business needs a blog, too. Firstly, you need to remember that a blog for a business is just a marketing tool. You can choose to use this tool or not, but like ALL of your marketing efforts, your cake business blog needs to have a defined and measurable purpose, be done consistently, and be an extension of your overall brand. Like any other form of marketing, it will take time to start seeing a benefit to it and to grow its readership. There are a number of benefits to blogging including improving your Google ranking, giving you a platform other than social media to share on, keeping your website content fresher, and helping you get more clients. That being said (and I know, I sound like a broken record here!) *blogging for business is a marketing tool*. It's a very effective one for a lot of small businesses and there are several cake makers whose blogs now help them earn a living, enough so that they need to hire other writers to help them blog. There are also a lot of misconceptions about blogging for small business, namely that each post needs to take a long time to write or be a fully researched essay, that you have to do it every single day for it to work, or that it's just a time suck.

I blogged for my small business very effectively - and no, I didn't do it every day, I didn't research for hours on each blog post, I didn't use ghost writers, and it did not keep me from running the rest of my business or having a life. It got me a lot of new business, it kept my existing customers engaged, and I found it to be one of the more fun aspects of marketing. However, like ALL marketing activities (here I go again!) - it had a purpose, I could measure it's effectiveness through statistics (and people commenting to me about it), I did it consistently and it was in keeping with my brand. I saw definite results from it because of that consistency. One of the major benefits to blogging is that you can time the posts to go out later on - so you can sit down and write ten of them and then time them to publish weekly so you're not needing to come up with a new topic every week. You can also use that content in more than one place. For example, you can blog about something, then post it across different social media platforms and include it in your newsletter. You can also recycle that content into the future. If you're having a quiet week, you can always post in social media, "Have you read my blog post about how to store cake?" with a link to that post. It's useful, good information and it should be shared - and because it already exists, you're not needing to re-invent it every time. You also fully own all the content you produce, so unlike social media where someone else gets to control who sees your stuff and when (and can delete it if they want to), you get to be entirely in charge of what your clients get and when they get it.

Blogging is just another way to communicate with your clients, so here are a few ideas for blog posts which won't take you forever to write, but which are fun, engaging content for you to offer your followers:

- Cake of the week feature - a picture of your favourite cake you made this week and a bit of back story about the event or the order

- Behind the scenes - some pictures of your staff working on something plus some back story about what is happening in that picture

- Some "food porn" - a close up photo of some yummy looking chocolate, a mixer going at high-speed, or mounds of fluffy swiss meringue buttercream plus some info about the ingredient shown

- A "how to" post - a guide for cake cutting, some tips on how to transport cakes, some tips on how to store leftover cakes

- Your new class timetable, highlighting a new class

- A short interview or feature on a new staff member

- Seasonal trends in cake - flavours, colours, or concepts which you're working on for the upcoming season

- A post about your next event or sale

- A feature about a charity you support

- A short picture tutorial about something you've made like a simple figurine

- An easy recipe you like (not one you sell, something you're happy to share like a family recipe.)

- A short video blog (time-lapse of a cake, holiday greeting from you, some "bakery life" type videos)

- A client testimonial along with a picture of the product you made for them

Blogging for your cake business is all about engagement, showing your customers and ideal customers a more personal side to you and your business. It does not need to be approached in the same way as a full-time blog would be, because at least initially it's just another way you do your marketing. If it helps you to do so, think of it like a longer status update - the photos need to be as good as you would put anywhere else and the content needs to be what people want to read about. Your cake business blog is an extension of your brand, so make sure you aren't publishing anything there that you would not be happy to publish elsewhere.

Blogs don't need to be updated every day to be useful or effective for your business. Just to prove this point - this very blog is only updated once a week. That's 4-5 posts a month on average. Your cake business blog doesn't need to have huge long articles - and in a small business, you don't want your readers to get bogged down in long articles anyway. You want them to read enough to engage their interest in you and your business. Blog content does not need to be perfect, but it does need to be relevant and engaging to your ideal client. Sure, you could let blogging become your only form of marketing and suck up vast quantities of time - but you wouldn't let any other form of marketing do that, would you?

So - should you start a cake business blog or do you need one in the first place?

Personally, I think a cake business blog can be a really effective marketing tool (because it's been proven many times), so if you're evaluating your marketing activities and this is something you're interested in adding into the marketing mix - then go for it! If you hate the idea, don't really want to add any more activities in, or just think it's not the right marketing tool for you or your clients - then don't. A cake business blog is just one of many, many tools you've got available in your marketing tool kit. Nobody is forcing you to do it (just like nobody is forcing you to Instagram, send out a newsletter or post in groups. Your business = your rules.)

CHAPTER 10

WHEN YOU REALLY NEED A HUG OF UNDERSTANDING

Many times throughout this book, I've mentioned the emotional side of what we do. Humans are emotional creatures, it's what makes us unique and interesting (and a little frustrating)! When you are the only person running your business, all the good bad and ugly falls into your lap for you to deal with. When I started the blog, I promised raw honesty and plenty of love and that's where these articles come from. Nobody runs their business by themselves or in a perfect world. Most of us have family, friends and circumstances around our lives which shape and define the boundaries of our business.

It might surprise you to hear that I don't think the business side of business (marketing, pricing, dealing with customers) is the hard part of what we do. I think the hardest part of what we do is the personal side. Having to explain to your daughter that you'll miss her game yet again because you have wedding cake to deliver. Forgetting what a night out with your husband is like because you are just too physically exhausted to think about getting off the couch. Feeling burnt out but having a whole calendar full of orders, when right now you don't even want to look at another cake ever again. Finding out one of your best online cake buddies has been talking badly about you to others. Finally starting your business up in earnest, only to find out you are unexpectedly pregnant, or your child gets sick or your Mum fell down and needs someone to care for her for a few months. This is life and this is business. It's messy. It's fun. It's chaotic. It's never boring.

When Life Happens

In August 2009, on an otherwise unremarkable Friday afternoon, I was decorating a Bollywood themed cake when my phone buzzed with a text from my younger brother. The text said that my Dad had collapsed at the gym. I wasn't too concerned at that point, as it was the middle of summer and my family live in a warm climate - so I thought maybe it was a heat exhaustion issue. I was worried, but not *worried*, you know?

I called and spoke to my siblings about the situation, but then kept on decorating. I had no choice. It was a Friday. The single busiest day of the week for cake makers.

Within an hour, my phone rang. It was my Mum.

She was calling to tell me that my Dad had died of a sudden, massive heart attack.

I honestly don't recall much detail of what happened right after that - I know my employee drove me home, I remember my husband coming home, and I vaguely remember getting on a plane within hours of that phone call.

I have no idea what happened to that Bollywood cake, or those orders due that weekend. I know only that I walked away from *everything* - my life, my kids, my chef job, my business - and went home where I needed to be, and I stayed there for over a month. At that point, I was extremely fortunate to have a one-day-a-week employee who could step in for me, and the business was small enough that she could pretty much handle things on her own (with email support from me from overseas.) I was very, very lucky in that respect.

Recently one of the readers of this blog emailed me to say that she finds herself unexpectedly (yet joyfully) pregnant with Baby #3 - and she's not sure how to keep a baking business going while she's "baking" a baby. After registering her kitchen, taking on orders, and climbing the hill to success, she's facing one hell of a big roadblock! (Adorable and fabulous as babies may be, they have a way of changing things just a wee bit.) (Boom-tish!)

Her email got me thinking about writing a post on how small businesses owners cope when life just gets in the way - and I'm talking life smacking you in the face with a heavy metal cake pan, not just the day-to-day drama of living.

The truth of it is, *you cope as best you can with the resources you have available to you at the time*. Major life events - be they tragedies or celebrations - are often unpredictable. LIFE HAPPENS, as they say. So what do you do *when life happens to you ... and you own a small business*?

Here's what I think:

Where you have a bit of lead time (like a baby, a sick parent, moving states):

Put in some plans for what you're going to do. Like for a pregnancy: don't take orders for the month before you're due, and the months after. For any major life event, start to educate your customers. The closer you get to the event, communicate a fair bit - in other words, be open and honest with them that this is a bump (ha!) in the road but that you've planned for it. NOBODY likes unexpected events, not least of which your clients who are depending on you. Make a plan for how you are going to manage, and how your clients are going to manage - and then tell them about it. Accept that you can't keep going at the same rate you are now - and start to slow down the wheels that are currently turning if you do not have employees who can fill the breach of your absence. ALSO - Do some planning for how to speed the wheels back up again once you are ready. What I wouldn't do is fall off the planet entirely. Slowing down is fine - stopping the momentum entirely is a bad idea (both for you and your clients.) Maybe you stop taking new orders, but you still post once a week on your blog, or you update on Facebook, or you share some pictures of your own baby shower cupcakes. Whatever. *Keep the lines of communication open* and TELL your clients and potential clients what the deal is - just don't disappear without a trace as that breeds mistrust.

Where you have no lead time at all (like in my own experience):

Just do the best you can with the resources you have available to you. Again, be open and honest and *communicate* with your clientele as much as you are able to. If they're used to talking to you personally and they're getting a call from your employee or husband - they KNOW something is not quite right. If you email every day and suddenly there is no reply for several days -they'll know something is amiss. Human beings, while sometimes cruel, are actually generally pretty understanding. In those days right after I lost my Dad, I have huge holes in my memory - but I know at some point I'd asked my employee to just hold it together for me until I was able to. She understood completely, and she rose to the challenge. BUT I made it a point to communicate with HER, too - every day I tried to call and check in, and when I realised I would be gone longer than I thought I asked her first if she could continue looking after the business for me. My clients understood. My employee understood. We still got their orders to them, and they forgave her if she was missing a few details or had to ask for their understanding or patience.

Above all else - remember that we're not brain surgeons, we're not scientists curing cancer, we're not the heads of State. We bake for a living. Is it important? YES (especially to your clients). Should we let people down? NO. But ... you know ... life happens. We can't always predict it. Will your client be angry that their wedding cake was made by someone other than you? Maybe. But ... ultimately ... when the cake hits the fan, *you are a person. You have a life. A sometimes unpredictable life.*

Sometimes we have no choice but to choose <u>ourselves or our families</u> over our business. There is NO shame in that. It's an entirely reasonable and entirely human thing to do.

Any client who does not understand that is welcome to find themselves another cake maker.

My Dad was gone. My family needed me.

I went home.

I have no regrets about it.

Cake can wait. Funerals - and babies - cannot.

We're In This Together

Every time you feel yourself getting pulled into other people's nonsense, repeat these words:

NOT MY CIRCUS,

NOT MY MONKEYS.

((POLISH PROVERB))

It's interesting, this concept of working together. On this very blog, I've advised you to both break up with Facebook[30], but also keep your support system around you[31]. It can be a really slippery slope, though -one minute your caking bestie is, well, your caking bestie ... and the next minute they are your sworn enemy because you disagree on that whole copyright thing[32]. This industry is full of women (and women are prone to drama), and it's also a very emotional, artistic, personal sort of medium that we work in. Daily, I talk to my colleagues, all of whom say that this industry has become an entirely crazy, unprofessional, bonkers place to hang out in. I talk to people all the time who say that they are ttthhiiisss close to just chucking it all in because it's not worth the headache. There are a lot of dramas happening out there, from arguments over what brand of fondant to use to people genuinely turning into mud-slinging back-stabbing she-wolves. I've run into that with this blog, too. I've literally had people say they won't tell people about this blog because they don't want "those bitches to get ahead". (Okay so that's vaguely flattering to me, but not at all what the purpose of this blog is.)

I'm going to call bullshit on ALL of that.

---

30   See *Breaking Up Is Hard To Do* in Chapter 9.
31   See *Who Is Riding In Your Sag Wagon?* In Chapter 10.
32   See *Cakes And Copyright* in Chapter 4.

I firmly believe that this is a community that needs to stick together, work together, lift one another up and educate one another.

Guess what?

WE ALREADY DO THIS.

We record, produce and create YouTube videos and written or photo tutorials because we believe in sharing and we want to learn from one another.

We write, edit, and publish blog posts and informative status updates because we believe in sharing and we also want to learn from one another.

We participate in sharing days, link love days and we re-gram photos because we believe in sharing and we also want to learn from one another.

We share links, shout out to friends, and tag one another in social media because we believe in sharing and we also want to learn from one another.

However, we also do crazy, crazy things like complain bitterly that others are undercharging, and agree to work for free out of fear of losing opportunities for PR, refuse to tell people that we went to a cool business class (ANY of them, not just mine), steal photos and claim them as our own, go to a class and then go on to teach the same exact cake, be unwilling to pay for things then complain when people don't pay us and so on and so forth. It's RIDICULOUS.

Why do we do that stuff? Mostly because we forget one thing: we're in this together.

YES, we're all struggling to differentiate ourselves in this crowded market.

YES, the new kids on the block are undercharging and undercutting us.

YES, being in business is tough as global economies get tough.

YES, there is always someone out there who will do it better, cheaper or faster than you will.

YES, being a small business owner is damn hard work.

YES, we are afraid that our competitors will take work away from us and, therefore, we won't be successful.

YES, we are afraid that if we say no to something which is unreasonable, there will be a line of people behind us willing to say yes.

Even with all of that, I think working together to create a happier, healthier culture in the industry will only be good in the long run. As a team we can educate customers, we can raise the bar on our skill levels, and we can bring more professionalism to the industry as a whole. We need to lift one another up, not tear one another down. Rather than say, "That stupid lady is only charging $30, no wonder I can't make a living," you should call that woman up or email her, introduce yourself and politely say, "I used to undercharge, too -but then I read this article/went to a class/heard someone speak/had a rude awakening and I realised that undercharging wasn't doing me any good. You might find it interesting, too." Maybe she'll listen. Maybe she won't ... but you've got to be brave enough to at least try.

We're in this together. It's our choice if we see that togetherness as a threat or as an asset.

I think it's time to start changing the culture of this industry.

Away from fear, and towards cooperation.

Are you with me?

I've Lost My Mojo. Now What?

Pour yourself a drink, we're having a pity party.

I recently read a post on the blog of Happy Cakes (http://littlecakesformyhappy. blogspot.com.au) on the topic of losing your cake mojo, and with the owner's permission, I'm re-printing some of it here. I think it's a fairly common issue among my peers at the moment:

> *"Do you find you lose your way sometimes in the cake decorating world? Or is it just me?? It's like I can't keep up with what's going on. The new crazes, the new products, the new styles and trends and the next big thing. There's a new cake decorator popping up every time I turn my head around. It's an insanely crazy busy world. Maybe it's just me. A cake doesn't seem like it can be any good these days unless it's 6 feet tall, balancing on a 45-degree angle, not to mention internal construction devised by a small engineering team!!*
>
> *It's like a macaron can't just be a macaron anymore, it has to be in a shape with painted detail. A cake pop isn't just a round ball anymore they're sculpted little masterpieces. Do you sometimes feel like you just can't keep*

up with the Jones's anymore? I'm struggling at the moment. People want these Ah-mazing cakes for a tiny amount of money and a cake can't just be a cake anymore, it has to be over the top cray cray. I'm a pretty simple girl and I think I like simple things. Don't get me wrong I appreciate all these beautiful masterpieces being created, but are they realistic for all of us. I don't think so. Well not for me anyway. I've lost my direction lately. Not sure why, but I wonder if it's cause I'm trying to keep up. Am I trying to keep up with the insanely crazy world of cake decorating? Maybe it's cause I'm comparing myself to all these amazing decorators. I've always strived to try new things and push myself, which is why I follow these amazing decorators, but I think maybe my need to become great like them means I have lost who I am as a cake decorator. It's a little overwhelming. I love making cakes, the joy that they bring people. The look on their face when they see it is my reward for doing what I do. I miss it to be honest. It's been a while. I feel like though my next cake isn't going to be good enough. Which is silly I know, but I feel like the pressure is on!! I mean it's just a cake after all, and there probably won't have been an engineering team behind it. I know the pressure comes from me."

I'm willing to bet that a lot of you out there read her sentiments, nodding all the while. It's a tough market out there at the moment. When you feel like everyone is getting ahead of you (or the trends are happening faster than you can keep up with), the industry can feel like the fun has gone out of it and it's all about the competition.

Too often in life, it's easy to look at someone else's "something" (business, 15 tiered creation, children, lifestyle ...) and get bitten by the bugs of envy, jealousy, frustration. It's human nature to compare and contrast ourselves to one another, but how do we move past it? Firstly, chances are that whatever they've got, they've slapped a big ol' pair of rosy glasses on before showing it to the wider world. Have you ever heard of a successful business which then goes out of business overnight? Or the neighbours who are sickeningly in love cuddly wuddly until they suddenly get divorced? Or the cake which looks great from the front, but not so great from the back? Yep. That's because there is ALWAYS more to the story - so firstly recognise that what you're envious of is just that: a version of a story.

Secondly, take a closer look at what they've got, and ask yourself: but do I REALLY want that? I used to be envious of another company that was growing at an incredible rate. When I looked a little closer, I realised that I might be envious of their growth ... but not envious of much else. I DIDN'T WANT to run a business that big, didn't want to work with my partner, didn't want to run my business from home, didn't want to focus all my energy on teaching, didn't want to have locations in several states - ALL of which were things that they did. Similarly, I might find myself envious of those kick ass cake makers who create these gravity defying, hyper-realistic cakes - but then realised that when I needed to do one, I didn't enjoy it very much ... and my customers rarely asked for them anyway. It's not my thing. So just check and see if what you're hankering for is really what you want for yourself.

Once you've done that, here's how to retrieve your mojo: go back to basics. Remind yourself why you are in business (again: it's not about the cake) and remind yourself of what you're good at and why your customers have chosen you in the past (and why they will likely choose you again). Yes, client's requests have gotten more demanding, and it can feel as though they are all wanting to get a little bit more but wanting to pay a little bit less. You can't change anything about that (at least not quickly) but you can work on: defining your niche, redefining your overall goals, getting clear about what values your business stands for, and what things in your life are important to you. In my own life, I have no real need to make millions of dollars or have a reputation as a cake maker of a certain style - but I do have a need to have a job which allows me to pick my kids up after school, afford their school tuition, AND which allows me to serve my personal goals of creativity, service and being inspirational. I've framed my business (and this blog) around those things, and so now when I look at other businesses and start to feel that flame of envy spark within me, I ask myself, "Yeah, but do I really WANT that?" Similarly, when I look at creations which are far beyond my skill level (artistic or construction) I admire them and think, "LOVE IT ... but it's not MY thing, " and I just keep on scrolling past. I can do this because I am very clear about what is important to me and what my purpose here is.

Lastly, remember that just because these things are available in the world, this doesn't mean that every customer wants them. Different strokes for different folks, right? Or as I often say in the Business of Baking on Tour (http://www. bizbakeontour.com), don't try to sell Ferraris to people interested in buying Fords.

So - for Leoni, my friend, and anyone else out there feeling like they've lost their mojo- go pour yourself a drink, think about what is right for YOU, and then go kick ass doing those things and leading that life which are all about your values, not someone else's. Heck, go and make a cake for yourself just to celebrate the skills you've got and to remind yourself of why you started this whole insane thing in the first place (and invite me over for a piece.)

In short:

Love your craft.

Love your clients.

Love yourself.

Be grateful.

Kick ass.

(and try not to beat yourself up about what the other guy is up to ... because that's really not your thing anyway.)

Should I Quit My Business?

I've spent many dark, lonely nights laying in bed looking at my bedroom ceiling. I'd be worrying about business issues or a lack of money and a little teeny tiny voice in my head would say, "You know Michelle, maybe you should just ... quit. Give up. Sell everything off. Move on." Not going to lie, many of those nights the very IDEA of not having to run a business any more filled me with **waves of relief**. I could feel my whole body RELAX just at the idea of not being a business owner any more. I would become almost giddy with excitement at the idea of never having to pay another business-related bill again or work on the weekend.

Sometimes I'd complain to my Mum about how business wasn't going as well as I'd like it to, and she would say, "Maybe you should just give it up. You don't need this kind of stress in your life." Complaining to my Dad was worse, "You know Michelle, some people just aren't cut out to run a business." Of course when they said that I'd get all angry and defensive and resolve never to complain to them again. Then that night, when it was dark and quiet and my husband was softly snoring next to me, **the voice would come back**. "Maybe they're right. This IS too stressful. I want a calmer life. I'm just plain exhausted. Maybe I should just quit my business." That wonderful feeling of relief would flood through my veins again and I'd think, "Right. This is it. I'm going to get up in the morning and start making plans to close the doors." Having decided that, I'd fall asleep with a smile on my face and with the tension having drained out of my shoulders I'd have a good night's sleep.

The next morning I'd get up, go to the shop and start doing the ordering, making the baking list, working on a figurine, mixing up a batch of buttercream ... and I'd forget entirely that I was meant to be getting ready to close the doors. I'd go happily along in my day, working in and on my business as though that late night conversation never happened. This same thing happened to me more often than I'd like to admit. It almost always happened during a crisis – either a financial crisis of cash flow, or an emotional crisis like a client complaint or staffing issue.

I'm guessing that story sounds kinda familiar to you, because most weeks I get at least a few emails which say something like, "Hi Michelle, I've been doing cake business for a year. I'm just not getting enough orders, I'm not making any money, my husband is not supportive at all, and I'm trying to take care of my toddler as well. It's all too hard! **Do you think I should just quit my business?**"

First let me say that without knowing ANYTHING about you other than what that message said, I'm in no way able to give you a simple yes or no answer to that. Now I know that most of the time, the people who get in touch with me are usually seeking permission to let their business go OR they are hoping I have some sort of secret sauce I can give them which will fix it all. Sadly, I can't give you either of those.

Second let me straight up say that if your main reason for wanting to quit is either, "There are too many cheap cake ladies out there", or "Customers only care about price", then quite honestly I think you probably should quit. People who are in this for the long-term (who approach their businesses truly from the head space of a business owner) would be frustrated about those two things but **neither of those things** would be the real reason they close down. Neither would be being "unhappy" or "it's just not fun anymore" because it's never that simple and you know it. Our lives and our circumstances are way too complex to use happiness as the measure of success. Businesses are like relationships. They take time and effort and not every day is rainbow unicorns and buttercream scented waffles.

This deep and desperate desire to close your business is something most business owners come across several times in the course of their careers. For some it's reaching the "grow or stop" phase of their business, when they've realised that they are utterly overwhelmed by everything. Those people usually have a ton of orders and are struggling to keep up. They at the point of needing to decide, "Do I hire someone? Find a bigger premises? Or do I just give it up because it's out of hand?" For others, it's the disappointment of having kept their business doors open a while and the orders are simply not coming in as they need them to. They are desperate for more money or more orders or both. Cake was SO FUN when it was a hobby but lately ... it's not feeling so much fun anymore because the stress or pressure of money has come into it. The third category of people who consider closing their business are people who have had a major life change which has led them to reconsider **everything** about their lives. Maybe they had a baby, lost a loved one, got diagnosed with an illness, moved location. NO matter which of those situations are yours, it very upsetting and scary when that little voice in the night starts talking.

If you're anything like me, when that feeling gets really bad you start acting like an irresponsible business owner. Secretly, **you're hoping that something massive** will happen to force your hand. You start to ignore emails. You won't answer the phone. You cut corners, make mistakes with orders, and kinda ... lose your shit for a little while. Eventually, you probably snap out of it and you're okay for a while ... but then you get tired or don't get orders or your child gets sick and this wonderful, glorious fantasy of walking away starts to seem more and more appealing. And thus, the cycle continues.

So - how do you find the answer to the question, "Should I close my business?"

(Also, let me point out here that I don't like the negative connotation of the word QUIT. It's a horrible word. It makes you feel and sound like a loser and ANYONE who's had a try at being in business is NOT a loser in my book.)

HERE'S WHAT TO DO: I THINK YOU NEED TO ANSWER THAT QUESTION WITH THREE MORE QUESTIONS. REALLY TAKE THE TIME TO ANSWER THIS. GO OUT FOR A COFFEE BY YOURSELF IF YOU NEED TO. MULL OVER THEM. CONSIDER THEM. LOOK WITHIN.

The first is: Am I feeling this way because of a temporary situation or have I secretly felt this way for a while and it has NOTHING to do with something temporary? Temporary things might be - physical exhaustion, complaining customer, a few slow months, lack of money, fear of marketing. More permanent things might be - families growing or ageing, major medical concerns, life changes like divorces or partners losing jobs.

The second is: Why am I doing this business in the first place? The answer is not "because I like cake", there has to be something way, way, WAY bigger than that. Running a business is not easy, and especially not in the beginning when it seems like you've got to be the one who builds the ship from scratch and then steers it too. There needs to be a BIG WHY for your business. *Just being passionate about decorating is a good reason to start a business but not a good reason to keep it going.* If you don't have a BIG WHY then that's probably contributing to your frustration and your desire to close because you can no longer feel or see the purpose for doing what you're doing, so it makes **all the problems feel big**.

The third is: The last thing I want you to do (stick with me here) - is close your eyes, look into your heart of hearts and imagine your life WITHOUT your business in it. Really think about what your life would look like in a few months from now, if you didn't have your business. Sure, you'll be less tired but I want you to think harder than that. Would you be missing it terribly? Would you be missing it a little but actually glad it's behind you? If you were to close now, would you feel as though you'd given it your all? Will you be proud of all that you achieved, or will you have regrets about the things you didn't do or didn't try to do? By the way, please don't be ridiculous about this whole visualising thing. Closing your business does not mean that every day you will frolic on the beaches of Maui in a red bikini looking smoking hot and throwing around hundred-dollar bills in the air like you just don't care. (I should know. That's what my vision looked like. Didn't happen.)

Sadly, I do not look like this.

If any of you are in a relationship, you'll know what I'm talking about, because choosing a partner is a little like this. The moment you realise you can't honestly imagine your life without them is the moment you know they are a keeper. So if you CANNOT IMAGINE your life without your business, that's telling you that it's not time to close yet, that there's still plenty of desire and effort hiding there under the frustration and desperation. It means it's time to change things for the better, take some time to think and plan, and work on making a better future for yourself. If you can EASILY imagine your future without your business **and it really doesn't bother you** ... then yes, it's probably time to seriously consider moving on.

So if you answer all those and think, **I really, really don't want to close** ... (my situation is temporary, I still have stuff I want to achieve, and I can't imagine my life without it), here are a few options for how to move forward from here. All of these fall under the heading of **getting shit done**:

- Scale back the business for a few months so you can re-group mentally. Be "booked out" for at least one weekend a month, or just "book out" for an entire month if you can manage it. You must give yourself the time and space to make a plan to move forward.

- Consider taking on a part-time job to supplement income (so your financial situation is not as desperate or pressured). I think bridge jobs are

BRILLIANT and I tell most people to get one if they can, even if it's only for a few months to help you calm the hell down. It also gives you the mental space to think a little more clearly. Sometimes you need to just **not think** about your business a little bit. When we live in our heads 24/7, it's very easy to get stuck there and turn mole hills into mountains.

- If before now you've never had a long-term vision for your business, only "I'm doing it because I love cake", then you need to DEVELOP a vision. You can do this by getting some mentoring, or doing some reading online about figuring out your business purpose and how to do it. You MUST HAVE a bigger picture or **I guarantee you will return to this very spot** in a few short months.

- Take a good, long look at your business and figure out which bits of it are not the best use of your time OR which bits give you the most grief. Then DO something to alleviate that. Outsource stuff, hire a part time helper, buy in those damn roses, just GET RID of stuff you do not need to do. Be absolutely ruthless in cutting crap out of your business. Scale down the number of products you make. Take one Saturday off a month. Declutter your business like you are Peter Walsh (http://www.peterwalshdesign. com) on crack.

- GET OUT. I'm not kidding on this one. Call a few friends in business (cake or not) and MEET IN REAL LIFE. Or join a small business networking group. YOU ARE NOT ALONE but I'm willing to bet that it feels like you are. Create a regular meeting with these guys - once a month for coffee on the first Tuesday night of the month. Make it a real thing and make it happen. You need the support of other business owners around you. Don't have anyone local? Create a Skype group. It's possible. MAKE IT HAPPEN.

- Do the **30 Days of Awesome** program (http://thebizofbaking.com/30-days-of-awesome). Imagine me encouraging your via email EVERY DAY for 30 days and believe me, positive stuff will start to happen for you. Commit to doing at least half of the activities - there will be no value there if you let them languish in your in-box. (And if you're reading this and you've got the class but it's stuck in your email somewhere, TODAY I want you to pick 2 emails from that set and take action on those.)

- If you feel this way ONLY because of a temporary situation (client complaint, etc.) then work out a way to solve that thing so that it never happens again or if it does, you have a method by which to deal with it.

- And once you've done all of that ... write a note in your planner for 3 months time, where you re-evaluate how you're feeling about things. If literally nothing about your feelings or situation has changed, then there are issues here which are bigger than you first thought and it's worth reading this post again. (Bookmark it!)

If you answer all of those and think, "**I'm really and truly done. I don't want to keep doing this**," (because my situation is NOT temporary, I have no freaking idea why the hell I'm doing this, and honestly YES I can imagine not having to deal with this thing - good riddance!), then first let me give you a MASSIVE virtual hug and tell you that I admire your bravery. Choosing to walk away is as brave a business decision as any you will make, truly. **There is no shame in choosing to change paths.** Let me repeat that. You are not a loser, a quitter, or a crappy business owner because you are deciding to change paths. You are simply choosing differently now. My tips for closing your business are:

- Take swift, decisive action. Pick a closing date and put it in your calendar in pen. Tell your loved ones the date. Declare it out loud to yourself, too.

- Don't literally walk away and leave customers hanging. Choose your "closing date" to be right after whatever the future-most order you currently have is. Between now and then, give it ALL you've got. You owe it to your customers and yourself to go out on a high note. If your last order is in excess of six months from now, then I would pick your closing date, find someone to take your orders over for you (whose work is on par with yours and who you trust), and personally call those customers and explain the situation. Give them the option of working with the new person, or getting a full refund from you. Don't drag this out longer than six months.

- Don't make any huge plans for the immediate future, other than taking some time OFF to just breathe. Give yourself the time and space to close this business down with dignity.

- Go speak to the right people (accountants, etc.) and make sure you do all the right legal and financial bits and pieces to close the entity.

- Decide on how you're going to answer the question, "Why did you close down?" because people will ask and I do not want you to feel like shit when they do. You know what, I don't care if you lie. It's not their business anyway. Come up with an answer you feel comfortable telling people. "I just decided to move onto other things," is a perfectly reasonable answer. Anything more is up to you and frankly, it's not really their beeswax anyway. Don't feel like everyone needs or deserves to know the whole story. Your business, your rules.

- Expect the following to happen: you will beat yourself up about the decision, you will suddenly get an influx of orders (because the Universe is funny like that) and you will doubt your decision and suddenly find your cake mojo returning. All normal. All okay. Just remind yourself of your closing date and the time off that which comes right after that. Then, take a deep breath, and don't let this "ummm ... maybe I shouldn't close," little voice in your head talk too much. If you let it talk, you will find yourself right back in the same "Should I close?" situation in a few months' time.

For many of us there are real financial considerations here, especially if the business supplements or supports our families. In BOTH scenarios (close or go on) I want you to put on your Big Girl Pants and TAKE ACTION about the money part of things. Go see the accountant, talk to your husband, figure out what money you have and what you need and start being a grown up about it. I found that REALLY REALLY hard but let me tell you, the feeling of relief when you KNOW what is going on with your money is really, really nice. It's like someone has rolled a big old boulder off your shoulders. **Knowing is better than not knowing. It helps you make better decisions.**

There are a whole lot of books I've read which say, "Just when you're feeling the worst about your business, that's when you're on the verge of a breakthrough." Some people call this an Upper Limit Problem (ULP), some people call it "the darkest before the dawn", and some people say, "as soon as you stop trying, that's when you'll get pregnant". You get the idea. Those are real things, which is PRECISELY why I want you to answer the questions above and visualise what life would be like without the business. I don't want you to make this decision just based on one day when you're having an "Oh @%#&$# it! This sucks!" moment. **I want you to take some time to really consider this stuff.** You've worked this hard, for this long and put in so much of yourself - believe me, when I say you can afford another few days or weeks to take the time to come to a proper, real decision about things.

Lastly - if you've been thinking about this and every week you find yourself making a new decision - this week I'm closing, next week I'm not and so on and so forth - then that tells me you've never really worked out your purpose for why you're doing this. **Having a purpose is what keeps you going when you least want to keep going.**

Unsupported

Recently someone wrote and asked me what to do when their family or friends don't support their business venture. This is a really hard one for me to answer because I have been blessed with an enormous amount of support from both family and friends. I even blogged[33] about the support thing[34] twice! I've been cogitating on this topic ever since because I want to give you all useful, real life advice on what seems to be a common problem.

Then this video landed in my inbox which gives you some brilliant advice on exactly what to say when your friends and family don't support you. It's a video by Derek Halpern from Social Triggers (http://www.socialtriggers.com/what-should-you-do-when-your-friends-and-family-dont-support-you/#more-4672) - and I think it's a bit of a genius. I recommend you make the time to watch it.

I love that video and the script it gives, but there is more that can be said - especially for an industry like this one, where so many businesses start on a kitchen table and start accidentally[35]. I've listened as so many of you said it's your husband or partner who does not support this venture, largely because a) it's not making any money, b) it's eating up all of your free time, c) you've become obsessed so the house is overrun with baking toys, and d) IT'S NOT MAKING ANY MONEY. I think the issue here becomes a lot about priorities, where you prioritise your business yet your partner either cannot tangibly see or emotionally understand what you're getting out of it if the dollars are not rolling in. It can be especially hard for a non-creative person to understand why you would invest so much time, effort, money and potentially heartache in something which does not seem to reap much in the way of tangible (hello- MONEY!) rewards.

I'm going to go out on a limb here and say the only people you need to use that script on are those who would potentially would be financially or emotionally affected by your decision to be in business. Frankly, the support of your friends is lovely and really nice to have ... but it's not their life that might be impacted. To them I think a simple and polite, "Thanks for your advice, I know you love me and I appreciate your concern," is sufficient. You shouldn't need to really justify it to them. Your husband, kids or parents ... that's a different story entirely. You really and truly NEED their help to get this thing off the ground, so it's them you need to get on board.

With men in particular (with apologies to the many men who read this blog), you

---

33   See *Who Is Riding In Your Sag Wagon?* In Chapter 10.
34   See *Don't Waste Good Chocolate* In Chapter 10.
35   See *Just One Little Cake Please* in the *Before You Begin* section.

need to take emotion out of it and make it all about facts and defined goals. "The extra income I bring in will mean we can take a vacation this year", "Here's my

list of costs and profit predictions, I've done the maths and believe I can make this work", "Let's sit down together and figure out how this might impact our family budget", and so on. "I'd like Thursday night to be my cake making night, can you please watch the kids? You can sleep in on Sunday mornings as a trade off." Basically - take your partner and say "I can do this, here's why, here's what I predict will happen, I need your help", and get them involved in it (as much as that's feasible). Be willing to compromise where you can because that's what families and relationships are often about anyway. Take the time to show them your plan (and that you actually *have* a plan) and make them feel a part of this whole thing. If you can show this isn't just some cutesy little baking hobby, that you're invested in it becoming a business, you're much more likely to get your partner on board with it all.

With all my heart and soul I say this - it's much easier to succeed when you have support from those you love. It's not *required*, but it's nice to have - and exactly like we need to educate our customers as to why it's worth buying from us, we need to educate those we love about why it's worth supporting us even if it's at some discomfort to them.

You believe in yourself.

Teach others to believe as well.

Confused In Cakeland – Parenting While In Business

Confused in Cakeland

Dear Michelle,

You're a Mum, blogger, business owner, teacher ... and I'm barely holding it together as a Mum and business owner. Seriously, do you have a lot of help, or do you never sleep? What's the deal? Am I just really bad at time management? How do you get all that done? What's the secret? Minions?

Signed,

Confused in Cakeland

Dear Confused in Cakeland,

I do not believe you can have it all. I think you can have some of it, most of the time, but not all of it, at the same time. That whole Superwoman thing is a myth.

The truth of it is, I work really hard at keeping all of those things going. My life is a fabulous, crazy, busy one ... but then I beat myself up about all the stuff I don't get done. Truly I often think about how much more I could and should be doing and I'm frustrated that there are not more hours in the day. You and me, we're not so different. I look at what other mothers or business owners do and I wish I could do what they seem to do so effortlessly.

Basically, I try to remind myself that most of the time, I just do the best I can with the resources I have. My house is messy, my kids need to remind me over and over to sign their school paperwork, I sometimes forget to eat proper meals (Slurpees and Oreo cookies are nutritious, right?), I skip the gym too often, I forget to make doctor's appointments ... you get the idea. I'm human. A very messy, sometimes grumpy, wonderfully imperfect human.

I have employees in my business, but at home it's pretty much just me (and a bit of hubby) doing everything - so I plan, I organise, I do my best to stay one step ahead of the chaos (by doing stuff like meal planning). Some days I fall over in a heap, other days I've got my act together. I'm a bit like the proverbial duck gliding on the surface of the water, all calm and serene ... underneath, I'm paddling like mad!

Thank goodness for Slurpees and Oreo cookies.

Yours in controlled chaos,

Michelle

Family Time

Today's post is going to be short, sweet and to the point because I've got all my immediate family here visiting from the United States. The last time my sister and her family were here was eight years ago!

People often ask me, "How do you do it all?" and the first thing I say to them (and in my Business of Baking on Tour class { http://www.bizbakeontour.com }, where I have an entire module about it) is this:

BALANCE IS BULLSHIT.

Some weeks, I'm a great mother/sister/wife/friend and some weeks, I'm a great business owner and on some weeks, I'm great at both. I'm simply not great at being both every single week, and I refuse to beat myself up about that.

This week, I'm choosing to be with my family and my friends and spend time away from my business. This week, I'm not going to be a great business owner who moves her business forward, makes things happen and earns a heap of money. This week, I'm just going to be a good mother, sister, wife and friend. I'm not attempting to balance anything at all and instead I'm pushing the scales all the way to one side.

The cliché is true - nobody ever lay on their death bed wishing they had made just one more cake, or wishing they had spent more time in the office. So this week, my lesson to you is simple: choose to have a life outside of your business. It can be so VERY EASY to get entirely sucked into the bubble which is your business. To obsess over money (or lack of it), plan world bakery domination and just give every waking moment to your plans while your relationships languish. Especially in a fast-paced, high-pressure, lots of competition environment like ours where it feels like if we are not CONSTANTLY creating new things, inventing new techniques, answering client emails within minutes of them sending one that we're going to miss out, or worse that we might fail. We get utterly *consumed* by our businesses, don't we?

I'm here to tell you that cakes (or macaroons or cupcakes) and dreams and plans will ALWAYS wait just a little bitty bit longer. Your children's childhood, your parent's growing older, your friends needing you … that won't wait. Ever. Those things march on no matter how many wafer paper flowers you make. A year from now, you might not remember losing that one order, but you will remember how guilty you felt for not making it to that family birthday party or friends' engagement. Yes, I do often tell you to take action and not make excuses, and yes, I do often tell you to find a way to do both life and business … and I stand by that advice. Today, I'm also telling you that it's okay to choose your life (to actually HAVE a life) once in a while and that it's vital to your long term well-being to do so.

Choose to make time for family and friends and to be a person outside of your business. Accept that this might mean you lose an order or two, or don't make as much money as you need or want to. Accept that it might mean that success will take you that little bit longer than you had hoped. Success can wait the few hours or few days you need to go on vacation, attend a family event, or call your Mum to have a chat.

Choose to have a life outside of your business, because your business does not define who you are.

And on that note, I'm off to play tourist with my family (and laugh at myself as my American accent comes back in full force and I suddenly stop ending each sentence with the word 'mate'.)

The Importance Of Self Care

These last few weeks has been HUGE for me on so many levels. My triplets celebrated their 14th birthday (which means cakes x 3, cupcakes x 3, extra cake for family dinner, events x 2 and so on), I got the world's most persistent head cold-turned-cough-turned-snotty-face, and I launched Confident Pricing (http://learning.thebizofbaking.com/buy/Confidentpricing) to the general public. There was more going on in my world too - my niece graduated college, my husband is changing jobs ... basically, it's been one hell of a ride and it's not over yet. As a result of all this, for the first time in over two years, I didn't publish a new post last Tuesday. This might not seem like a big deal to you, but **to me, it was a HUGE deal**.

Last Monday, as I lay in bed feeling like now was a good time to invest in Kleenex shares, I realised I didn't have a post ready to go. I felt horrible about it. I kept thinking, "I should get out of bed and write something", but then I'd look at the alarm clock and realise I'd dozed off for 30 minutes since I had that thought. I eventually made the decision that I needed to sleep and heal more than I needed to write a blog post and that's exactly what I did.

When you own a business, **it can be SO easy not to engage in any self-care whatsoever**. I suck at taking care of myself. I wear clothes that need replacing (and OMG my bras are ridiculously pathetic), I don't always make the best food choices (hello there, Oreos for breakfast!) and generally I don't take care of myself as best I should. When you've got orders to fill, blogs to write, kids to feed, marketing to do, events to prepare for and ingredients to buy, self-care has a way of just falling off the To Do list entirely. Women are particularly bad at this, because it's in our nature to care for others, nurture others before ourselves, and sacrifice our own comfort or joy for other people. Financially too, when the decision is to buy groceries or pay for a decent haircut, most of us won't hesitate to cancel the hair appointment.

You should not underestimate the importance of self-care because it's the kind of small investment which pays off HUGELY. There is nothing which makes me happier or more motivated to kick business butt than getting a decent haircut and blow dry. I feel SO much better and lighter and much less exhausted and crappy. I swear those few hours I spend in the hairdresser's chair make me feel like an entirely new woman. So we all KNOW we need to look after ourselves better, but with time and money in short supply, managing to fit in self-care is hard to do.

Here are my top 3 tips for looking after yourself better:

1. Before leaving your appointment of choice (hair, massage, manicure, personal trainer, whatever your thing is), **make an appointment for the next session**. I guarantee that if you leave with the intention to call later and get it done, it won't get done because life will get in the way. Make it a part of your usual routine, even if it's 8 weeks between appointments. DO NOT LEAVE there without scheduling in another appointment.

2. **Pre-pay for stuff when you can.** If you see your hairdresser is having a special, or you come across a Groupon offer for a spa day - BUY yourself a gift certificate for that thing and hang onto it, so you can use it when you most need it (which is probably when you're most cash-poor and feeling sucky.) Also, put money aside for self-care. It doesn't need to be vast sums, $5/week will do just fine. **Make having money for looking after yourself a priority** and find an easy way to make saving that money possible. My family uses YNAB software (which I highly recommend, it's changed our lives (http://ynab.refr.cc/BTZ8VPP)) and in it there is a budget line for haircuts (because haircuts are my thing.) And while I can't

claim this is legitimate tax advice in any way, I've heard of hairdressers being listed as "consultants" on plenty of business tax returns.

3. Before I launched Confident Pricing, I knew that it was going to be something I wanted to celebrate, because I've worked really hard on it. I also know that I often **forget to stop and give myself a "YAY YOU!"** in the midst of the controlled chaos which is my life. When I made the "To Do" list for the launch of the class, I added in "make and pay for mani/pedi appointment" and I marked it as a high priority item and vowed not to ignore it. Last Friday, I went and got pampered for almost 2 hours - and walked away with sparkly fuscia toes and sparkly blue nails (no judging please. Secretly I am still a teenager. It's an awesome way to live.) Every time I look at my hands or toes now, I smile and give myself a little mental, "Yay you! You did it!" and it's making me feel pretty damn good - so step three is, **if you KNOW something big or difficult is on the horizon, put self-care on the To Do list as though it's just another job that needs to get done as part of the event**.

Self-care does not come easily or naturally to me. I'm not a 'girly girl', I don't wear make-up (much to my Mum's annoyance), I don't get regular massages or waxing or whatever. I'm so low maintenance that I'm like the cactus of the female world - BUT I still know that I like to be rewarded once in a while, I do like to maintain standards, and that if I'm not looking after me, nobody else will. It doesn't matter what you choose to do as part of your self-care routine, just DO IT. **Make self-care an essential part of your regular business routine because it's easily one of the best business investments you'll ever make.**

Who Is Riding In Your Sag Wagon?

My Dad used to be a long-distance 'weekend warrior' cyclist - one of those overweight but enthusiastic lycra-clad old men you see travelling in packs on Sunday mornings in most big cities. He loved "biking" as he called it, and tried very hard to get us kids involved in his sport. I was the least enthusiastic child in this pursuit, but being a good Dad, he offered me to "ride in the sag wagon" instead so at least we were doing something together. The sag wagon in the cycling world is the vehicle which follows behind the pack of cyclists and (among other things) holds all their gear like spare tires and luggage, and picks up any cyclists who have "sagged out" of the trip.

In other words, when you can't last the distance, the sag wagon picks your sorry butt off the road and helps you get to the finish line with your bike chucked in the back.

I've always promised honesty in this blog so here it is: the last couple of months have been pretty tough for my business. Blame it on the rain, on the economy, on the season, on the industry being over saturated; blame it on Marcia's getting braces - the fact remains that for a few months, business has not been the easiest road to cycle down. Luckily, things are turning around and I'm steadily heading back down the track - but it has got me thinking about how invaluable my own business sag wagon has been to me.

Today I want you to think about your own sag wagon, and think about the people, things, or other resources you've got that are going to help when it feels like your feet can't push those pedals not even one more revolution up that hill. I didn't grow my business - or this blog - alone: I did it with a sag wagon full of things I could not carry and people who were willing to let me rest awhile while they drove.

Here's who (and what) rides in my sag wagon:

- My partner: Not just because he is great at deliveries, can give me technical engineering advice on cakes, or because he's great at folding aprons. He makes it on this list because he believes in me WHEN I DON'T. You *have* to have someone who has unfailing faith in your ability to succeed. You've got to have someone outside yourself who cheers you on, commiserates when things go wrong, and who encourages you to be better every day.

- My product: At the heart of it, I believe in our products. I know without doubt that my team and I produce some great stuff. When I'm having a crappy day, the products we produce and those we've produced previously stand up as examples of what I - and this business - are capable of. I've been known to sit down, look through our portfolios and say to a team member, "Seriously, we make some awesome stuff!" You have got to totally believe that what you do or how you do it is truly fabulous and that it's worth people buying it. If you don't think anything about your business or your product is truly remarkable, who else will?

- The numbers: For a long time, I hated doing financial stuff (okay, I still do.) At the end of each month, I add up the income we earned and submit that info to my bookkeepers. The numbers do not lie. Either they inspire me to think of new things, or they remind me that I need to stop whining because the situation is not as dire as I think it is. There is comfort in numbers. Do this weekly if you need to. Become friends with the finances even if it feels like they are the playground bullies who will push you off your bike when you ride past.

- Feedback: I've got an email folder labelled "Awesome Stuff" which is where I put all the thank you emails, photos of kids eating cake, and copies of online reviews I've gotten. Feeling saggy? Re-read that stuff. Not only do YOU think your product is great, total strangers do, too.

- Oreos: Self explanatory.

- "Oooh Shiny!" things: When I'm feeling my most out of energy, I'll often bring an idea out into the light which has been sitting in the darkness. I'm one of those people who always has a good idea for something but nearly never gets the chance to try it out. Everything from how to use a piping tip in a different way, to a new business idea, to a new product. I write all these brilliant ideas down and get excited about them and tell the whole world about them, but then lack the time to pursue them. When I can't push the pedals anymore, I rely on my creativity and the excitement I felt about those ideas to propel me forward into innovation. Maybe in those scribbled notes there really IS a germ of an idea which will lead to something big. Maybe not - but the sheer excitement of bringing an old idea into the light and looking at it again gives me the burst of energy I need.

- My hands: Like you, I got into business because I loved to decorate cakes. For me, baking (not just decorating) is like a form of therapy, so the slow times are when I bake stuff I like, not stuff I have to make for a client. Muffins for my kids' lunches, a recipe I tore out of a magazine, the recipe in that cookbook I got as a birthday present but never opened. Creating something with my hands and then enjoying it is a GREAT way to pick one's butt off the side of the road because hot chocolate chip cookies can pretty much restore anyone's faith in the world.

- My colleagues: Never underestimate the power of a decent latte and lunch with a friend who is in the business, too. Nothing feels as good as decent bitch-and-gossip session with someone who just "gets it".

All those things - and all those people - are right there in my sag wagon, ready and able to help when my muscles are screaming out in pain and I get a flat tire *and* the bill for my new bike is overdue. It's all good and well to have the most amazing decorating skills, the most wonderful clients, the whizz-bang website and fifty thousand Instagram followers -but even with all of that, you're going to have times when the energy reserves get low and you'll need someone or something to give you that little nudge up the hill.

I left one crucial item off that list. It's the easiest to forget, the hardest to appreciate but provides the most forward movement of all and that's this: ME. The knowledge that I am actually a *passenger* in other people's sag wagons is perhaps the most powerful motivator of all. The knowledge that I didn't get to where I am without inspiring at least a few people along the way goes a LONG way to making me find the energy to continue innovating, continue trying, continue riding that damn bike no matter how much my butt hurts. You have the resources in your wagon in the first place because *you did not get this far alone.* Other people rode alongside you, up ahead of you, or are only a little ways behind you in part because you climbed on the bike in the first place.

It's not a marathon, it's not a sprint, and **there may be no finish line** - so it's really just about knowing that you can keep riding as long as you have the sag wagon not far behind.

Who is riding in your sag wagon these days?

How To Avoid Making Mistakes In Your Business

One of my earliest "paid" cakes.

I recently read a post over on my friend MJ Valentine's blog where she wrote a letter to her 15-year-old self (http://mjvalentine.com/live-love/gay-okay-things-id-say-15-year-old). It inspired me to write a letter to the Michelle who was just thinking about starting out in business - I thought I might give her a hand and help her avoid a ton of mistakes. If I could go back in time, she probably wouldn't listen to anything I have to say (she's stubborn as hell, and prefers to learn how to do things the hard way) but ... I'm going to give it a try.

Dear Michie*,

(*"Michie" is what I call myself in my head. This is how I'll know this letter is from me, because I don't allow ANYONE else to call me that.)

Another really early cake. Don't you love my gaping ribbon and fabulous backdrop?!

*Hello from your future self, the self who is now on the OTHER SIDE of that "I'm going to own an amazing cake shop" dream goal. I have to tell you, sister, you did some pretty damn spectacular things. **You did it. You actually did it.** You created the shop which only existed in your head. You made a WHOLE HELL OF A LOT of people really, really happy, you met some amazing cake people, you influenced and inspired a lot of people. You also ate wwwaaayyyyy too much chocolate, but that's how you deal with stress so I forgive you. Now that I've been there, done that AND got the dirty aprons (and t-shirts) to prove it, I thought I'd give you a bit of guidance so that the road from there to here isn't quite as bumpy. Here's the stuff I wish you had known way back when you were secretly buying and hoarding one cake toy at a time (and one glass jar at a time) for your dream cake shop.*

Stop Beating Yourself Up *- Life is way too short to constantly give yourself a hard time about the stuff you haven't done yet, or the things you should be doing faster or harder or better. You're always feeling like you won't be as successful as those cake gods, or other business owners are doing better than you are financially, or you feel like a fraud every time you teach someone how to pipe a buttercream border or ganache a cake. Cut out that bullshit right now. It's a waste of time. Instead, know that you're doing the best you can with the resources you've got, and that's better than most people. It's time for a bit of self love.*

This is me about 3 years into my business.

Get the Client Database Happening from DAY ONE *- Grow your tribe really, really early on. As soon as you read this, in fact. Collect client information and especially* email addresses because this is going to be VITAL to the growth of your business, and later on it's the one project you really regret not doing properly. You have got to have a way to consistently contact your fans and clients and a proper database is the single best way to do it. This is non-negotiable, so listen to me on this one, okay? Grow your tribe. They love you and your product, so you've got to be able to tell them about it.

Take Time Off - You can afford to do it, and I promise that you won't lose that many orders because you take a week off twice a year. Your mental health will be WAY better if you do it. Let me assure you that therapy costs a lot more than a week at home sleeping and eating properly does. You need to just remember to breathe, and the best way to do that is to build in some time off to your schedule. Whatever orders you may lose over those two weeks are worth less than the investment in your own well-being.

It's Going to Be WAY Harder - and WAY BETTER - Than You Think - You're one of those over-achiever people who makes things happen no matter what, so it's going to be a hell of a shock when you realise no amount of hard work is equal to success. You're still going to work more hours, pop more anti-inflammatories, and feel like you've been run over a bus more times than you can count. The good news is, you'll also be so loved, so inspired, so supported and so grateful for all of it that you'll forget the painful bits and keep coming back for more (a bit like childbirth for some people). You'll also be glad that you realised early on that it was more about business than it was about cake, and the investments you've made in your business knowledge were worth it ... even if some days it still feels like you have no idea what the hell you're doing. You're doing it for the love AND the money, and that's why it's both harder and better than you imagine.

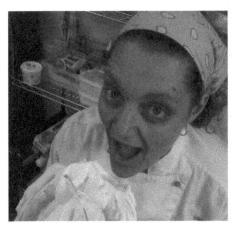

This is me in year 6 of my business.

Let's Talk About The Money - *Remember that piece of paper where you wrote down every single start-up cost and expense of the business so you knew how much money you needed to start off with? You big nerd, you even included a pack of garbage bags and a bottle of dishwashing liquid! TRIPLE that amount. Not because your maths was wrong, but because you forgot to leave yourself a financial safety net and that causes you more stress than anything else ever will. Hire the bookkeeper REALLY early on (stop trying to do it yourself), remember that the tax you have to pay is a good thing (because if you were not earning real money, you would not be paying real taxes) and learn as much about money, finance, pricing and general numbers as you possibly can, because (as you will later say to your students): THE CONFIDENCE COMES FROM THE NUMBERS. Don't be afraid of money, about checking your bank balance, about asking clients for what you are worth, about needing to ask for financial help. Make friends with "the whole money thing" even though it freaks you right the heck out, because there is no shame in wanting or needing to make a living. None-what-so-ever. "Starving artists" are really just people who didn't bother to make friends with the money. Money is not scary if it allows you to pay for the kids' school fees and invest in the business. You need to THRIVE, not just SURVIVE so make friends with the whole numbers and money thing.*

Don't Let Fear Rule Your Decisions - *Every single time you were afraid of something but did it anyway (introduced a new product line, moving to a bigger premises, hosting an international teacher, started a blog) it worked out. Not always in the way you hoped (that one international teacher didn't end up as fab as you hoped ...) but the lessons you got from it or the opportunities it created made feeling the fear worth it. Your naked cake idea is going to take off, moving to bigger premises works out really well, starting a blog was a good idea ... it all worked out okay even though you were scared. Learn to make cupcakes (!!), get in on that whole dessert bar thing and go with that chocolate dipped everything idea you had, hire the business coach, take the accounting class. Pay attention to your gut and then jump in - too many times you either created or saw a good idea or trend or class you wanted to take or do, then you dragged your heels out of fear and missed the boat as a result. Just. Do. It. Stop being afraid because, dear Michie, that's an utter waste of energy and emotion.*

You're Going to Plan to Succeed, and Still Fail (sometimes) - *Although your big plan was to sell the business when you turned 40, something WAY more awesome is going to come along way before that which will fulfil you way more. So - make the endless plans and To Do lists, and then don't fall apart if the plans don't always go right, or if there is a fork in the road or you need to make a bigger decision before the time you planned to. I've learned that there is no real thing as failure,* *there's just a whole lot of lessons to learn ... most of which are more valuable then you will realise right then and there. You're going to make money, lose money, screw up orders, create masterpieces, feel like a failure, feel like a goddess, make some pretty poor decisions and some really genius ones - but you're also going to come out a better person for ALL of it. Just accept now that sometimes, you'll screw up. Ehhh. It happens. You'll move on and keep on going. Some early product development ... which I should have actually followed through on. Mmmm, homemade s'mores!*

Some early product development ... which I should have actually followed through on. Mmmm, homemade s'mores!

Let's Talk About the Money (again) *- It will take you being in business for several years for you to work out WHY you are in business, because at this point you still think it's about cake. It's not. It's about making people happy, and those people include yourself and your kids. This means your business needs to make money - real money, not just pocket money. Take bigger risks with your money in terms of investing more in the business right from the very beginning, but also, make sure that safety net is there (at least 6 months of rent and wages) so you're not going to freak out about it. Having the safety net means you make less fear-based decisions, you have the freedom to invest where you want to, and it fixes up the really big fat tax problem you created somewhere around Year 6 of the business. I'm saying this again in the hopes you'll listen to me: <u>make friends with the money. Better the devil you know! (really)</u>*

The Cake Will Fall Over *- There is a 6 tier (3 double barrel) wedding cake which will fall over in the back of the car with a sickening thud. There will also be a 3 tier* red velvet cake where the bottom tier totally explodes AT THE VENUE, as well as some figurines whose hands fall off while you are setting it up in front of the bride. You'll also spell a few names on cakes wrong, random cake bits will fall off, break totally or fall over, some cakes will just never ever stand up straight, and you'll have a couple of clients who complain or offend you so much that you cry. There is that one REALLY crazy lady who ... ahh, actually, I'll let you discover that one for yourself. Oh, and driving away from a wedding cupcake tower set up, you'll back into the groom's son's car and smash in the whole side panel of it less than an hour before the wedding starts. Very embarrassing. I promise you that every time, you'll seriously feel like crap about it, but every time you'll get up and keep going. I promise, you survive every one. 100% of the time. It always ends up being about how you deal with it more than it is about what actually happened.

My very first fondant wedding cake, first figurines, first sugar flowers – my final year pastry school project.

Here's the thing, Michie. Every step you take in your business, you're going to come up against one really big roadblock: YOURSELF. The problem is never the lack of money, lack of time, lack of confidence or customers who only care about the wrong things. The problem is simply that sometimes, you'll be indifferent, sometimes skeptical, sometimes procrastinating, sometimes worrying the heck out of things. It's the choices you make even though you feel those things which will lead you to <u>this moment</u>. I'm going to let you in on a secret from the future. This moment (the one I'm writing to you from) is the one where you've sold the business as you planned, you're raising your kids as you would like to, you're getting to hang out with amazing people, and you finally get to be the writer you wanted to be. You are actually living the life you wanted for yourself. **You did it. You really did it.** It's not perfect (would be nice to lose 10 kilos, make more money, finally learn to sew, fix up the house a bit blah blah blah) but you know what? This moment and this life? It's a life of love, adventure, gratitude and sweetness - which is precisely what you're aiming for, cake shop or not.

There is so much more I could warn you about, Michie - the employee who quits on you with no notice, the dodgy landlord you have to deal with (and it costs you a bomb to sort that out), the advertising you paid a heap for but it netted you nothing ... and so on. The thing is, there is so much more BRILLIANT stuff I could tell you about, too - the mothers who cry tears of gratitude, the little kids whose faces light up when they see their cakes, the other business owners who tell you that you inspire them to be better, the people from all walks of life that you will meet. I can't tell you all of it, though, because you've got to get back to learning by doing and I've got to keep on keeping on, too. I've got so much I still want to do! Actually, that's my last lesson (and maybe the hardest) - don't be so damn impatient. Things have a way of happening exactly how and when they were meant to.

And, as always, be grateful. Not everyone gets to make a living doing what they love. You will. Every single day, make sure you stop for a moment and just be grateful about it. Breathe.

Love (and a whole lot of chocolate buttons stolen from the 15 kilo bag),

Michelle

Don't Waste Good Chocolate

One of the most fabulous resources your business can have for free (but which is utterly invaluable) is a mentor. I'm not talking about business coaches (although they are valuable, they're not free.) I think you've really got to have more than one mentor, but you've got to have one at the very least.

Before I carry on about why this is so important, I want to tell you two stories.

In real life, I teach a class on the basics of how to run a cake business. I've run this class quite a few times now, and at the start and end of every class, I tell the students that they have open access to me at any time. I invite them to call me, text me, email me, Facebook message me, or if they want to, call and invite me out for lunch. I'll give them my time, my knowledge and my unwavering support ... entirely for free. Basically, I'm happy to help them out and *I really mean it*. (By the way - I make that offer for the same reason I write this blog. Because I wish someone had offered it to me way back when.)

In all this time and all those students, only ONE person has taken me up on this offer. Now, business coaches (the real kind) would tell me that because I don't put a price on my time, these people don't really think it's valuable and so they don't take me up on the offer.

Bullshit.

These people don't take me up on it because they're afraid to, or embarrassed to, or somehow just don't want to make that call which says, "Hey, Michelle? I could use some help here." Asking for help is SO HARD to do, and especially to do it to someone we might look up to, or someone who has already achieved what we're wanting to achieve ourselves (yes, I'm assuming the lack of phone calls is not because secretly they all thought I was an ogre). Plus in an industry as saturated as this one is, it takes a very brave person to stand up and admit to needing some support - because everyone around you seems to be doing it all so *effortlessly*, don't they? (Bastards!)

Basically, my phone is much quieter than I would have thought.

My second story is about how being brave enough to ask for help netted me the best business advice I ever got. When my cake business was still just a bit of (edible) twinkle in my eye, I sat down in a cafe to write down some ideas about my future dream business. I ordered a hot chocolate and a gingerbread man (yes, okay, secretly I'm 12 years old. Whatever. Don't hate.) Anyway, I was looking at the gingerbread man packaging and saw an address on the back - and it was a couple of blocks away from the cafe I was sitting in. Long story short - after my snack I drove there to see if I could get a job (nothing ventured, nothing gained, yes?) The owner wasn't in, but I got given her name and number. I called her, but instead of asking for a job I kissed her ass a little and told her how much I admired her (true) and asked if I could buy her a coffee and get some insight into owning a small baking business.

Much to my shock, she agreed and we booked in a time to meet.

To make a long story even longer, she reneged on her offer. I went to meet her, she got kinda suspicious and weird about it and basically, just let me hang around her for ten minutes, before she kicked me out (which she nicely but firmly did.) In that ten minutes, I got more useful, practical, invaluable advice than I'd ever gotten before or since - and that's advice which *I now teach you and teach my students*. I jokingly refer to her as "the ten-minute mentor" because that's how long the relationship lasted.

Since then, I've acquired and nurtured relationships with all kinds of mentors and each of them has brought a facet either to me or my business which just wasn't there before. I've got one mentor who is twice my age, and has never owned a baking business in her life ... but she knows a hell of a lot about being a working mother, and keeping it real while doing so. I've got one who I met through my business and she works in one of the country's biggest PR companies - she gives me PR advice, I give her cake advice (because she decorates as a hobby). I've got mentors who are small business owners both in and OUT of this industry and they all bring different things to the table. Most of this is pretty informal. I'll call one of them and say, "Hey, I've got this crazy idea - can I run it past you?" or "I want to start a PR campaign but I don't even know what PR means - can I buy you lunch?" Over time I developed these relationships and I call on these people when I need them - sometimes we'll meet regularly (once a month usually) and sometimes only when the need arises. You would be astounded at how much free advice is out there if you just have the balls to ask for it.

I talked about having people in your sag wagon[36] a few posts ago. These are similar people but they ride in your BUSINESS sag wagon. They serve a slightly different purpose but they are just as important. I recently somewhere that this is a bit like having your own "war council" to call on in times of change.

What these stories are demonstrating is that asking for help is scary as hell, but asking for help might also give you some of the BEST resources which money

---

36   See *Who Is Riding In Your Sag Wagon* in Chapter 10.

CAN'T buy. Open your eyes to the people around you who might be useful to have as mentors. They won't all be bakers. They might be small business owners. They are probably <u>not</u> related to you, and they are probably <u>not</u> your immediate friends (although they might be helpful to have in your corner, too.)

Here's what I'm saying: pick up the phone and ASK FOR HELP. Be honest. No, don't call your immediate competition and ask them for business advice - but maybe call someone with a business you admire who seems to get things done in a way you feel is similar to how you'd like to conduct yourself. The worst outcome is that they will say no, the best is that they will be flattered enough to give you their time (and hopefully more than ten minutes' worth). Mentors - in all shapes and sizes, in all industries - are by far one of the best investments you can make in both yourself and your business. Make the time to find some and nurture those relationships and I think you'll find that the reward for them is as big as it is for you. There is nothing more wonderful than the giving and receiving of love and help - even in a business arena.

Stop texting. Stop Facebooking. GO make a call. You might get something out of it, you might get nothing ... but without making the call, it's a bit like leaving the expensive chocolate on the shelf to just gather dust.

CHAPTER 11

WHEN YOU NEED SOME TOUGH LOVE

Whoever said small business was easy was clearly sniffing a lot of confectioners' sugar in the back room.

This whole small business thing is hard work – but the pay-off is enormous and I'm not talking about money here. I learned so much about myself in the course of running my business. I also believe that the lessons and experiences you will have in business will shape the rest of your life whether you stay in business or you don't. Me, I learned invaluable lessons about what I am truly capable of, about skills I didn't even know I had, about friendship, about love, about money, about what things I can tolerate in myself and others and what things I can't.

Mostly, I learned that if anyone is going to get this thing off the ground, it's me. The joy and the pain of being a small business owner is that YOU are always the person in charge. I've learned that being the Boss Lady is incredibly freeing and incredibly terrifying, and sometimes I feel both those things in the same moment. If you're feeling more terrified than freed, this is the chapter for you.

Five Thousand Macarons

Your brother in law is going to put your website together for you, and you can't take orders until it's done ... but it's been months now and it's still not done. You want boxes which are a certain shade of pink but you can't find them anywhere, and you don't want to put your cakes in the same white boxes that everyone else does. Your child is only in day-care one day a week, and every time you get to the end of that day, you still have the same list of jobs which did not get done. You're waiting on a special cutter to arrive from overseas. You need a bigger mixer and you've spent months waiting for the one you want to go on sale. You need a bigger oven, but you've looked at twelve different models and you still can't decide which one to buy.

Does any of this sound familiar?

You are sure you've got a great business idea, you know your product is fabulous, and you really want to get this thing going. So what's the problem? Well, the oven is not right and the boxes are not pink and ... yeah, right. What you really are is stuck because you're afraid of succeeding. Over the years, I've had the great honour of people asking me to mentor them in small business, and without doubt most of the time their questions and "problems" boil down to a fear of success. The funny thing is how often their comments and questions seem to have nothing to do with success at all. For example: What if I get an order for 5, 000 macarons and I can't make them all? I can't get the perfect (insert tool) for my cakes, so I can't start taking orders until I import those. My packaging is taking forever to get designed and I don't want to go to market with cheap-looking boxes. I can't ... but what if ... I still need ... there aren't any ... are all sentences people say when what they're really saying is, "I'm terrified I might succeed, and so I'll come up with lots of excuses as to why I can't even move forward."

A really classic example of this was the French cake maker who told me she lays awake at night worried about how she will cope with massive orders, given that her oven can only make 24 cakes at a time. I asked her how many customers she currently has - and the answer was ZERO. So she was worrying about coping with big orders when she didn't even have a single order yet ... and she genuinely could not see that this was a problem. It's the OVEN which was the problem - of course.

It sounds funny, doesn't it? To be so worried or afraid of succeeding that we end up paralyzed and unable to move forward. What all of us are afraid of is neither success nor failure - *we're just afraid of change*. We're moving our own goalposts and that's a scary thing to do, isn't it? We surround ourselves with comfortable circumstances and then, even though we say we want to change, we don't. It's HARD work, this changing business -committing to forward movement, committing to taking action - all of these are things which stress us right the heck out. I think sometimes we don't even realise that we are sabotaging ourselves by being afraid - we wrap that fear up neatly in the worry of oven sizes, or packaging, or not having exactly the right logo. We're really afraid of the changes this will mean to our lives, the fear of not being as 'good' at what we do as we think we are (or others tell us we are), the fear of being the boss (and all the good OR bad which comes with that.) We're afraid of what our lives might be like if we do succeed - because *that* life is different to *this* life, and *this* life is the one we're used to.

If you're reading this and thinking, "She's full of it. Of COURSE, I'm committed to succeeding and of course I want to make it work! I just can't get the things done which I need to! It's got nothing to do with fear of success!", then do me a small favour and give this exercise a try. I've asked you in the past few weeks to really think hard about your business and the reasons behind being in business in the first place. Here, too, I'm going to ask you to think back on that answer AND think about the reasons why you may not be moving forward.

First, ask yourself: Am I not making progress because my (packaging/logo/whatever) is not right? Is my business really going to either succeed or fail because of this issue?

Second, remind yourself your earlier answer to the question: What is my reason for being in business? Then go back to the first question: is not having the right (packaging/logo/whatever) actually keeping me from fulfilling that actual purpose or is it something else? (Hint: It's not about the "stuff".)

So how do you deal with this fear? How do you remember that it's not about the boxes, the oven, the fancy cake pans? This is where the hard yards come in. You remind yourself WHY you're doing this - and you stop worrying about the stuff which isn't going to get you moving because the thing is just to GET MOVING. It's not to say that those smaller concerns are not valid. Of course they are - but in and of themselves they are just <u>not a good enough reason to be stuck</u> where you're stuck. Stop giving the little stuff the power to rule your life.

Once you remind yourself why you're in this game to begin with, I want you to think (in detail) about what life might be like when you succeed. Really think about what that might be like - and not just the good stuff. Think about the added responsibility. The Saturdays which won't be your own. The money you'll make, the freedom you'll have, the joy you will feel every time a client beams a big smile at you and says, "It's amazing! Thank you! You're a genius!" The times you'll have to deal with big bills but no orders. The good, the bad, the ugly of your new venture. Close your eyes and imagine that life. Get real and get honest about it.

Then ask yourself if the packaging, the oven, the (insert limiting item here) even appear in those mental pictures except in a small supporting role. If they don't - then it's time to put those things aside and choose progress over stagnation. In the early stages of business, it's so very easy to get stuck on the details - but the details are not going to move you forward and what's more, the details have a very annoying habit of stopping your forward movement entirely.

Rather than leave you with an example (because most of those I've mentioned above are in fact, mine anyway ...) I'm going to leave you with this simple thought:

Without <u>progress</u>, you will have neither failure nor success. The details will work themselves out if you remain focussed on the bigger picture. Commit to the bigger picture. Don't commit to the details.

So, today I want you to make progress - what, if anything, is currently holding you back - and what you're going to do about it? Be brave.

Detours Not Roadblocks

I'm going to give you the gist of this post right here at the beginning.

If you can work on:

1. Figuring out what your problems are, and then
2. Some possible ways to solve them, and then
3. Actually move forward on trying out those solutions

You'll be miles and miles ahead of most people, including your competitors.

You need to become the GPS that recalculates it's route when things don't go exactly from Point A to Point B as they were meant to or you'd like them to.

Have you ever had a friend who asks you for advice, doesn't take it, tells you why your advice is no good, but then a short time later they come back to you asking for more advice? I'm finding the same experience is true of being a business mentor. I've got people who are brave enough to ask for advice (which I really admire them for, that takes guts) ... they then get the advice ... then write back and tell me how my advice *can't possibly work*. Often they then list a whole lot of new problems to add to the first list. Then they want advice on this new list, which they get from me, and then again I get told my advice *won't work*.

I'm not saying my advice is always right, nor am I upset that they don't take it. I'm just sometimes left wondering if what they wanted was advice, or what they wanted was someone to listen (which I'm happy to do), or if maybe, just possibly ... it wouldn't matter if it was cake or widgets or umbrellas, these people are *simply not going to succeed in being business owners.*

Harsh, I know. But here's why I'm wondering that: At some point, no advice in the world is going to help you move forward until you <u>decide</u> that it's time to move forward. I do not mean to belittle these problems at all. They're real. They're challenging. They feel like enormous roadblocks to your success. There are sometimes a hell of a lot of them. They can feel insurmountable, they really can.

Here's the truth of it - the difference between those of you who will be successful and those who won't is this:

> The ones who act like a GPS and find <u>DETOURS</u> around the problems will succeed.

> The ones who only find ROADBLOCKS ... and a few more roadblocks ... and still a few more ... **will not** be able to move forward. Their journey ends right here, stuck on the side of the road.

Problems are real, problems are painful, problems will always be there in different degrees. At some point, you need to *make the decision to find the detours*.

So once you've decided to stop feeling crappy about all the problems you have, and try to find some detours around them, how do you do this when it's all just so overwhelming?

Here's how to be a GPS:

> **STEP ONE:** Sit down with a mug of tea or entire bottle of wine or a sleeve of Oreos, and make a no-holds-barred list of your business problems. ALL the ones you can think of. From little ("I can't find decent packaging", "My chocolate cake recipe is inconsistent") to big ("I owe my suppliers 20K", "My family is not at all supportive of my venture") and everything in between ("My local council is being a pain in the butt about registration", "I've got a lot of local competition undercutting me.")

> Then drink some wine or dunk some Oreos or chant or whatever makes you feel a little bit calmer, because it will have taken some real, serious energy to have let all that out of your brain and onto paper. It might look like a heck of a lot of problems.

> **STEP TWO:** Look at that list and order NOT in terms of which problem *feels* the biggest, but which one is really and truly the biggest roadblock to your *long-term* success. The thing which, without it being solved, *you can't really move onto any of the other problems* on your list because this

one is the linchpin. Be honest here. This is where you feel the fear[37] but move ahead ANYWAY. Detours, not roadblocks.

STEP THREE: Another sip of wine, oreo, chanting, etc. ... then go and make a list of possible detours to that ONE roadblock, even if some of the detours seem a little outlandish ("Marry George Clooney", "Win the lottery"). Just come up with a list of *possible* solutions to your big fat problem. Don't be limited by possibility (I'm pretty sure George is taken). Just let it all fall out of your head onto the bit of paper (or screen). Be creative, be brave, THINK HARD.

STEP FOUR: (and this is the HARDEST thing of all) - put away the wine and Oreos actually take some of those detours. Get rid of the truly crazy solutions and try out some of the reasonable ones. Work at solving this big ol' problem of yours, in whatever way you can. It might take a while to solve it, it might require several detours before you get there, it frankly may never get solved entirely the perfect way you hope it might. But without at least looking for the detours in the first place, you'll just get stuck back at the roadblocks. Just work on solving PROBLEM NUMERO UNO. For now, don't worry about all the other ones on your list.

It's not that the problems aren't real or aren't significant. They absolutely are.

It's that you have to be willing to look for a solution to at least one problem, or you'll just get overwhelmed by all of them.

So.

Deep breath.

Do this:

1. Figure out your problems.

2. Come up with some solutions for the biggest one of all.

3. Try the solutions out.

I make it sound simple, don't I?

Successful business owners really do this. They look for detours, then take them (and thus leave their competition in the dust). They do not sit on the side of the road looking pissed off because their GPS led them down a street which ends in an

---

37   See *Five Thousand Macarons* in Chapter 11.

alleyway.

Find DETOURS.

Feel The Fear And Do It Anyway

I'm telling you these stories for one reason and one reason only - to show you how sometimes doing the thing which scares the heck out of you is usually the Universe telling you that this is *exactly* what you should be doing. By nature I am NOT a risk taker. I'm a very driven, highly motivated go-getter but I am no fool. So I research the hell out of just about everything, I think (too much) about the options, and I even PLAN conversations in my head about stuff. I even think about what might happen after the fact, if my plan doesn't work, and what might happen after the fact if my plan DOES work. I am very quick to make decisions, but usually because I've already thought about or researched about fifty billion possibilities in my head first.

So I'm not a risk taker - but I take massive leaps. I rip the bandaid off as quickly as I can because I'd much rather be a doer than a thinker.

Here's my story.

When I was 20 years old, I came out here to Australia to do a one year study abroad program. Six months later, I was engaged, and nine months after that I was married. I had NO intention of coming here to meet a man (at the age of 20 I had already decided I was going to be a spinster aunt anyway). More than the crazy of getting engaged to someone you don't know very well, along with the deal came the move to Australia because my fiancé was a Melbourne boy who would not survive living anywhere else (or so he claimed). So at age 20, I decided to marry someone and move to an entirely different country for him. Oh, and he's a lot older than me, was my first "serious" boyfriend, I didn't know another soul here other than the other international students, and I came from a very close-knit family. So I decided to uproot everything I knew and loved, and just ... marry an old guy I barely knew and follow him to a country with funny accents and strange foods. What the ... ? (And in case you are wondering, no, my parents were not at all impressed.)

About a month into our relationship, I recognised that things were getting serious, so in a very Michelle-like fashion, I wrote down a list of questions, the things that freaked me out the most about this relationship. "Do I love him enough to make this choice?", "How do I feel about the age difference?" and so on - there were about 6-7 questions. Then every week that went by, I answered those questions and I wrote the answers down. As our relationship grew (and we went through ups and downs, as relationships do) the answers would change and ran the gamut from HELL YES to OH DEAR GOD NO.

As the weeks wore on, I found it harder and harder to answer those questions. Not because I didn't want or need the answers, but because I realised that in the greater scheme of things, they weren't going to actually give me the answers I wanted. The answer I was looking for HAD ALREADY BEEN ANSWERED simply because I cared about this man enough to bother creating a ridiculous list of questions. I already knew the answer, I was just seeking validation from the questions - a validation that would never come. The truth of it is, making that decision scared the shit out of me. This was huge. I was making a long-term choice, with potentially far reaching and life changing consequences.

It's fair to say these guys are pretty life changing ...

Admittedly, I got lucky. We're still very much in love, we have great kids, I took one hell of a gamble and it paid off. Not all my decisions are like that (wouldn't it be nice if they were!) What I learned from that (and subsequent leaps) is that it's when you feel the MOST scared, the most excited, the most oh-my-god-what-am-I-thinking about something ... that's when you should probably do it the most. ALL of the people I've interviewed for this blog had to do the same thing - make the leap from their stable, normal jobs into being full-time decorators and bakers. ALL of them. I can assure you they were all scared out of their sweet little minds when they did it - but the important thing is, they DID it.

So if you've read the Tour website (http://www.bizbakeontour.com) through a bunch of times (and have had it rolling around in the back of your mind ever since), go ahead and write down the list of reasons you are afraid to come along with me. Because I thought about this (of course), I probably can name a few of those fears for you. So I know, the amount of money is scary, taking the time off is also scary, and you might even be scared that Sharon and I will stand there in judgement because of what you have - or have not - done thus far with your business (we won't). You're probably also scared of what Sharon and I might ask you to do - namely, examine your business idea, examine your business dream, answer some very hard questions about what you want to do or why you do it. If you find any of those parts scary, it's because somewhere in your heart of hearts, <u>the decision has already been made</u>. You KNOW that you want to move your dream to the next level, and here we are asking you to get the HELL out of your comfort zone and face the reality of actually DOING this thing.

Dreaming is SO much easier, isn't it? Nobody asks hard questions, tells you to take time off work, or charges you for the pleasure. Dreaming is <u>safe</u>. Dreaming is <u>easy</u>.

Dreaming won't get you anywhere but warm and comfy in your bed (which is a nice place to be, but not really a good place to decorate cake. Ever slept in a bed filled with sprinkles? Very uncomfortable.)

I can tell (because I was you, not that long ago) that reading this post alone is probably making you feel a little defensive. A little uncomfortable. A little ... annoyed with me for saying that you've got to listen to that inner voice and take the leap you've been avoiding for so long. Maybe even a little annoyed because I'm asking you to spend some money ON YOURSELF and get your business out of your head and into the real world (and nothing irritates people more than being asked to spend money AND spend money on something which is scary to even think about.) And maybe ... just maybe ... you think it's uncool that I write this blog for free and yet here I am, asking to get paid for this thing.

That's the second scary leap I said I'd tell you about. I decided to launch this class and charge for it when nothing like it had ever been done before, not here in Australia nor anywhere else. I've chosen to invest real money (which I don't have too much spare of, let's be honest here), and a whole lot of time and a whole lot of love in this thing. I can tell you that I keep getting told that nobody wants to do live courses anymore, that 'everyone' just wants to do online videos for $19. 99, that nobody can afford to take a weekend off to do a live course. I've also been told that I don't have a big enough audience, I picked cities that are too small, cities that are too big, I priced it too high, I priced it too low, it's not possible to do a live AND an online course, and so on and so forth. Oh man oh man, if I listened to all of those, this thing would never have gotten off the ground. (A bit like my cake business.)

So I called my friend Sharon and I told her we should do this crazy thing, and then I've worked my butt off to bring it to fruition. And, you know, it might not work as well as it does in my head ... but I'm going to do it anyway.

Why?

Because I believe in dreaming big, and also DOING big.

I also find that scary as hell. Seriously. Every time I do anything to do with this course, it scares me (and I spent a lot of time thinking about that fear.)

<u>I do it anyway.</u>

The alternative - to not do the things which I believe in - well, that's not really an alternative, is it? And - sitting here and saying to my kids or my friends or family I didn't even try is WAY SCARIER than trying and failing.

So, I write this post (and I hit the publish button) a little bit afraid of what might happen if the course sells out, and a little bit afraid of what might happen if it doesn't.

I'm feeling the fear - and I'm doing it anyway.

It's the fear which tells me that this is exactly the right thing to be doing.

Feeling Inadequate

SUCCESS
it's not always what you see

Do you ever look at cake pictures and think, "I'll never be that good!"?

Or, do you ever read about those business people who appear to 'have it all' and think, "There's no way I could manage doing all of that!"?

Or, does it seem like you're working your butt off in your business and getting nowhere, while someone else doesn't appear to be working as hard but they also appear to be raking in the dough?

This is a highly competitive industry with a lot of really talented people in it. I am not at all surprised that we sometimes feel inadequate or that lack of confidence is the main reason we do not pursue our dreams. It can be hard to look at your cake and compare it to someone else's - regardless of whether that someone else is a 'cake god' or just your nearest competitor. It becomes even harder when you've got a good idea but a lack of confidence keeps you from executing the idea ... and then a short while later someone else announces that very same idea to great fanfare. You then of course spend ages beating yourself up about not coming out with that idea when you had it, and then also feeling proprietary about it, "But it was MY idea! I was there first!"

Oh, how I wish I could bottle up confidence and sell it to you all, or be a bit like the Wizard of Oz, and hand you all a big fat stack of medals and that would be enough to give you courage. Sadly, that's not an option, so instead here are a couple of things which help me every time I think I'll never measure up.

1. I remember that appearances are just that. Appearances. You never truly know what is going on underneath the surface. We don't know how hard someone is really working, how much they are sacrificing, how much money they borrowed, and what their relationship is like. Any of us who have been shocked by "the perfect couple" getting a divorce knows that the only person who knows what's happening ... is the person themselves. Don't focus too much on what "everyone else" has, because remember that they are simply showing you what they CHOOSE to show you. I can't tell you how many times friends would call me and say, "I'm so jealous, your business is doing AMAZINGLY!" because of what I'd posted on Facebook, when in truth I was wondering where the hell the money for the rent was going to come from.

BE KIND,
FOR
EVERYONE
YOU MEET
IS FIGHTING A
HARD BATTLE

2. Encourage one another. One of the best ways to make yourself feel better is just to do a kindness for someone else. So next time you see a picture someone else has uploaded and you think, "Oh my god, that's a total train wreck!" instead I want you to comment with something good about it, or a nice and polite suggestion for how they might improve. We ALL started somewhere and the best way to get kindness is simply to give kindness. Just like we don't know the truth behind the people we admire, nor do we know the truth behind the people whose creations we think are terrible. You have no idea if they spent all night on that or not, or if because they have arthritis they can't physically roll out that fondant any thinner.

3. Be brave, or as I like to say, "Feel the fear and do it anyway!" so post that photo, make that offer to your clients, jump in and have a conversation with your hero, try that new technique. Just take a big fat deep breath and DO stuff. And while I think 3 clichés is too many for any one blog post, I'm

going to add one more: **You will LOSE100% of all the races you don't enter**. And I know (because you take the time to read this blog) you are many things but you are not a loser. NOT. So get your butt out there and get stuff done, in as many baby steps as you need. Post just one picture. Ask just one question. Email just one person. JUST. DO. IT. (and there's another cliché. Sorry.) Believe me when I say that the more you do something the easier it gets to do it ... and anyone at all who has made a sugar flower knows that the first one is ugly as sin, the 50th one is damn near perfect.

4. Print this post out somewhere and either stick it up on a wall, or fold it and put it in your handbag and re-read it when your confidence it at an all time low. WHY? Because I want it to serve as a reminder that you are not the only one out there feeling this way. **You are not alone**. Anyone working in a creative industry struggles with self-doubt, lack of confidence, feeling inadequate. Some super well-known cake people will email me with, "I've got this idea. Do you think it's okay?" - and guess what, I send those same emails ALL the time. I look for reassurance from friends both in and out of this industry because I'm human and I too want someone to look me in the eye and say, "You're good enough, and what's more, you're getting even better." It's totally okay to feel that way (because we all do), I'm just here to tell you that those feelings cannot paralyse you. You are not alone.

and lastly ...

5.   Go visit Cake Wrecks (http://www.cakewrecks.com). Have a bit of a giggle at those disasters, and then look at a Sunday Sweets post as well and be inspired. You're doing this for three reasons. First, because sometimes it's nice to take a step back from our own crazy and have a bit of a giggle. Second, it reminds you that everyone starts somewhere, and everyone makes mistakes. Third, because instead of looking at pictures and being intimidated by them, you're better off being inspired by them. Don't think about not measuring up, think about aspiring to be like the people you admire and realising that they started somewhere too. One of the main reasons I ask the people in the Real Stories series (http://www. thebizofbaking.com/search/label/Real%20Stories) to include a picture of their own cake is to inspire you all. Here's a secret I'm going to let you in on. I ask them to do it because I know they are going to go and read the post about themselves. I know they're going to cringe at that photo. I also know they're going to scroll down and see how far they've come and in that moment, the pride is going to outweigh the embarrassment. I do it to inspire the very people who are in those interviews in the first place.

     If Cake Wrecks isn't your thing, go pull out the photo of the first cake you made. Smile, laugh, shake your head and go, "How could I have ever thought that was any good?!" and then go look at the cake you finished last week. Maybe you thought last week's one wasn't any good either, but I'm willing to bet it looks a heck of a lot better than that first one.

6.   I wanted to end this post with, "And stop caring what other people think, " but that's not great advice, because I actually DO want you to care what people think. The only difference is, the only people whose opinion I want you to care about is YOUR CLIENTS. Not other cake decorators, not your Mother, not the cheap cake lady down the road. You're in business to serve yourself and serve your clients, and those are the only people whose opinions matter. If your opinions are more about beating yourself up than lifting yourself up, then I want you to return to #4 and re-read it.

Don't be intimidated. Be inspired.

In It For The Love AND Money

WHEN YOU BUY FROM A MOM OR POP BUSINESS,
YOU ARE NOT HELPING A CEO BUY A THIRD
VACATION HOME.

YOU ARE HELPING A LITTLE GIRL GET DANCE
LESSONS, A LITTLE BOY GET HIS TEAM JERSEY,
A MOM OR DAD PUT FOOD ON THE TABLE,
A FAMILY PAY A MORTGAGE, OR A STUDENT PAY
FOR COLLEGE.

OUR CUSTOMERS ARE OUR SHAREHOLDERS AND
THEY ARE THE ONES WE STRIVE TO MAKE HAPPY.

THANK YOU FOR SUPPORTING SMALL BUSINESSES!

Share if you agree!

Can someone please tell me, when did it become not okay to want to make a living? I keep seeing all these articles about how you should only do work you're passionate about, telling us that if you really love it then the money shouldn't matter, how if we love what we do then it isn't really 'work' at all. I've seen social media posts from cake companies nastily referring to other cake companies "only in it for the money" as though that is some sort of dirty evil secret.

And yet, I see post after post after post complaining that clients are not willing to pay us what we are worth, that cake toys and classes are expensive, that we are being undercut all over the place, and that "we're closing our cake businesses down because we're simply not making any money to survive."

Wait ... WHAT? So it can't be about the money (because it's just not cool to be about the money), and yet the money is the problem with this industry. Does anyone else see the issue with this? It's not about the money but apparently it's all about the (lack of) money?

I'm going to be the one to say it loud and proud:
IT'S ABOUT THE MONEY.

Passion does not pay the bills. Last I checked the grocery store does not take passion as payment, nor does the mortgage company or my kids' school.

There is a perception in this industry that it's not okay to actually want to make a real living out of creating edible art. That somehow if you're not doing it for the love, that's not okay. Maybe it's because we are all expected to be "starving artists" but honestly, I'd much rather be a well-fed artist who can continue to create art than a starving one who needs to stack shelves in order to stay alive.

Of course, it's not nearly as black and white as that. This industry -or any industry- is not ALL about any one thing.

Those of you who have read this blog for a while now know that I think your business needs to have a much big purpose than just creating gorgeous cakes. My own mantra has always been, "I'm not in the business of cake, I'm in the business of happiness" ... but please note, that's the <u>BUSINESS</u> of happiness. I love the craft of making cake, but unless I'm fully committed to making money from it, then there is no reason for me to be in the business of it. I might as well keep it as a hobby[38].

A lot of people tell me they are NOT actually in business, that they only make cake for family and friends and/or that they only charge people for their ingredients and/or that they only do it because they really love it. I don't have a problem with that ... except of course when that person has a Facebook business page, has business cards, or is telling people to pay them more than the ingredients actually cost them. As an example, are you really going to your sister and saying, "Okay, so I added up my receipts, and for ingredients I paid $19.88," and then expecting her

---

to really only give you $19.88? Oh, and if it's for the love, why do you even use the words "charge them" for ingredients? A **charge** implies _a fee for the purchase of goods_, doesn't it? So which are you? In business or not in business?

From others I hear, "I'm in business, but I'm not doing this for the money."

Answer me this: if you were not in it for the money ... why are you building your website, baking macaroons, teaching, working out your prices, writing tutorials, creating and selling retail products? Why on earth would you bother with the crazy messy of being IN BUSINESS if you were not in it for the money? Are you telling me you work 15 hour days, have a bad back, answer emails at 1 am and haven't slept late on a Saturday morning in 5 years because IT'S JUST FUN?

If so, you've got a very warped idea of fun my friend.

It would be very, very nice to have a sugar Daddy, win the lottery or find a money tree which would allow me to just give everyone free cake, teach everyone for free, and invent and give away products for free. That's not going to happen, so instead I made my business about making money. No, not millions of dollars, but enough money to pay me a decent salary so I can afford the groceries and the school tuition and the cake toys. I defined my level of success in **many different terms** but one of those was money. Let me explain that in more detail. I make no secret of the fact that I really value education and I wanted my three kids to go to private school. Private school costs THE BOMB and times three it's like a NUCLEAR bomb. So at the very least my business had to make enough money to pay those tuition fees (and let's not forget the books, the uniforms and the field trips too.) Judge me as much as you like, but <u>I had to be about the money</u> **because I needed the money** to pay the fees of the school ... because that's important to me. Does it make me elitist to want to send my kids to private school? Maybe, but so what? Perhaps my definition of success was just to be able to make enough money to buy instead of rent my house, afford a vacation once a year ... or just buy groceries without having to price compare. It doesn't really matter where you would spend that money or how much of it you want to make, what matters is that you are honest and real about **needing to earn that money in the first place**.

This week I spoke to a brilliantly talented cake maker who said to me, "All I really want is to be able to go to the grocery store and buy what I need without having to think about it." For her, it's not at all about elite things like private school, and yet she is coming to me because she's just not making it financially. So ... try and tell me again that what you do is not (at least a bit) about the money.

You are probably in this for MANY reasons - perhaps lifestyle, artistic expression, love of cake, passion - but if one of those is not money then **you have no business being IN business**.

How To Be Stubborn

One of my very good friends pegged me as a 'Tigger' personality almost from the first moment we met. He is an 'Eeyore' personality, so where I am inclined to be bouncy and cheerful, he is inclined to plod and mope. It's just who we are. I am famously terrible at being grumpy or sad or mad for very long amounts of time. Mid-arguing with my husband I have been known to say, "I'm sick of being pissed about this. Can we go get ice cream now?" or "You're really irritating me, the only way to fix it is if you give me a cuddle then grovel a bit and I'll get over it." I'm bad at holding a grudge, and I'm always inclined to see the good in people, or find the lesson in the hard experience, or just be really grateful that I've got what I've got. There are plenty of days when doing all of that is really, really hard work. I am no Little Miss Sunshine (how terribly annoying that would be), it's more that I would just rather search really hard to see the good in things than dwell in the bad things.

I recently read this passage by Elizabeth Gilbert (she's the author who wrote "*Eat, Pray Love*") and when I read it I thought, YES! That's exactly what I am. Stubborn as hell (just ask my Mum. She'll confirm that for you). Like a dog with a proverbial bone, I'm nearly never willing to let go of trying to make things good or right or happy or at the very least - tolerable. On the days when it feels like your business is going to drag you right down into the abyss - you just need to remember this Thriving Lesson: BE STUBBORN.

Ms Gilbert says it far better than I ever could:

> "*There are days when I wake up at 5 am, and for some reason the madness is right there waiting for me, like it's been sitting by the side of my bed all night. The disappointments, the anxiety, the regrets, the insecurity, the anger, the second-guessing — all of, waiting for me, with a greasy smile. Like: "Wake up, sucker! We can't wait to mess with your mind and give you a horrible day!"*
>
> *Mornings like that happen to me more than you might ever guess.*
>
> *I fall into spells of living where I can't seem to take a correct step or a wise action. I've been depressed, anxious, confused and deeply ashamed of myself — often enduringly, often all the same time. More recently than you might imagine.*
>
> *Follow any of that stuff to its natural destination, and one will find life to be bleak and sorrowful, indeed.*

*But you know what? I'm fucking STUBBORN, people. I will fight that shit.
I insist on pursuing enjoyment and meaning in the life that I have been
given — even when some of the times I feel half crazy and totally uncertain.
I fight for the light. You give me a crack of light the width of my pinkie, I'm
going to try to squeeze myself through it, if it kills me. I will find something
good around me, I swear to God, and I will hunt it down eat it — sometimes
literally (pizza). I will make myself go out in the world and look at something
beautiful. I will demand that I find a way that day to commit an act of
kindness on someone. I will insist on trying to create. I will not be ashamed
to call up my old therapist and be like, "Listen, I need a tune-up here, " and
ask her to try to help me put my head on straight, rather than spinning
in a vacuum of uncertainty. I will spend hours trying to find a goddamn
inspirational quote that actually does its work on me. I will grab myself by
my own hand and say, "Listen, kid — screw up as much as you want: I AM
HERE TO LOVE YOU." And I won't let go.*

*You think those Happiness Jars that I talk about all the time are all about
light and gladness and easy rays of sunshine? No — my Happiness Jar is a
ninja weapon of stubborn defiance against the creep of despair. So is my
relentless commitment to living a healthy creative life — a creative life that
doesn't worship darkness. So is my stuttering, semi-effective meditation
practice. So is my tithing. So is my travelling. So is my care and feeding of
my own curiosity. So is my hunt for divinity. So is my daily attempt to wring
some forgiveness out of my soul — for myself, for others. (And then to try
again the next day, if it doesn't work today.)*

STUBBORN.

*It's a word that saves my life every day, and has given my life whatever
worth it's got.*

Because without it? Nothing good will come. "

She's right.

You've just got to be stubborn as hell sometimes because the alternative is to
survive ... but only just.

So ... in a baking business context, how can you be stubborn?

- BAKE. MAKE. CREATE. The very act of working with one's hands is immensely therapeutic. The smell, the feel, the intensely heady and wondrous potential of flour, butter, sugar and the chemistry which makes it all come together ... this is where the magic lies. Make a recipe for the hell of it, not because it's been ordered by someone. Bake ugly cookies with your kids. Cook something for dinner which is NOT sweet and NOT baked but maybe is a bit of a challenge or a bit of an indulgence.

- Flick through photo albums of past creations and reminisce about the client's reaction, your sense of satisfaction in completing the order, or just how damn grateful you were when it finally got delivered. Laugh at your dodgy early attempts at things (I have a basketball cake which makes everyone laugh, it looks entirely deflated).

- Read testimonials from happy clients.

- Sign yourself up for a class - and not necessarily one about baking or business. The pursuit of knowledge is all-empowering and motivating.

- Go back to your Final Cake Design thinking to remind yourself of the bigger reason why you're doing this in the first place.

- Go read Cake Wrecks (http://www.cakewrecks.com). There is very little in life which cannot be solved with laughter.

So when you're having a crappy day, week, month? Just be stubborn.

Or as I like to say:

> Love your craft.
> Love your clients.
> Love yourself.
> Be grateful.
> Kick ass.

(Be stubborn while doing all of those.)

The Stories You Tell Yourself

The stories you tell yourself are interesting ones, aren't they?

My prices are too high, so I don't get any orders.

I live in a rural area, and people here do not value cake.

Nobody is willing to work for me.

All business owners need to work super hard and a bunch of crazy hours.

I love my work so much, I don't care if I don't get much of a weekend.

I'm unrealistic about how much money I can make from cake.

Nobody makes a real living out of making cake.

It's just a hobby.

I have no idea how much money this business is making, hubby deals with it all.

Small business is all about sacrifice.

Most of the emails I get are from tyre kickers. People only care about price.

I'm not a good enough cake decorator to teach others.

If I don't offer to deliver on Sunday, I'll never get any wedding orders.

I need to be open seven days a week.

If I don't answer those emails right away, I'll lose orders.

I'll never be as good as (insert cake god name here).

I don't care if I ever make any money from this, that's not what it's about for me.

I have to keep my prices low, otherwise, nobody will order from me.

The cake lady down the road is getting all the orders because she's so cheap.

It's too expensive to register my kitchen, and I'll never get caught.

Sometimes, I feel like a complete fraud. My pictures make my cakes look better than they are.

I'll never be truly successful.

I'm not good enough to charge proper prices.

I'm doing it just because I really love it, not because I want to earn a living out of it.

You get the idea, don't you?

In our heads, we write a thousand and one scripts every day, and those scripts dictate how we run our lives and therefore our businesses. We don't think we're good enough, so we don't make the effort to market our businesses enough. We don't want to lose any orders, so we answer emails at midnight and say yes to the psycho lady (even when our gut tells us to run like hell.) We are afraid of people rejecting us, so we under-quote and WE KNOW IT. We claim that we do what we do just because we love making cakes, yet moan that it's impossible to make a living from this. Every single day, we tell ourselves whatever story we need to tell, in order to justify our actions or *our lack of actions.*

Isn't it time you started writing a different story?

You And Beyoncé

Image source: www.billboard.com

This industry has a very low barrier to entry (your Mum just needs to give you a couple of bucks for a cake and BOOM you're in business) so there are a heck of a lot of businesses currently operating out there. This week on the Business of Baking Facebook page (http://www.facebook.com/bizbake) I asked you what you think is the difference between those baking businesses that will be successful and those that will not. The vast majority of answers were variations on a theme but the gist of it was this: the difference between success and failure is having business skills. How to cost out your products, how to price accordingly, how to handle your accounts, how to ensure you get a decent hourly rate, how to market your product, understanding customer service ... and so on. Of course product and raw skill come into it, but overall the people who responded overwhelmingly sited **business skills** **as the key difference between success and failure**.

I especially loved Tanya's comment (she closed her business last year for several reasons) who observed that when she comes back to it, she will, "... spend way more time on the numbers and less on browsing new techniques."

Oh Tanya, you just said in one sentence what it's going to take me a whole blog post to express.

As business owners, we invest in our business in so many ways- in new equipment, in taking technique-based classes, in hiring staff, in advertising, and of course in time. Every day we choose to invest something in our business somewhere. So why is it that *the one thing we should invest in the most* - our business skills - we invest in the *least*? I will freely admit that I used to be guilty of this a lot. It was

WAY easier and WAY more fun going to a class about modelling chocolate than it was going to a class on how to keep correct tax records. It was WAY more "doable" and WAY more within my comfort zone to spend 2 days, $2000 and a flight to Sydney to attend a class with a famous cake maker than it was to spend time learning from a business coach. It was WAY more fun to watch 2 hours of YouTube videos on piping cookies with royal icing than it was to listen a 2-hour webinar about marketing and advertising.

You know what? I did all of those - both business classes and technique classes - and there's no prize for guessing which classes paid themselves off a hell of a lot faster than the others. There's also no prize for guessing which of those classes will be of use to me long after I hang up my apron for the last time.

Before the amazing cake decorating teachers who read this blog get upset, I want to clarify that in no way am I suggesting you shouldn't take technique classes. Of course you should - they're fun, they expand your skill base, and they can be immensely useful. I'm just saying that you've got to be investing in things in addition to technique classes if you're planning on succeeding in this industry. You've got to be investing in your business skills. It's a vital part of your training as a business owner.

One of the purposes of this blog is to help you come to the (sometimes painful) realisation that if you're taking your business seriously, you've got to be a business owner as much (if not more) as you are a creator of wonderful things. Let's face it, we'd all rather be playing with fondant than playing with calculators (although I do know how to make a whole lot of rude words using only the numbers on a calculator, that gets kinda boring pretty quickly. Not surprising when I learned that skill back in the third grade, really.) THIS IS THE CRUX OF IT: Business owners need to have business skills.

The good news is, business skills can be learned. The bad news is, you've got to find some time in your already crazy life to learn those skills.

Let me frame this in another way.

The biggest investment you're going to make in your business isn't going to be in your commercial kitchen, in your television advertising, in that massively gorgeous oven or in the figurines class you took last winter. The biggest investment you're going to make is the one you make IN YOURSELF. How you choose to invest in yourself as a business owner will depend on a whole lot of things - what you can afford, what you have time for, what skills you lack, what you need more of. For some of you, the investment might be in hiring an employee that frees you up to do some business development work. For some of you, the investment might be in a business class or some coaching. For some of you, the investment might just be time - time to work out what the next steps of your life look like in and around your business.

You must choose to invest in yourself as a business owner. It's much more important - and the value will last a whole lot longer - than investing in yourself solely as an artist.

This week I saw a meme which said, "You have exactly the same number of hours in each day as Beyoncé does", and while I'd really like to laugh that off and complain that I might have the same hours, but I don't have her financial resources and her staff members, I can't deny the truth in it. We all have exactly the same amount of hours to spend in each day. It's how we choose to spend them that makes all the difference. Let me repeat: *you need to choose to invest in yourself as a business owner*.

Oh ... and as for Beyoncé? She's an insanely crazy mega-talented singer ... but so are thousands of other beautiful people out there (all you need to do is watch American Idol, The Voice or X Factor to see just how many talented people exist, and that's only a small fraction of them). Yes, Beyoncé is an insanely crazy mega talented singer, but she's as successful as she is <u>because she's one hell of a clever businesswoman</u>.

There's a lot we can learn from Mrs. Carter.

Timing is Everything... Or Is It?

One of the most read and (to me) most vital posts I've ever written is called The Final Cake Design[39]. I reference back to it pretty often because I think it's the single biggest lesson I ever learned in this whole crazy business thing, and it's the thing I lean on when I am most filled with self-doubt (which still happens. I'm human.) I've actually got a heap more to say on that topic (big surprise, right?) but today I'm going to address the question - can the final cake design change? In other words - what if right now I'm happy with making some pocket money from my business, but I know that once the kids are a bit older, I've saved more money or the cake-zombie apocalypse happens, I'd like to take it to the next level? What then? What if a golden opportunity comes knocking but I'm not ready for it? What if something bad (or good) happened, and the timing of my plan is different now? Isn't NOW is the time to own a baking business? If I wait, will I miss the boat?

Or in short: can I change the Final Cake Design?

The short answer is NO, the longer answer is YES. The 'NO' is because I asked you to think BIG and think HARD about the whole reason behind why you're in business at all. I specifically said not to worry about the product, the shop, the scale of the thing (yet). I just talked about thinking over why you want to be in business and what it's going to be about for you. So in theory, that reason won't really change very much as it's on a much higher level than the decision to open a shop or not.

However, the path you take to get there, and the timetable you follow are highly likely to change. So for example, if your reason for being in business is to actually enjoy your job and get some work/life balance ... that end goal stays the same, but this year you (for whatever reason) need to keep the business at home, and next year you can start looking at ramping it up so you can leave your existing day job behind once and for all. Or if your reason to be in business is to be famous ... that end goal stays the same, but this year (for whatever reason) you stay in your current premises and next winter you invest in some PR, you start submitting articles to cake magazines and seeking television appearance opportunities. It works the other way, too - you suddenly come into some money and can move the timetable forward a bit because you have the financial means to do so. You get made redundant from your job and suddenly you have the time you wanted to give the baking business 100% of your attention. Time is elastic in that way and you can speed up or slow down the creation of your business as life circumstances change.

---

39   See *The Final Cake Design* in the *Before You Begin* section.

Let me be brutal: I'm not giving you permission to put things off until forever, to sit around thinking rather than doing, or spend forever waiting for the right time. There is never a 'right' time for anything in life. I'm saying that you are perfectly entitled to make decisions based on what else is happening in your life, and that sometimes opportunities do not always come along to the timetable you hoped or wanted them to. Sometimes opportunities come around a lot faster than you wished for, too.

Let me give you a real life example. A few weeks ago I had a mentoring session with someone who found out that the "perfect" shopfront became available in her neighbourhood and it would be empty within a few short months - way earlier than she ever planned to get her business out of home. She asked me if I thought it was a good idea to take the lease out on the shop. She's already needing to knock back orders because she's got too many requests, she's frustrated with the business encroaching on her personal life and space, she's overwhelmed by the amount of work she currently has and the time/space her home-based business is requiring, and her kids (3 of them) are pretty young. Is any of this sounding familiar? Because it certainly sounded pretty much like my life used to!

In her mind, the shopfront potentially relieves a bunch of those issues (space, time, ability to grow and earn more.) It's so very tempting, isn't it? My advice to her was this- think about what life with a shopfront might be like - for example, how many hours it needs to be open and how you're going to staff those hours, plus the finances of building a kitchen and keeping it afloat until you make a profit - and then look at your life and see if the timing is right. Is NOW when you want (or can) take on the responsibility of leasing a shop, or is this something more doable when the kids are a little older? In other words, now might be a *great time* or a *terrible time* to take on this opportunity and I can't answer that for you, but I CAN tell you this much: opportunities have a way of coming your direction whether you plan for them or not. So by all means, do some thinking and planning ... but also, let go of the need to have things happen to an exact timetable.

To give you a non-business example, I remember when I decided to start my family, I'd do all these calculations in my head, "If I get pregnant now, then I will take leave in October, which works well for work as that's the quiet time ..." or "If I go off the Pill next month, then get pregnant the month after that, that means the baby will be born in Winter, which is good because ... blah, blah blah." Let me assure you that thousands of dollars and many medical procedures later, I no longer cared one single iota when that baby came, I cared only that a baby would come AT ALL. *Time became much less important* to the end goal.

I've taken an enormous amount of leaps without thinking about the timing too much (I went to culinary school when my three kids were toddlers, my husband was out of work, and I was in a high paying but soul destroying job at the time ...) so it's not that every decision needs you to research the hell out of it before leaping. I'm just pointing out that *time is elastic and opportunities appear and disappear daily*. Accept that you can choose to take action or NOT take action and that the world will continue to spin at the same speed as it did before you made your decision. You are not "missing out" on something amazing ... and even if you are, something more amazing is probably waiting for you around the corner.

You can change things. You can grow them, scale them down, re-assess and re-structure things. You can alter your path, take an entirely new route, speed up to warp speed or choose to stop moving forward entirely. The Final Cake Design probably won't change (it's far too big to be affected merely by a change of direction) but the road there and the time you take to get there can change dramatically. That's totally okay. You're not missing out on anything.

The finish line is still the finish line. You'll get there.

How to Lose Weight And Still Eat Chocolate

The only comparison shots I've got! Left: A few months ago. Right: Six years ago. Not the most flattering outfit but you get the idea. Now the embroidery starts over my shoulder, originally it started at my ankles. I had to wrap the sari around an extra two times for it to fit this time. (and yes, my husband has also lost some weight!)

Five years ago I decided to change the course of my life dramatically, and over the course of two years I lost 70 kilos (154 pounds). (That's like losing an entire supermodel holding a big handbag.) I've now kept that weight off (plus a bit more) for three years. It might surprise you to know that in all those years, I ate chocolate pretty much every single day and I still do.

Here's the interesting thing about losing weight. LOSING it is actually the really easy part. You're all excited about your shiny new gym card, you love your bright pink running shoes, you can't wait to program your Fitbit, you went and got the cutest pair of gym pants ever, and you've told everyone you know that you are "being good". You've got a goal weight in mind, you've set up some mini goals along the way, you've got a reward scheme set up for each goal, and most of all you're motivated and excited and you are going to DO THIS THING! You are losing weight, getting fit, and things are looking pretty damn fabulous both emotionally and physically.

Fast forward three months. The weather has turned cold so you end up staying in bed and, therefore, missing your Zumba class. Your fancy water bottle broke when you dropped it and you haven't had the chance to replace it. It's Valentine's Day, Christmas, your birthday, Mother's Day ... and you allowed yourself to indulge on the holiday (and then just kept on indulging). You've either hit the dreaded plateau, or the scale has started to move in the wrong direction entirely.

Fast forward three months. You managed to stop the food train before it raced to the bottom of the hill, you got back on track and replaced the water bottle, found a way to exercise on cold days (hooray for Zumba DVDs) and the scale is back to moving in the direction it's meant to. Before you know it, you've hit your goal weight!

You go out to dinner to celebrate. (oh, the irony.)

Fast forward three months. You've ticked off the mini goals and gotten the gold star for the big goal, the runners now look a little tatty and the plastic on the gym card has started to peel at the corners. You can't remember the last time you looked at the My Fitness Buddy app you used to track your weight loss on.

Fast forward three months. You're now heavier than when you started a year ago.

Wait. What? What does that scale say?! What the hell happened?!

What happened to all that excitement, motivation, enthusiasm, drive? What happened is that you forgot that your life continues for a long time after you've reached goal weight. It's about what you do AFTER you get to your goal that's much more important. You've still got to exercise and eat right and be involved with your body EVERY SINGLE DAY. Yes, of course, since you're not actively looking to lose more weight you can be a little more relaxed, drop the intensity down a little, allow a treat or two without beating yourself up about it. But there is no way you can get off that treadmill permanently and expect to maintain your new svelte figure. Even supermodels have to work at keeping those bodies looking the way they do.

If you haven't worked it out already, losing weight and owning a business are very similar life experiences. It's what happens AFTER all the fun stuff of setting up the business which is important. You get so excited in the beginning – designing logos, ordering business cards, signing up for wedding expos, searching out new packaging, buying lots of gorgeous vintage cake stands and telling everyone you know that you are starting a new business. It's such an incredible adrenaline rush, isn't it?

Fast forward three months. You haven't gotten quite as many orders as you had hoped, the ink on the business cards wasn't quite the right colour, a few of your cake stands got borrowed and never returned.

Fast forward three months, and three months more, and three months more. Your business (like the numbers on the scale) has gone up and down like a yo-yo. Sure, there were a lot more ups than downs, you still love what you do, this whole thing is still awesome and you're still mostly motivated ... but it doesn't seem to have an end point. The goal was to open the business (or open the shopfront), and you did that. Now, what? Honestly, sometimes in business, it can just feel like an endless slog of rent which needs to be paid, bills which need to be managed, and cakes which need to be baked, products which need to be created, marketing ideas which need to be put into action. Those things, for as long as you'll be in business, won't ever go away ... much like holiday eating binges, cold winter mornings that keep you from the gym and sleeves of Oreos won't go away either (much to my disappointment).

I've often said that going INTO business is the easy part, STAYING in business is the hard part. Those of you who have been at this for a while will know how true that is.

In the coming weeks, I'm going to introduce a new feature to the Business of Baking ('Thriving Lessons') – posts which are aimed at helping you stay on the treadmill, but will still allow you the occasional sleep in on a cold morning. I can't pretend like it's all about some magical, mystical "work/life balance" thing (because whoever invented that expression was just trying to piss us all off, really) but I have learned a few tricks along the way for staying motivated, moving forward, and keeping on with the business of keeping on. I hope you'll find this new feature useful. I don't have all the answers (not to weight loss either) but I can share a few things which have kept me moving forward on days when I'd much rather be in bed (literally.)

It's what happens AFTER you've reached the goal which is - in many ways - more important than the actual goal itself.

Bringing a fancy water bottle along is optional.

Stop Multitasking

This past weekend, I went on a Mum and Son's Scout camp with my boy. I am not by nature the camping type (generally speaking, I only ever want to sleep under 5 stars ... like the ones at the Hilton). I really prefer a hot shower, cold sheets, not having to build my own accommodation for the night and a toilet which actually requires flushing. That being said, I packed up my woefully ancient (um, falling apart and a bit musty) sleeping bag, prayed it would not rain and there would not be bugs, and away we went.

I had to put in a lot of work to make that weekend happen. I had to start my cake work a day early so I could leave earlier on Friday, I had to make sure someone was in my shop on the weekend to handle pick-ups and enquiries, I had to work out delivery logistics and kid logistics and put in a fair amount of planning to make sure I could go. It wasn't a huge deal, but it definitely took a bit of effort to make it happen. Here's the really great part about my weekend: not a single person there (other than my son) knew what I did for a living. I got to <u>totally escape</u> being "the cake lady", "my friend who makes cakes", "the small business owner", and "oh, you're that cupcake lady, right?" The other great part is that other than a SINGLE text to my husband to ask if all the pick ups had gone okay, I didn't do anything work or sweets related unless you count incinerating a whole lot of marshmallows on the end of a slightly wonky stick.

I cannot tell you what a gift it was to just totally abandon my work, my skill, my passion, my life, my vocation. I live, breathe, eat and am sometimes almost consumed by my business and my blog and yet getting the hell away from those was a joy I've not felt in a long time. I realise that might sound a little odd -

because if I love it so much, why am I so grateful that I got to leave it behind? Well, there are two reasons for that. One, my son deserved every minute of that time to be all about HIM and not about cake. My kids already spend a fair amount of time competing with my business for my time and attention, and in this case, there was nowhere and nothing more important than letting my son strap me into a harness so I could fling myself down a steep incline, screaming while he laughed at what a wuss I was. (Oh - and he also discovered that his Mum is NOT superwoman. I have zero archery skills. As in, it took me so long to find my lost arrows in the grass several feet behind and away from the target that I actually had to call in a Scout search team to help me find them.)

So firstly, it was just divine (although a little embarrassing with those arrows and all) to wear only the ONE hat of being a Mum. That nearly never happens for me. I live my chaotic life at crazy speed and I wear the title of "Kick-Ass Multitasker" like a badge of honour so I'm never only wearing one hat. What a rare and fabulous gift, to only have one thing to concentrate on for 2 and a bit days. Secondly, being entirely unplugged from my business was like having a mini mental vacation. I spend SO much time in my head and in my business's head. Even when I don't know I'm there, *somehow I'm still there* ... and this was a brilliant opportunity to just NOT BE THERE both physically and mentally. I didn't have any brilliant ideas for marketing or new designs, I didn't suddenly find inspiration while singing, "She'll be coming round the mountain when she comes", and I managed to avoid talking about what I did for a living all weekend long. I did not multitask AT ALL. Nobody knew me as anything other than a crappy archer and an embarrassing mother.

- I spent those two days being ONE thing: a mother.

- I spent those two days caring about ONE thing: my son. (Okay, I just lied. I also cared about the bugs, in specific hoping there would be very few of them.)

- I spent those two days revelling in this ONE thing: the quietest mind I've had in a very long, llllooonnng time.

Today's thriving lesson: STOP MULTITASKING. Find at least a day (if you can't afford a whole weekend) and entirely unplug yourself from the role of the aspiring business owner, the decorating teacher, the cake lady, the failing or the succeeding business owner. Put in enough planning and effort to allow yourself to do so without guilt or worry and then actually go. I'm not talking about going on a Facebook diet for a few days or putting your phone on silent. I'm talking about really truly walking away your businessperson self and going back to just being ...

you. The you who is a Mum or Dad, a sister, a friend, a whatever-you-are. JUST BE YOU for a while without ALSO having to be business person or cake person.

It's a little funny that in a blog about running a baking business I'm telling you to run away from being a baker or business person ... but I think sometimes the best way to thrive (in business and in life) is to go back to basics, even if only for a short while. You were a person long before you owned a business; you will continue to be someone long after it's over. Every once in a while, walk away from your business and touch base with the YOU, who was there before and will be thereafter. Just be ONE thing for that time. It's hard to do, but worth it to maintain your sanity.

Bugs, rides on a flying fox (and musty sleeping bags) are entirely optional.

Healthy, Wealthy And Wise – Part 1

I've been reading so many encouraging emails and posts from students and readers of the blog who are (finally!) getting control over their business and personal lives. It's really wonderful to hear that you're exercising several times a week, have cleaned up your diets, and (I love this!) have instituted "no business Sunday. " For so many of us, trying to keep track of a household, maybe a job, maybe kids, maybe elderly parents AND a cake or cookie business means that there simply are not enough hours in the day to think about looking after ourselves, too. In my earlier article, "The Importance of Self-Care"[40] I admitted that I'm kinda crap when it comes to looking after myself.

Shortly after writing that article, I realised that most of my self-care was situational - meaning I did it when I had big things coming rather than doing it as part of my everyday life. Since then I've changed a lot about my life and lifestyle and I'm sharing some of those today in the hopes that it helps you find time to be a little kinder to your body. Sadly, most of us only do this stuff AFTER our body (or our soul) breaks down ... and then it's usually a case of too little, too late.

I've since made some huge strides in becoming more healthy, wealthy and wise and in this 3 part series, I'm going to share with you the exact things I do to make my life (and thus my business) a whole lot better. . . without masses of effort, time

---

40   See *The Importance Of Self-Care* in Chapter 10.

or money. **I'm not ashamed to admit that I'm lazy, easily bored, cheap and time poor. So if I'm all of those things and I can make this stuff happen, you can too.**

HEALTHY

Eat

I make no secret of my love of sugar and all things sweet. I don't think I'll ever be able to give it up entirely. Earlier this year I discovered that I have really low iron levels (to the point the doctor asked, "How are you not fainting all the time?"), low Vitamin D and a whole lot of other general wellness things were out of whack. This is NOT OKAY. So I went and got the iron transfusion, starting taking vitamins, made the effort to get more sun. I then decided to take a closer look at my diet and here's what I found (or rather, didn't find!). In any given day, I'd have ZERO fruit or vegetables. ZERO. My diet was basically all carbs and protein. I hardly drank water (lucky to get maybe 2 cups a day and one of those would be tea/coffee.) Most days, I'd eat 2 tiny meals and then after 4 pm, it was like all hell broke loose and I would consume almost all my calories between 4-10pm. Basically, I was a hot mess!

I can't say I've got it perfect now, but I CAN say I'm getting a heck of a lot better. I've cut down sugar quite a bit, I'm reintroducing fresh fruit and vegetables, I'm taking my vitamins as I should, and I'm drinking lots more water. My kids and I have started to make smoothies for breakfast to increase out fruit/veg intake. When I get home from the US, I'm going to start the 30 Day Green smoothie

challenge created by the gorgeous girls at Simple Green Smoothies (<u>http://</u>
<u>simplegreensmoothies.com/30-day-challenge</u>). I didn't do this to lose a bunch
of weight or be some sort of poster girl for a healthy life. I still want my Oreos,
dammit! I did it because I'd let things slide WAY too far and I was feeling sluggish,
tired and just overall kinda gross. It was time to get my healthy mojo back and
each day I'm doing that a bit more that's another day I'm better than I was. Added
bonus, I've realised that the better I eat, the more creative I am. In the last few
weeks my productivity has increased ENORMOUSLY and I'm way more focused and
overall happier.

**My tip: Don't wake up tomorrow and decide you're going to be on an all vegan,
organic, paleo, unicorn poop only diet. That's never going to work in the long
term. Pick ONE thing you want to get better on. Get better on it till the new
normal is that you're good in that area. Then pick another thing. Also - invest in
a sexy 1L (24oz) water bottle. It makes drinking all that liquid a lot less boring.
Plus all that water means you will pee a lot. My tip: don't take your phone to the
bathroom with you.**

Get Your Ass Moving!

I've been a gym goer for a long time ... but here too things had slid backwards.
Either I didn't go as often, or when I DID go I'd kinda half-ass my way through it.
You know what I mean. Sitting on the stationary bike barely spinning those wheels
while scrolling Facebook. My scrolling was faster than my pedalling. Yeah, not so

much cardio effort there! I ditched my gym and decided to get moving outdoors. We've got a dog and he was a great excuse to get moving, so three to four times a week I'd take Teddy out and walk for about an hour. Except of course walking is kinda BORING. I downloaded some e-books and listened to a chapter each time I walked him. This had the advantage of me keeping walking (so I could get to the end of the chapter) but after a while, it stopped working for me. I found my walking had slowed to the pace of whoever was reading. Again, no cardio action happening. I was happy with this for a while, but started to feel that it was less like exercise and more like a way to just kinda ... hang out with my dog.

I decided to re-do the Couch to 5K program (C25K). I'd done it ten years earlier and loved it, so I thought I'd try again. Last time, I had to do this with a stop watch. This time - HOORAY - there are apps which do it for you (I use the one by Zen Labs ... it's free (http://c25kfree.com)). So I'd get up, shove my earphones in, start the app. . . and head off around the neighbourhood. I'm just about to complete Week 8 and I could not be prouder of myself. Bbbbuuuttt ... this is me. Bored again. I downloaded the Rock my Run (http://www.rockmyrun.com) app (free!) and it made a massive difference to the experience. I'm an 80's girl so I pretty much downloaded all their 80's mixes so I could rock my way around the neighbourhood. These days, I'm C25K 3 days a week and 2 days a week I walk for 45-60 minutes. Some weeks I only manage the runs, other weeks I'll get out there 7 days a week. Some weeks I repeat one of the weeks because I felt I didn't give it my best effort. Not going to lie, I don't run as much as I kinda lumber along. I'm slow. I'm uncoordinated. I dress kinda "homeless chic" when I run (tatty t-shirt, pathetic yoga pants, hoodie). The point is, I'm MOVING!

My tip: All the things I use to exercise are FREE with the exception of my earphones and my shoes. I find the "bud" style falls out of your ears, the "over the head" kind are uncomfortable (even headbands give me a headache) so I spent less than $20 to buy some which hook over my ears. I love them. With shoes - go and buy a decent pair to whatever value you can afford. I wear New Balance880's but you can wear what works for you. Added bonus: you can take your shoes and your earphones with you wherever you go. Cheap and easy.

What little things do you do to improve your health and fitness? If the answer is "nothing. I suck", that's totally cool. We've got to start somewhere. After reading this, pick your ONE thing you're going to improve on, even if that one thing is "reduce my coffee by one less cup a day". Just like our businesses are a work in progress, so are our bodies.

Healthy, Wealthy and Wise - Part 2

WEALTHY

In last week's post[41] I talked about how I got my eating and exercise back on track, and in today's we're going to learn how I got my financial life back on track, too. Money is something women do NOT like to talk about. The vast majority of us secretly wish someone else would take care of it. ALL of it. I'm talking about money in our business and money in our personal lives. Some of us find it confusing just to pay bills, so the idea of having investments is several steps too far out of our comfort zones. Many of us don't have as much money as we would like or need, so having to deal with it makes us sad, angry or upset. I would seriously freak out when it came to discussing money and I spent a lot of time wishing for a lottery win or certain that if I had more money, my entire life would somehow be sprinkles and rainbows and I'd be skinner too. My attitude to money and wealth changed a lot once I read the book '*Get Rich Lucky Bitch*'. I ended up doing Denise's LB Bootcamp (https://yu103.infusionsoft.com/go/lbb/emzeegee) and have not looked back since. My relationship with money is a work in progress but it's a hell of a lot healthier than it's ever been.

However, attitude isn't everything (although it's a big part!) There is a reasonably large age gap between my husband and I, so when we got married he took care of all things financial - not because I couldn't, but because to my mind he was older and wiser and had already been managing this for some time. Why should I bother when he's got it all under control? Except, of course, **he didn't have it under control at all**. We'd get final notices because he forgot to pay or plain lost the bill.

We'd pay a lot of late fees for the same reasons. I'd open the mail and have a full on panic moment because bills were always coming in unpaid and then I'd fight with him about his incompetence - how freaking hard is it to pay a bill?! It took me ten years but eventually I took the bull by the horns and took over all our financial affairs. Turns out he was relieved to hand it over!

The good news is, I learned to just suck it up and handle the bills. I didn't like it, but I liked it a lot more than getting late notices. The bad news is, I sucked at money managing and budgeting was a foreign concept to me. Along the way, I also changed careers and opened a business ... while he changed jobs more times than I've kept track of. In short, we weren't keeping it under control whatsoever. No late notices, but still no money for vacations or "extras" like new tires for the car - either of those would send our finances into a tailspin from which it took years to recover. Ironically, my business finances were damn near perfect - because early on I knew it wasn't my mojo so I hired a freaking fantastic bookkeeper and accountant and we worked on it all together. Sure I made mistakes there, but those were born of ignorance not ignoring it.

So my husband and I tried a bunch of different tactics. Excel spreadsheets. Financial advisors. Fighting about it. Opening lots of bank accounts and putting money in a bunch of places. NONE of it worked in the long term for us. We just always felt like we were treading water, and most of our efforts at organisation were too hard and frustrating. Plus let's be real here, when you feel like you're broke you feel like you have NO MONEY to manage anyway. About eighteen months ago I heard about budgeting software called YNAB (You Need a Budget) (http://ynab.refr.cc/BTZ8VPP) and we signed up for it a year ago. It totally changed how we do things, and I'm really proud to say that we don't fight about money and we've got money in savings for when we want to go on vacation or change the tires. I still mostly do the day-to-day management, but now we do our finances together rather than either of us sticking our heads in the sand about it. This is a MASSIVE step forward for our family and our marriage.

Is that the end of the story? Of course not. Was the point just to tell you about Lucky Bitch and YNAB? Nope.

I think it's time for you to step up. **Get involved in your family's finances**. If you don't want to deal with the day-to-day stuff, I understand - but that's no excuse for not at least UNDERSTANDING what your situation is and where things are at. Do not wait until you lose your job, the marriage dissolves, someone dies or you have a sudden need for cash. RIGHT NOW take some control over your money. I would hope that if you're a long time reader of this blog, you're already taking control over your business accounting. If you can manage it there, you can manage it at home.

When my Dad died, my Mum was left totally adrift with no clue how to handle their finances. A Dad of a friend went into hospital, and because he was unwell and away from handling his affairs, they uncovered his massive gambling habit and a mess of a financial situation. Another friend's husband passed away and she uncovered thousands in credit card debt she didn't know she had. I know of at least two women stuck in marriages that are slowly killing them because they have no money of their own, kids to feed and no way of supporting themselves or even knowing what their financial rights are. **DO NOT let this be you. Pull on your big girl pants and GET INVOLVED in your finances. We no longer live in a time when money is "secret men's business, " and ladies, you have NO EXCUSES not to become empowered in this area of your lives. I know it's scary. YOU CANNOT AFFORD TO IGNORE IT ANYMORE.**

If you are strong enough to own business, or have dreams of someday doing so, that means you also have the strength within you to get your financial affairs in order. You do not need to learn to trade stocks, invest in property, have a ton of savings or be born into wealth for this to be important. TODAY, make a time to sit down and figure this stuff out. I say this in my pricing class (http://learning. thebizofbaking.com/buy/ConfidentPricing) and it applies to your personal life too - **If you don't control your money, your money controls you.**

Healthy, Wealthy and Wise - Part 3

WISE

You might not know this, but I personally read and respond to every email I get, and one of the best parts about that is the incredible stories many of you have shared with me. In today's post, I wanted to share with you some of the bits of wisdom I've learned from running my own business and from listening to stories of you running yours.

- We like to think the cake industry is about cake, when in reality it's not about cake at all - it's about people. It's about the people who buy it and the people who make it. Everyone you meet along that spectrum, from the customer who is demanding to the supplier who overcharges you to the colleague who thinks you are a threat rather than an ally ... they all have a story which shapes how they behave and what they say. There is ALWAYS a back story, and we would be much better people if we remembered that instead of taking everything so personally all the time.

- You are all a lot stronger than you give yourself credit for. ANY of you reading this who have a business of any kind - a small one, a big one, a failing one, a succeeding one, one that makes cookies or one that makes 8 tier wedding cakes regularly - you're out there. You're doing it! Maybe in your mind it's not fast enough, good enough, too hard, too easy ... blah blah ... the point is, YOU ARE DOING IT. Chances are most of you doing it have other demands on your life, be those personal (kids, elderly parents), physical (bulimia, a dodgy back), or mental (anxiety, shyness, depression). The thing is YOU ARE DOING IT. This makes you all kinds of awesome in my book. You are strong. You are capable. You've got this thing.

- Given what I said above - that everyone has a back story, and that everyone is stronger than they think - **I still very much believe that it's entirely possible to make a living (and a good living if that's what you're aiming for) in this industry.** I do not believe customers only care about price. I do not believe that the industry is too saturated. I do not believe that people will never pay what you are worth. I do not believe that only people on TV are making money. In fact I do not believe most of the bullshit the nay-sayers say - the stuff they say because them themselves are TOO AFRAID to try. I believe we are ALL capable of success, and the evidence is there in my inbox. The emails include stories of, "I have more orders than I can handle" and "I finally quit my day job!" and "I got the keys to my new store today!" and "Someone asked me to teach them!" And yet, you'll still meet people who say it's too hard to make a living. SCREW THEM. **It's possible**.

- Lastly, I wrote an article a while ago ('*Cake Business Lessons from 2014*') (http://thebizofbaking.com/cake-business-lessons-from-2014) and I think it's one of the best (if least read) articles I've written on this blog thus far. It's one you should print out and refer to when things are feeling a bit too hard.

To succeed in life AND in business, you need to be all three of the things I've been talking about - Healthy, Wealthy, And Wise. That being said, "health" does not only refer to eating kale all the time, "wealth" is about way more than money, and "wisdom" is something you acquire each day you get to be on this earth.

Choose to make those three a priority - more of a priority than improving your piping skills - and you'll get further than you ever thought possible.

CONCLUSION

WHAT HAPPENS NEXT?

Dear Cake Maker,

Running a business (cake or otherwise) is likely to be one of the most rewarding and most challenging things you've ever done. Maybe you picked up this book, got halfway through, and got totally overwhelmed so you skipped here, to the last page, in the hopes of finding the keys to cake business success. (I do that with fiction books ALL the time. I'm impatient to find out what happens at the end.)

Let me help you out, by distilling the entire book into one "cheat sheet" of what I believe are the most important things I've said so far. These are the lessons I really hope stay with you as you continue your cake business adventure. They are in no specific order – it's all important.

1. *Your Business = Your Rules. One of the benefits of owning your own cake business is that you get to call all the shots. You decide how to do things. Absolutely it's important to get advice, read, learn and grow more, but ultimately how you choose to do things is up to you. There is a LOT of advice out there, so you've got to absorb that stuff, process it and then do things in the way that suits you and your business. Your business is a reflection of who you are. Make it reflective of the best parts of you, not just a copy of someone else's ideas of what that should be.*

2. *Marketing isn't optional, and it has to be a consistent effort. I know you don't like it, wish you were better at it, want more time to do it, and so on. I get that, I really do. I just want you to commit to doing it consistently, in whatever way you are comfortable and able. Don't sit around waiting for clients to magically appear. They won't - or at least, not enough of them will to keep your business going. You just have to keep on plugging away at marketing. You must market your business. Must. Yes, the industry feels very saturated at the moment. There will always be people who are more skilled than you are, or charging less than you are. So what? That's nothing new. The difference into the future isn't going to be if you can out skill or under-price them. The difference will be that you'll out-*

market them. We've all seen companies with mediocre products or crappy service succeed, and they do so because they market well. I'm not saying be mediocre or give bad service, I'm saying you cannot underestimate the importance of marketing to your business. So you hate it. That's nice. I don't care if you hate it, you've still got to do it.

3. *A rising tide lifts all boats - make sure your tide is made up of people who will encourage, push, teach and help you. Not the whiners, the complainers, the ones who will look for roadblocks and convince you that you can't get past them. Not the people who themselves are too scared to make changes so instead they complain and belittle. I would strongly encourage you to cull those people, groups or organisations out of your life which no longer serve you. You don't need them. You've got growing to do, and if what they say is already not sitting well with you, you've outgrown them. Sure, we all have a good complain once in a while (it's human nature) but if the people around you are only ever doing that, you don't need them. It's time to say "buh-bye" to the time wasters and energy suckers.*

4. *Haters gonna hate. Let them. You've got more important things to work on and care about. Your time and energy are your MOST PRECIOUS resources, so spend them wisely on the people, projects and things that deserve them. Would you rather enter into a half hour argument online with someone who is never going to order from you, or spend that half hour having a coffee and a laugh with a friend who loves you? Or spend that half hour marketing your business, working with a business coach, or doing some research into a new product? I'm going to say it again: Your time and energy are precious - don't waste them.*

5. *If you don't plan to succeed, you won't. I mean this in EVERY aspect of your business. We spend too much time on the micro-management of our days and not enough on the long-term planning. You need to not only think about the bigger picture but plan for it, otherwise all you are doing is living day-to-day and order to order. You need a bigger plan, and you need to work out how you're going to get there and then JUST DO IT. Even if that plan only spans the next 6 months, at least it IS a plan. Running a cake business with no plan is like having a 3D cake with no internal structure. It's highly likely to crumble. (By the way, I now offer mentoring sessions to help you do this, or work on your pricing or marketing. More information can be found here.)*

6. *Life happens. Cakes fall over. Employees get sick. Kids break arms. Orders*

for 5, 000 cookies come in. Clients ask for stuff last minute. It's never about the event, it's about how you deal with it. So, when unexpected stuff happens, do this: have your freak out moment, then get right the hell up and get to work on solving that problem or coming up with a Plan B, C, or D if that's what's needed. Then: learn from that experience, and change the way you do things so that if there's a next time, you'll be better prepared.

7. Policies, procedures and systems around your business aren't optional. A friends and family policy, deposit and refund policy, standardised recipes, a schedule for your week, a baking list. . . these things save your butt when everything goes to hell. Even if you own a home based cake business that only needs or wants one cake order a week, you've got to systematise and formalise all the things you can. If nothing else, it will free up a lot of your time and give you some confidence - both things we all need more of.

8. It's absolutely about the money. It is also about a lot of other stuff, but it most certainly is about the money, otherwise all of us would be doing it for free. You cannot complain that clients do not understand your pricing or won't pay what you're worth, but then turn around and tell me you are doing a bunch of things for free or cheap because you're really "only doing it for the love. " If you don't think it's about the money, then I think you need to re-examine what the words "in business" actually mean. Business = the exchange of money or goods for other money or goods, in other words, business is by definition a profit making venture. If you're not in it for the money, then why on earth would you sign up for the stress, the crazy customers and the late nights?

I need money to feed my kids, pay my mortgage, and buy cake tools and go to classes to up skill myself. I can't do any of those with love alone. I believe business is about a LOT of things (including love) but it's about the money because that's what business actually IS. Anything else is a hobby, an interest or a pastime, not a business. You can support the industry, teach your skills, "give back" to the industry, help people out, socialise with cake makers and make cakes for people without charging a SINGLE cent - you don't need to be in business to do ANY of those things. So if you're REALLY not in it for the money, DO IT ENTIRELY FOR FREE and let the rest of us get on with earning a living to pay our bills. Stop acting as though it's black and white -that we must be about one OR the other. When did it become shameful or wrong to want to make a living AND do it for the love? Guess what? It's not. By the way, I think many people who *say they aren't doing it for the money say that as a means of protecting themselves from their fear of failure. If they go into business, and then don't make money, then they can always claim they "weren't in it for the money" in the first place and save themselves some embarrassment. Personally, I'd rather give it one hell of a try and fail than only half try. As the saying goes, you will lose every single race you do not run. Me, I'd rather come dead last than not run. (By the way, I don't want to lose. I'd much rather win. But you can't win if you don't enter the race either.)*

9. *Stop wasting money on stuff you won't actually use, truly enjoy, or grow from. Cake business owners suffer from "ooh shiny!" disease a LOT. There are a lot of really cool videos and cake tools out there. You don't need them all. You need to prioritise the ones you want versus the ones you just need or feel sucked into by your peers. Just because something is cheap, that doesn't mean you should have it or need it - sometimes it's better to save up for the bigger thing which will last longer than buy the cheap thing over and over. Your spending should be an investment and not just an expense. You're going to get a lot more long-term value and happiness out of hiring a bookkeeper than you will buying more $9.95 videos you'll never watch or shaped cake pans you'll never use again. I'm all for a little bit of indulgence (hello there, my Oreo friends) but just giving in to every whim isn't indulgent, it's foolish.*

10. *There have to be boundaries. The only way to have a life AND a cake business is to have boundaries. Stop answering your phone after 6 pm, don't take orders via text, don't work on Mondays ... whatever. Decide what your boundaries are and then live by those boundaries and teach your clients about those boundaries. You've made the time to run a business, this means you can make the time to have a life, too. Let's be real here. We work in cake. We are not brain surgeons. This doesn't mean we are not important or we don't service the world in an important way, because we do. It means that when it comes to cake, nobody is in mortal danger so "emergencies" are not really emergencies. Their order CAN and WILL wait till Monday morning for you to call them back. Just because they forgot they have 100 people coming over in an hour, that's really not a good enough reason for you to miss your husband's birthday party or your daughter's concert. Choose to have a life outside of your business, and do that by setting boundaries.*

Like I said, being a small business owner is hugely rewarding and hugely challenging, but I believe the lessons we learn doing it stay with us for a lifetime –

long after the cake gets eaten and the oven gets turned off.

Let me leave you with this thought:

> There are only 3 directions one should go in life (and in business);
> **ONWARDS, UPWARDS OR FORWARDS.**

I invite you to come along with me for the ride, whichever direction you choose. (Take note: 'backwards' is not one of the options.)

For further resources, additional articles and to get in touch with me personally, please visit thebizofbaking.com – I look forward to hearing your story.

With love and a whole lot of rainbow sprinkles,

Michelle ☺